W9-AMB-796

BONANZA

A VIEWER'S GUIDE TO THE TV LEGEND

By David R. Greenland

Foreword by David Dortort, Creator and Producer

Dedicated to my wife, Cleo, who never complained
when I went riding with Ben and the boys.

Acknowledgements

I am deeply grateful to David Dortort for devoting such a considerable amount of his time to the realization of this project. During the course of several conversations, he provided me with much new information and corrected many old misconceptions. Without his encouragement, the book may not have been possible.

For help beyond what was asked of them, I want to express my sincere appreciation to Mitch Wood and especially Paula Rock.

Special thanks to Gary Yoggy, particularly for "Three Queens Full." And to Andy Klyde, whose own book on "Bonanza" I eagerly await.

For various forms of assistance and consideration, I would also like to thank Christopher Andersen, Mary Ann Bauman, Chris Capone, Ed Colbert, Deirdre Culpepper, Bruce Dinges, Robert Dutton, Richard Fry, Dan and Chris Gill, Michael Gordeuk, Karen Gray, the Kisers (Wayne, Tim and Ruth Ann), Bruce and Linda Leiby, Margaret Magrini, E. Helene Sage, Richard Stanford and Darlene Smyda.

While all photographs, research material and memorabilia are from my personal collection, I must thank Jeff Kadet, Milton T. Moore, the Movie/Entertainment Book Club, Paul Parker, Simon Parker, and Toad Hall of Rockford, Illinois.

For my parents, this is 2+2.

And to Harriet Carlson, Barry Craig and Paul Greenland, whose contributions of time, effort, patience, equipment, etc. can never be adequately repaid. Everyone should have such a cheering section.

—-David Greenland

Library of Congress Cataloging in Publication Data

Text © copyright 1997 by David R. Greenland

All rights reserved. No part of this book may be reproduced in any form or by any means without prior written permission by the publisher, except brief quotations used in connection with reviews or essays written specifically for inclusion in a magazine, newspaper, and/or electronic media.

Publisher:
R & G Productions
PO Box 605
Hillside, IL 60162-0605

Book design and production: Wayne, Tim and Ruth Ann Kiser

Printed in the United States of America

First Edition, 1997

Special queries regarding sales or special orders should be addressed to:
R & G Productions
PO Box 605
Hillside, IL 60162

Foreword

by David Dortort
Creator and Producer

Just as a long-dormant volcano doesn't erupt suddenly and spontaneously, but only after a considerable passage of time during which the constantly changing physical forces and elements deep within it need a boiling point that can no longer be contained, so does a concept for a new and original creative approach require a sufficient period of gestation and inner turbulence before it can manifest itself as a fresh and novel vision. Nothing springs from the head of Zeus without due contemplation.

So it was with "Bonanza." After agreeing to do so, I wrote the pilot script for "Bonanza," and then I waged a rather intense battle to shoot the show in color rather than the customary black-and-white, thereby introducing superior filmed color television for the very first time into the living rooms of America and the world. From its very first frame, "Bonanza" was photographed in vibrant, living color at the pollution-free 7,000-feet above-sea-level altitude of Lake Tahoe. The world of television broadcasting and equally significant, of television advertising, was never the same. Where there had only been black-and-white, now there was a veritable rainbow of gorgeous color. Naturally, NBC dubbed itself soon thereafter as "the rainbow network." Marshall McLuhan, the great guru of the message and medium of television, proclaimed that my actions were responsible for one of the giant advances in the rather brief history of television until that time.

But the truth is, the concept for "Bonanza" did not fully occur to me all at once, in a blinding instant of creation. Yes, as a devoted student of American history from my college days on, I was keenly aware that the role, the image, of the gunfighter–the man who settled disputes and dispatched evil-doers with the lightening speed of a gun–had been blown out of all proportion to its actual role in the history of the West, and by all of Hollywood's Western film and television product since the days of "Bronco Billy." And, yes, I was guilty of doing pretty much the same thing with "The Restless Gun," because it was the unswerving tradition.

No, "The Restless Gun" did not vary all that much from the norm, and furthermore, it was not an original creation of mine, but basically an adaptation from a radio show written by someone else. I was aware that the true history of the West was fundamentally quite similar to the history of all great migrations on our planet over the eons of time, and that was the epic story of people embarking on a long and dangerous journey, men, women and children, and even more children born under the most difficult and hazardous of situations enroute.

It was the story of people seeking a new beginning, new land and homes, imbued with the hope for a better life for themselves and their families. It was the story of sinking one's roots in the new land, the plow that broke the plains, and the tragic subjugation of the previous inhabitants, the Native Americans, because it was believed that they had to make way for the building of homes and farms, of schools and places of worship. It was the shameful story of the slaughter of the buffalo, the brief glory of the fur trade, and as Bernard DeVoto so succinctly noted, man's unbridled lust for the mineral riches of the earth–gold, silver and copper.

However, for me, the most immediate reason for shedding the image of the gunfighter was because he was, essentially, a loner, one man who by himself took care of a problem affecting a struggling community or an isolated ranch. He did it by dint of his courage, his nobility, and his awesome speed in drawing and firing his six-shooter. Sometimes with a sidekick, always mounted on a spirited horse, he accomplished his deed of valor, modestly accepted the thanks of those he had helped, and rode out the way he had come in. It was a workable formula–the hero as rugged individual–and it was the basic plot-line for many a noteworthy movie, as well as a number of early television Westerns.

But it had little, if anything, to do with the actual life of a flesh-and-blood human being. We never knew where he, or in some rare cases she, came from, who they were and what they had done before they suddenly came to life on a Western landscape. Not one of them had been born in the West, but other than some vague, occasional hints, we never knew about their families or why they came to the West in the first place. Even the need for an answer was deemed highly questionable. Don't let anything get in the way of the action, the confrontation, the gunfight.

The problem with that, as television played to an ever larger audience, was that one man couldn't do it all alone. At least not to the total satisfaction of the audience. In addition, on a more practical level, if the one-man show became a hit, the actor who played the part would be booked into all manner of celebrity-seeking events, such as rodeos, and state and county fairs. Often, as in the case of John Payne in "The Restless Gun," he would depart on a Friday morning or even a Thursday evening and not return until late the following Monday afternoon. The fees paid for these guest appearances were most appealing–almost impossible to turn down–not to mention all the attendant acclaim. Though "the show must go on," it became the producer's problem to "shoot around the star," making do with the lesser actors and scenes shot mostly in very long angles which didn't work too well on the small screen of the television set.

It was frustrating. Here the show was built around one man, and that man could be maddeningly absent while you tried to make sense of what you were shooting. That was when I vowed that if I was ever called to produce another show, there would be more than just the one man to carry the freight.

That call came soon enough. After two years and seventy-eight episodes, almost always in the top two or three of those of the national ratings, Payne and the studio–the Revue Productions, subsidiary of the monolithic MCA–agreed to disagree and end the show, due to rather bitter, well-publicized differences about money and bookkeeping practices. John chose to take the settlement money and run, leaving me, at least temporarily, whistling in the wind. However, no sooner had the second season finally ended than NBC, obviously impressed with the quality and high marks that "The Restless Gun" had achieved, invited me to take them, for the first time, into full-hour, prime-time programming. The first thing I did, naturally, was come up with a format that had four leads–a father and his three sons.

Both Michael Landon, who had been in the pilot of "The Restless Gun," and Dan Blocker, whom I hired as an extra, and then, recognizing his vast talent, cast in several larger, eventually guest-starring episodes, were easy choices to make. I wrote the part of Little Joe Cartwright with Michael in mind, and Hoss, "the gentle giant," for Dan. Lorne Greene and Pernell Roberts completed the cast, but not without a fairly bloody battle with NBC. The executives at NBC, to a man, said they had never heard of any one of my four selections, and it would require, at a minimum, "established" actors with well-known marquee names to induce sponsors to step to the plate and pay for this high-budget production, for "Bonanza" was to have extensive distant location shooting, as well as the higher cost of filming in color.

They especially objected to my using Dan Blocker to play Hoss, on the grounds that a large, fat man, as opposed to a tall, narrow-waisted man, would never be accepted by the fans as one of the stars of the show, and, furthermore, there was no precedent for that kind of casting. Well, as David Greenland will relate later on, it wasn't all wine and roses, but I finally won that battle, as I did the subsequent one on pioneering color in filmed television.

In the first season, my main preoccupation was with establishing the background for "Bonanza," combining, as had become my personal trademark, the carefully

David Dortort had been writing motion picture and television scripts for many years before "Bonanza's" debut. Prior to that, he had a pair of novels published as well as a number of short stories. He had been elected to three successive terms as president of the television branch of the Writer's Guild of America, West. With the half-hour show, "The Restless Gun," he became the first writer to produce a television series. "Perhaps," he says, "because of the surprising success of that program on NBC, due in some measure to my writer's instinct for story and character rather than all-out stunts and action, NBC invited me to lead them into full-hour, prime-time programming."

researched, factual history of a time and place with a necessary mixture of fictional characters and story lines. A strong part of my make-up and education demands that I treat the facts of history as meticulously and honestly as possible, since I know that children and young people will be watching. My personal credo is that education should be an important aspect of entertainment, and that anyone who is granted the privilege of access to the public air should carry along with that a sense of responsibility, to tell the truth and not unduly twist or sensationalize the facts.

The discovery of the richest strikes of silver in history on the Comstock Lode at the eve of the Civil War and the almost simultaneous onset of the great pioneer migration to the West, qualifies as one of the most colorful and significant chapters of the American Story. Not only did the incredibly pure bullion pouring out of the Comstock play a decisive role in the outcome of the Civil War, but some of the great dynastic fortunes of that age that are still with us today had their beginnings there, also. To mention just one of many, a miner named George Hearst, who fathered a son he named William Randolph, was one of those who hit it big on the Comstock.

Setting the stage, establishing the main characters, teaching an important history lesson, was the primary business of the first, and possibly the second, season of "Bonanza." But after General Motors and its Chevrolet division purchased the full hour and moved it to its Sunday night at 9:00 p.m. flagship time-slot, which commenced a historic additional 12-year run–nearly all of it spent in the top runs of national TV viewing–the emphasis gradually began to shift. Though the Comstock never entirely faded, more and more it was overshadowed by the emerging vision, the vision of the Ponderosa, home to the Cartwright family.

Now, at long last, we are back to the gestation process and the subsequent volcanic eruption with which we opened this sermon. The creation of the great mythical Ponderosa Ranch was in some ways, I believe, "Bonanza's" crowning achievement. Yes, we gave a fine "father image" to the world at a time when it was desperately needed. Yes, we brought forth an ethical and moral code that stressed the importance of morality, of good, decent behavior, of kindness, compassion and charity to less fortunate neighbors and weary, foot-sore pioneers, of love–strong manly love–and understanding and mutual respect between a father and his sons, between brothers. We stressed the importance of family, of caring and supportive family, breaking with the tradition of the loner and his gun. We tried to correct the often infamous treatment of minorities in the American Story. We taught that the customs, the modes of worship, the languages of so-called "foreigners" should be treated respectfully and not made the butt of distasteful, stereotypical humor. We insisted, usually against the network's wishes, that Western heroes could laugh, enjoy one another, have fun, even conjure up wild, practical jokes, just as much as everyone else. It didn't always have to be grimness and sudden death.

But all this notwithstanding, there was always the Ponderosa, the land that had to be nurtured and cared for, the great, majestic trees, the ponderosa pines and the redwoods that needed to be protected and preserved. America doesn't suffer from a dearth of heroic Western figures in its past. But where are the magic places, the mythic settings that are the potent stuff of dreams? Where is the place we think of when we long for Paradise? Search as we may, the simple answer is that America doesn't possess any such place, not a single one.

Other civilizations have Shangri-La, Camelot, Valhalla, Elysian Fields, the Garden of Eden, the Promised Land. But in these United States there is nothing comparable. Mythical heroes in abundance, but mythical spots–where? Try to think of one.

Slowly, even subliminally, the concept for such a magical place began to take shape. It took perhaps the first two or three years of the show, but as the vision grew steadily stronger and clearer in my mind, all the pieces began to fall into place. I returned again and again to what is arguably the best-known and most treasured legend in the English-speaking world, the poetic, legendary place called Camelot, home to King Arthur and his Knights of the Round Table. Slowly, we began to envision the Ponderosa as America's Camelot–the good king and his gallant knights supplanted in our democratic republic by the good father and his steady sons.

In the decade of the 60s, with the nation torn and despairing, with more and more families falling into a kind of dysfunctional abyss, we felt passionately that somewhere there should be a message of hope, of kindness, of understanding. A house need not be a dismal, unhappy "house divided;" rather a house could and should be a "house of love." At the Ponderosa a father loved, respected and helped his sons. Brothers loved, respected and helped one another. And the Ponderosa was a place to be cherished, nurtured, protected from harm, a sanctuary for the helpless, the innocent, the unjustly accused. The Ponderosa's message was universal. As the concept of a better, happier life took hold, or perhaps because of it, the show gained more and more strength until "Bonanza" was crowned the number one show in the world several years running.

No one understands all this more, perhaps, than David Greenland. It was and continues to be a constant source of wonderment and encouragement to me when David Greenland and literally thousands of others have said wherever my wife and I travel, in all the far corners of the world, that "We grew up watching 'Bonanza' every Sunday night. Every week without fail my family and I gathered around the television set and watched 'Bonanza.' We waited for it all week long."

And many, truly in mind-boggling numbers, have taped every single one of the more than four hundred episodes. They remember every story. Some, like David Greenland, can recite the names of the individual guest stars, even the director, as well as some of my closest associates, most especially Kent McCray, my good right arm for so much of "Bonanza."

On the Ponderosa we were a happy crew. Most of the crew, most notably our chief cameraman, Buzzy Boggs, and our astonishingly gifted composer and conductor, David Rose, among so many, were with me for all of our history-making 14-year run, surely one of the longest, if not the longest run of any hour-long dramatic show in the history of television.

Of our multi-talented actors, Lorne Greene, Michael Landon, Dan Blocker and Pernell Roberts, and let us not forget the beloved Hop Sing as played by Victor Sen-Yung, I cannot say enough or too much. But David Greenland, in the body of this book, takes up the cudgels for me with remarkable insight, sensitivity and penetrating observation. I am truly indebted to him for an outstanding piece of work, as I am forever indebted to my dear wife, Rose, and my darling children, Wendy and Fred, for their love, their steadfast support, their ceaseless, never-ending encouragement.

Finally, my salute to good, loyal David Greenland. His knowledge of "Bonanza" is as encyclopedic as it is wonderful. It is my fervent hope, dear reader, that you will enjoy his book as much as I did.

David Dortort
Los Angeles, April 1997

Contents

Introduction

by David R. Greenland, Author

A young boy, persuaded by a group of his peers to shoplift paint for model airplanes, is shamed into changing his mind when confronted by the images of his heroes staring at him from a display of lunchboxes.

A teenage girl, never comfortable with the knowledge that she is adopted, bursts into tears of joy the night Ben Cartwright decides to adopt Jamie Hunter.

A high school freshman, attracted to a girl whose last name is Cartwright, dubs his strategy to make her notice him Operation Ponderosa.

Those are but three of the countless stories "Bonanza" fans have shared with me during the writing of this book, and they illustrate far better than any cold statistics the impact of the show.

"Bonanza" did not become the most popular Western in television history simply because it was the first network series to be broadcast in color. Nor was it due to the enormous appeal of one of the most versatile casts ever assembled. While those were definitely contributing factors initially, what ultimately sustained the show's widespread following for nearly fourteen full seasons was a sense of humanity the majority of its contemporaries lacked. This quality resulted in "Bonanza"'s ability to transcend the Western genre and become one of the few long-running shows to actually improve with age. Name another program whose tenth season, for example, was better than its first. For that matter, name all the prime time dramas which ran longer than "Bonanza". To date, with the exception of Gunsmoke, there aren't any.

It is fascinating to look back and see how effectively "Bonanza" was constantly being reinvented, not out of creative desperation but by creative design. The cast was capable of handling drama and comedy with equal ease and no loss of credibility, occasionally within a single episode. There seemed to be no limitation to the imagination behind "Bonanza", and because it was one of the first "period" shows to incorporate contemporary issues—racism, domestic violence, mental illness, political and religious corruption, ecological preservation, social injustice, the plight of war veterans, the generation gap—it retains a certain timelessness.

Lorne Greene, 1966.

Critics who accused "Bonanza" of being unrealistic and overtly romantic evidently did not subscribe to the belief that the most admirable drama usually aspires to depict life as it perhaps ought to be. Doing so often takes more courage and inventiveness than is required for holding a mirror up to man's shortcomings. We have the evening news to remind us of them. True, "Bonanza" did a great many stories concerning life's darker realities, but it always tried to offer a promise of hope, however small.

By the time "Bonanza" ended its original run, it had been seen in nearly ninety countries by an audience estimated to exceed 400 million. Thanks to syndication, the series is among that select group which has never been off the air and is always being shown somewhere around the globe. It continues to be a huge hit in Germany, Japan, Italy and Egypt, as well as domestically. With new gen-

David R. Greenland *is a free-lance writer, musicologist and television/film historian who has had a lifelong interest in the Old West. In addition to writing screenplays for commercial video productions, his work has appeared in several publications, including* Classic TV.

Bonanza: A Viewer's Guide to the TV Legend *is his first book.*

A former resident of Los Angeles, David was born in Illinois and remembers seeing "Bonanza" *for the first time on a black-and-white set in 1961. He currently lives near Chicago.*

erations discovering it, the viewership for "Bonanza" may conceivably be larger now than when the show was cancelled. Consider these facts:

In 1987 the Family Channel's acquisition of over 160 episodes not previously released in syndication (including the never-rerun final season) was rightfully considered a major media event.

Since 1988 there have been not one but three updated TV films based on the original series.

In 1990 "Bonanza" was the only Western among Entertainment Weekly's list of "TV's Best Golden Oldies". That same year, The Cable Guide named the 1972 episode "Forever" #3 on a list of "TV's 20 Hardest Hitting Homicides".

In 1993, the same year NBC aired a one-hour retrospective of the series, the readers of TV Guide voted "Bonanza" "TV's All-Time Best Western".

A photo of the original cast appeared on the cover of TV Guide in June of 1996 when the editors selected the show's debut as #29 out of "The 100 Most Memorable Moments in TV History".

"Bonanza" websites on the Internet have carried as many as 30,000 letters in a single year.

Plans are underway at Universal for a possible feature film, and there has even been talk of a Broadway musical, as improbable as that may seem.

References to "Bonanza" in sitcoms, movies and commercials are almost too numerous to mention and show no sign of letting up. The show is an undeniably large slice of Americana.

The idea for this book first occurred to me in the late Seventies and was an off and on effort until 1994, when I was finally able to connect with David Dortort. Prior to that, my research was limited to old magazine and newspaper articles, hazy and often contradictory recollections from former production people, and brief discussions with guest stars who either could barely remember being on the show or considered their appearance merely a job they were fortunate to get. An ad I placed in one of the entertainment trades in 1981 elicited almost no response, sadly enough, and because this book is a tribute to the show and not an exposé of anyone's private life, those who were only willing to speak "off the record" were of no help. More often than not, they had some ancient grudge to air or wanted to share useless information only readers of supermarket tabloids would find valuable. Needless to say, I made no use of such material. Those primarily interested in little more than backstage gossip–usually inaccurate– are advised to look elsewhere.

In general, books about television shows fall into two categories: those which concentrate mainly on behind-the-scenes anecdotes while treating the episodes themselves as incidental, or those which simply slap together stale information and pictures. I have attempted to avoid both classifications, and I hope the reader will find the effort worthwhile.

—David R. Greenland
February, 1997

Publicity shot for Christmas on the Ponderosa album, 1963.

11

CHAPTER 1

The Production

The Western, like jazz, is one of the few original American art forms. From the writings of Zane Grey and Louis L'Amour to the paintings and sculpture of Frederic Remington, the heritage of the Old West has influenced nearly every level of artistic expression one would care to name, particularly on film. Between 1926 and 1967, Westerns comprised a quarter of all feature films produced in Hollywood, including such universally acclaimed classics as "The Searchers," "High Noon," "Shane," "Ride the High Country" and "Red River."

Although the Western made the inevitable transition to television, that trail was blazed by juvenile cowboy heroes, not visionary filmmakers. The simple, sanitized version of the Old West presented by Gene Autry, Roy Rogers, Hopalong Cassidy, the Lone Ranger and others was highly entertaining to children but offered little to the mature viewer except perhaps a passing wisp of nostalgia.

The "adult" Western did not appear on home screens until the fall of 1955, when CBS converted a three year-old radio program called "Gunsmoke" into what would eventually become the longest-running prime time drama in the history of television. Two years later, and for the next three seasons, "Gunsmoke" was the highest rated show in the country, and its success did not go unnoticed by the competing networks. By 1958, there were two dozen Western series on the air, half of them ranking in the Top 25 but very few as worthy of repeated viewings as "Gunsmoke."

The genre reached its saturation point in 1959, with nearly thirty series consuming over seventeen hours of programming each week. Naturally, very few of these shows were consistently creative, and some which are fondly remembered today have not aged well. Even those justifiably regarded as classics–"Have Gun–Will Travel," "The Rifleman" and "Maverick" among them–were clearly low on inspiration before their final seasons. Virtually all the newcomers of 1959 are now forgotten, and only one would become a legend, thriving even as the television Western began to fade because it was

Second season publicity shot, 1960.

more than a Western: "Bonanza."

Contrary to the generally accepted myth, "Bonanza" was not specifically created to help sell color television sets. More accurately, NBC wanted to enter the arena of in-house production rather than relying totally on outside companies for its programming, and was unconcerned with the problem its parent corporation, RCA, was having marketing color sets. Considering the current popularity of Westerns, the choice of which type of show to make was a logical one.

At the time, NBC was carrying "The Restless Gun," a half-hour series in its second and final season. The show, featuring film star John Payne as an accomplished gunfighter who, in a novel twist, tried to avoid violence whenever possible, was one of the better Westerns on the air. However, Payne, weary of the weekly grind and involved in a legal battle with Universal Studios over profits from the show, did not want to do a third year.

David Dortort, a successful writer personally asked by Payne to produce "The Restless Gun," was Hollywood's first writer/producer, as well as a three-time president of the television branch of the Writers Guild of America West.

He was also the obvious candidate to lead NBC into prime time television.

Dortort, who was planning to exit MCA (Universal) because profit participation did not

13

then extend to writers or producers, jumped at the opportunity. NBC told him he could create whatever he wanted.

"The network came to me early in '59 and asked if I had an idea for a show," recalled Dortort. "I told them I thought I did, but that I also had about a dozen episodes of 'The Restless Gun' to complete. I had initiated a policy of doing two per week, which didn't leave me with much time for anything else.

"Even so, I thought of 'King Arthur and the Knights of the Round Table,' the whole concept of 'Camelot.' The British knew it was fictitious, part of their folklore, but most Americans thought it was true. I thought, 'Maybe it's time to create for Americans the equivalent of 'Camelot.' Not with knights, but using the great story of our whole westward expansion, the great and heroic struggle of the pioneers. That should be celebrated. And so that's how the concept of the Ponderosa came about. Instead of having the good king, I'd have the good father, and instead of the knights, I'd have the loyal sons."

If it seems unlikely that this fresh approach to the Western could have originated with a Hollywood producer it is because David Dortort does not fit the stereotype. In addition to being a literate man who enjoys poetry, the theater, and opera, he is regarded among his colleagues as one of the few people in the industry possessing genuine integrity.

Born in a tough section of Brooklyn in 1918, Dortort was more interested in learning than joining street gangs, eventually enrolling at the City College of New York when he was only fifteen. One subject that fascinated him was geography, and this knowledge would later prove useful on filming locations. In fact, the "Bonanza" crew came to refer to him as "The Guide".

When only seventeen, Dortort surrendered to an urge to experience life firsthand, roaming the country during the depths of the depression.

"I saw thousands of people on the road," he recalled. "They were more friendly than they are now. I rode the rails, stayed in hobo jungles, saw the World's Fair in Chicago. The further West I went, the more the beauty of the country began to open up–Wyoming, Utah, the Continental Divide. That's when I started to develop an interest in our country's history, particularly the history of the Old West."

Stopping in Las Vegas, which was then just a railroad junction, Dortort was picked up by the local sheriff for loitering. During the course of a two-hour conversation, Dortort discovered that the pot-bellied constable was a lonely man grateful for the young man's company.

"At the time the country was being terrorized by the notorious bank robber, John Dillinger," Dortort remembered, "and I asked this sheriff what he would do if Dillinger came by. He stood up, strapped on two guns and said he'd be ready."

The lawman arranged for Dortort to hitch a ride with a trucker delivering potatoes to Los Angeles. "I was wearing a thin shirt, and it was freezing in the high desert, so I had to huddle under a blanket in the sleeping area of the truck."

In Los Angeles, Dortort helped the trucker unload the 100-pound sacks of potatoes before going to stay with an uncle in Hollywood. "My family had been to California when I was only about five years-old, so this was really my first time there."

Dortort eventually returned to college, becoming the editor of the school's literary magazine and graduating in 1936. Before he was thirty, he sold a novel entitled "Burial of the Fruit," based on the grim days of his youth. Though the book was a critical success, sales were unspectacular. Nevertheless, he managed to get the opportunity to adapt it for the screen, but the resultant script was judged too violent.

Undaunted, he went on to write screenplays for nearly two dozen feature films, including the Westerns "Reprisal" (1956), with Guy Madison (TV's Wild Bill Hickok) and Felicia Farr (a future Mrs. Ben Cartwright), and "The Big Land" (1957), with Alan Ladd.

Perhaps Dortort's best work was the screenplay he co-wrote with Horace McCoy for 1952's "The Lusty Men," a modern day Western starring Robert Mitchum. "Until that time," Dortort observed, "the only contemporary Western figures in pictures were Gene Autry and Roy Rogers, singing cowboys. But those films had nothing to do with real working people on ranches." Already his desire to put a fresh slant on the familiar was evident.

Dortort's idea for a western drama was stimulated by the story of John Sutter's sawmill and the 1848 gold strike in the Sacramento Valley. Dortort planted the Cartwrights, including Little Joe played by Michael Landon, there to begin their adventures. He said of Landon, "He's the most highly intuitive young actor I've ever seen."

Dortort also wrote prolifically for several early television anthology programs such as "Suspense," "Climax!" (which earned him an Emmy nomination for the 1954-55 season), "The 20th Century-Fox Hour" (a 1955-56 Emmy nominee for his adaptation of Walter Van Tilburg Clark's classic "The Ox-Bow Incident"), and, perhaps most significantly, NBC's "Fireside Theatre." For the latter, Dortort wrote a story entitled "The 36th Star," concerning Abraham Lincoln's efforts to make Nevada, then part of Utah territory, a state loyal to the Union, thereby achieving the three-fourths majority needed for a constitutional amendment to abolish slavery. This slice of history would later provide the plot for an episode of "Bonanza."

Dortort based the "Bonanza" "back story" on events concerning the historical figure, John Augustus Sutter, a colorful Swiss biologist and botanist who also happened to be a bankrupt merchant and self-appointed captain. Sutter migrated to the rich soil of California's Sacramento Valley in 1839, determined to plant breadfruit trees to help feed the world's growing population. He persuaded the Mexican governor of California to grant him 50,000 acres of land in a valley where the American and Sacramento rivers met. Here, Sutter built a stockade which became a gathering point for overland immigrants who had completed the exhausting trek across the Sierras. Among these weary but hopeful travelers was, Dortort imagined, a former seaman and his two young sons. Their names: Ben, Adam and Eric "Hoss" Cartwright.

But the Cartwrights were not destined to

15

The Cartwright homestead was nestled among the stately Ponderosa Pines of the Sierra Nevada mountains.

remain in the valley of the Sacramento for long. In 1848, Sutter's partner, James Wilson Marshall, discovered gold at the site of a sawmill the two had constructed, and the inevitable rush of prospectors was a disaster. The gold-hungry mob trampled several hundred acres of wheat Sutter had expected to yield up to 40,000 bushels, stole his livestock and eventually caused him to lose his property.

After his neighboring land was also ruined, Ben Cartwright decided to move up into the Sierra Nevada Mountains and build a stronghold no one would destroy. When he first saw the majestic Ponderosas (from the Latin word ponderosus, meaning weighty), pine trees which grow only 5,000 feet above sea level and reach a hundred feet or more to the sky, Ben knew immediately what he would call his personal empire.

In 1859, a decade after Ben and sons built the Ponderosa, Henry T.P. Comstock, a Canadian wanderer who had arrived in the Nevada territory

three years earlier, accidentally got caught up in the greatest single mineral strike in history. This discovery of 400 million-dollars worth of almost pure silver subsequently became known as the Comstock Lode–in essence, a bonanza–and led to the birth of Virginia City. It also formed the basis of a television classic.

"I was, of course, thrilled that NBC was going to allow me to create whatever I wanted," Dortort said. "The more I thought about the show, the more things fell into place. As an avid student of American history since my college days, I wanted to do something besides the gunfighter myth, which was only a very small portion of Western history. What about the real people who settled the West, who struggled with all the hardships? What about the women who had to give birth without a hospital or a doctor? I was interested in telling the whole pioneer story, the story of the people who sank their roots, who built their homes, who built their churches, who built their schools. What about them? And I decided to portray all of this by creating a mythical folk story, in a sense America's 'Camelot'. We have no history like that. We have the Revolutionary War, we have the Civil War, but where's the great idyllic legend? There isn't any. So, in a way, I created that. And all over the world, people picked up on it, because it's a story that's universal."

In addition to avoiding the traditional "gun-fighter myth" perpetuated by most Western series and films, Dortort wanted to bypass the typical dusty cow towns as often as possible, concentrating instead on what he called "the glories of the West–the lakes, the mountains, the breathtaking vistas, the cool clear air." He envisioned his brainchild as "a great living pageant" which would be shot on location at Lake Tahoe. And unlike any other network series, it would be filmed in color.

Dortort's proposals met with immediate opposition from NBC. While they were at least willing to consider using Lake Tahoe as a location on a limited basis, they turned thumbs down to shooting the series in color. The RCA warehouses filled with unsold color television sets had nothing to do with the network's business, he was told.

"NBC didn't care about RCA's color sales problem," recalled Dortort. "All that mattered to them was the additional cost of producing a show in color. They said it would be too high, that the lab processing took too long, that no one had enough experience to do it. I said, 'You're asking me to go up to the Sierra Nevadas, one of the most beautiful spots in the country, with the snow-capped mountains, the magnificent lake, the evergreen forest, the bluest of skies–and shoot all this in black-and-white? It's sacrilegious. I won't do it. You've got to shoot it in color.' And they said, 'We can't, there's no way.' So I told them to forget about the show. I just couldn't do it. Their attitude didn't make any sense."

Fortunately, the network finally agreed to do it Dortort's way, but not before he offered to participate financially in what was essentially a gamble. Five years earlier, when NBC became the first network to broadcast color signals, only one percent of the homes in America were capable of receiving them, and that number had not increased as rapidly as RCA had anticipated. Color programming was a desperately needed commodity, and

Dortort knew it if no one at NBC did. Seven years later, programming on all three major networks was in color.

There was one more corporate obstacle for Dortort to surmount: NBC rejected his idea to cast relatively unknown actors in the leading roles. That, the network argued, was certainly no way to attract an audience, especially when a large viewership was required to justify the show's being in color. "Television makes its own stars," Dortort countered, rightfully so. Apparently NBC had overlooked current luminaries such as Jackie Gleason, Lucille Ball, James Arness and countless others who were but minor actors before coming to television. "I told the network I knew my people, I had written the parts with them in mind," said Dortort. "If Marlon Brando, who was then at his peak, would do the show, I'd change my mind. Otherwise, either go with my four guys, or let's forget the whole idea."

Again, NBC went along with the stubborn producer, whose instincts resulted in one of television's most memorable ensembles.

The network was pushing to get the show into production as quickly as possible for the Fall 1959 season, leaving Dortort precious little time to write

Much of the series, especially the interior scenes, was shot at Paramount Studios in Hollywood. This photo was taken at the studio in 1967.

a script for the pilot. By day he would work on the remaining episodes of "The Restless Gun" at Universal, then spend the evening writing the first segment of "Bonanza" in the office of an NBC vice-president, Fenton Coe, assisted by Coe's secretary, Joan Sherman.

The production facility Dortort requested was Paramount Studios, the only major studio still located in Hollywood proper. It also housed the only two-story Western set not resembling a generic cow town, which is what primarily attracted Dortort. This set, which "Bonanza" used for Virginia City through the 1969-70 season, was eventually seen in episodes of "Gunsmoke," "Have Gun-Will Travel," "Mannix" and most of the films made with aging Western veterans by producer A.C. Lyles in the mid-to-late-Sixties. It was also used for "The Trap," a crime drama Lorne Greene appeared in shortly before "Bonanza." When Michael Landon utilized it for several episodes of "Little House On the Prairie" in the late Seventies, the set had obviously become rather shabby. By 1979, twenty years after "the debut of "Bonanza," it had been demolished. Spared by the wrecking ball was the barn in which Cecil B. DeMille filmed "The Squaw Man" (1914), the first feature film to be made entirely in Hollywood. On "Bonanza" it was seen infrequently as the freight station. Paramount donated the structure to Hollywood Heritage, Inc., which used it as the Hollywood Studio Museum.

Unlike Universal and Warner Bros., Paramount in 1959 was not very involved with television or outside production companies. Consequently, NBC paid dearly for rental of the lot, which included not only the Western town but Stages 16 and 17 as well. It was on these soundstages that the interior sets for "Bonanza," including the Ponderosa, were constructed after being designed by Paramount's Hal Pereira, Earl Hedrick ("Bonanza's" art director and artist of one of the world's most famous–though geographically incorrect–maps) and David Dortort. Decoration of the sets for most of the show's run fell to Grace Gregory, who kept them in a perpetual state of flux by bringing in pieces from antique shops and flea markets.

Although credit was given to veteran Hollywood makeup artist Wally Westmore during the

The Virginia City set at Paramount Studios was used occasionally between 1974 and 1978 by Michael Landon's biggest post-"Bonanza" success, "Little House on the Prairie."

"Bonanza" days at Paramount, development of makeup which would photograph correctly for color television actually fell to his brother, Frank. Wally, who wanted nothing to do with television, made Frank work in what was little more than a shack located far from Paramount's makeup department. Even after the makeup was perfected to the point where red would not photograph as orange or purple, for example, there were problems due to the intensity of the arc lamps used to illuminate the interior sets. The heat was ruining makeup, wardrobe, and reducing the shooting schedule from seven or eight pages per day to as little as two. Clearly, a solution had to be found.

"Alex Quiroga, who worked for Fenton Coe and had been trained as a color technician in the wonderful color labs of Berlin, had a meter to mea-

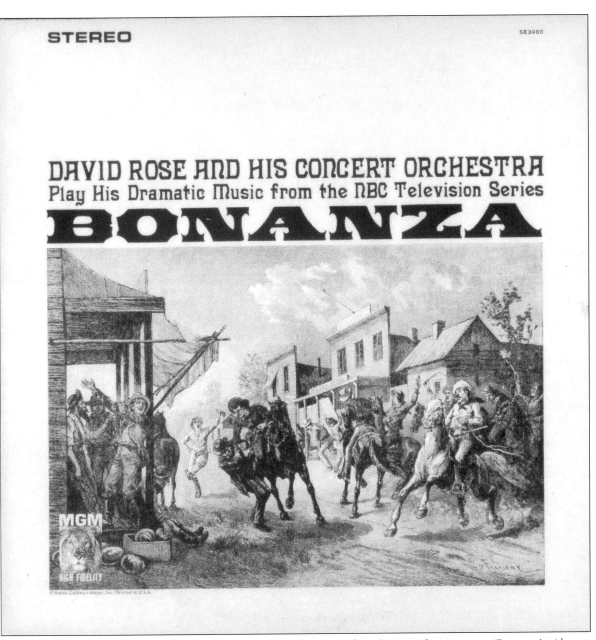

STEREO

DAVID ROSE AND HIS CONCERT ORCHESTRA
Play His Dramatic Music from the NBC Television Series
BONANZA

MGM
HIGH FIDELITY

"For quite some time, I have been wanting to record an album of my music from the NBC television series, 'Bonanza,' said orchestra leader, David Rose. "I checked with MGM Records and received the go-ahead, and then I got the blessings of David Dortort. I knew that over a period of two years and some sixty shows, enough basic music material existed to make several albums; however, some of the themes were underdeveloped, having been written for short scenes. I thought it would be easy to select material suitable for commercial recordings and to develop those themes which required completion. How wrong I was! Making the right choice of basic material turned out to be a time-consuming job. I finally selected eleven themes I had composed for various 'Bonanza' television shows, plus the title song which was written by Jay Livingston and Ray Evans. I spent the better part of two months developing my own compositions; then, I got to work orchestrating all twelve completed tunes."

sure arc lighting," Dortort recalled. "I suggested to him that we try gradually reducing the number of arcs from ten to two. Paramount was indignant, didn't want us to do it. They said we might as well shoot in black-and-white, which only requires one arc. I told them, 'Fine, we'll go elsewhere.' But I had the crew behind me all the way, so the studio relented, and we were able to make the actors more comfortable and our entire operation more productive. As a result of our experimentation, Eastman Kodak was able to develop a faster type of color film."

In 1970 Capitol Records released this album, containing music from two Dortort projects.

Although proud of what he has called his "tight crew of marvelous professionals", Dortort differed from most executive producers by becoming closely involved in nearly every aspect of "Bonanza." Not only did this extend to helping solve various location, technical and story perplexities, he took an active hand in the areas of casting, wardrobe and, notably, music.

Alan Livingston, vice president in charge of NBC's television programming during the preparation of "Bonanza," also happened to be the brother of Jay Livingston, who along with Ray Evans had composed several classic songs, including "Silver Bells," "To Each His Own," "Golden Earrings" and a trio of Best Song Oscar winners: "Mona Lisa," "Que Sera, Sera" and "Buttons and Bows." In short, Alan wondered if maybe Jay and his partner would be interested in taking a stab at writing the theme song for the network's new Western. Though they were not given many suggestions as to the exact nature of the show, Livingston and Evans said they would give it a shot if they could publish the song themselves. NBC agreed, and royalties from the theme eventually made the the songwriting team's upfront fee of $1500 look like pocket change. Of the many recorded versions, the most well-known are probably the instrumental by guitarist Al Caiola (1961) and vocal renditions by Johnny Cash (1963) and Lorne Greene (1964).

Dortort did not think much of the lyrics, which were not heard publicly for more than four years, but approved the use of the music as long as veteran musician David Rose could score each episode without having to incorporate the Livingston-Evans theme. Rose, who passed away in August of 1990 at the age of 80, was an award winning composer and conductor who will no doubt be best remembered for penning the camp classic "The Stripper." Beyond that, he was Red Skelton's longtime musical director, wrote the hit "Holiday For Strings," and won Emmy awards for a Fred Astaire special, "Bonanza" and two for "Little House On the Prairie." He also composed the themes for Dortort's "The High Chaparral" (first used in an episode of "Bonanza"), Landon's "Father Murphy" and "Highway To Heaven," as well as two short-lived Western series on other networks, "Dundee and the Culhane" and "The Monroes."

In a highly unusual move, Rose not only wrote original scores for each individual "Bonanza" episode, he used an orchestra of over thirty pieces to record them. Needless to say, the overall effect was nothing short of cinematic, contributing to the show's reputation as a movie for television before the concept even existed. Years later, Michael Landon, who used Rose on all of his projects, called the man "a genius" with an uncanny

20

knack for knowing precisely how a scene needed to be scored.

In 1961, Rose "spent the better part of two months" selecting music for a "Bonanza" soundtrack released on the MGM label. Among the twelve cuts was "Ponderosa," a wistful tune almost as recognizable as the show's famous theme, as it appeared in every episode for most of the series' run. Shortly after the album was released, Rose revealed that he considered "Bonanza" "the best thing I've done musically." Sadly, there was never another Rose soundtrack despite the abundance of exceptional fresh material added over the years, including a stirring new theme called "The Big Bonanza" used during the twelfth and thirteenth seasons.

In addition to David Rose, "Bonanza" benefited from the musical skills of such talents as Harry Sukman, who scored "The High Chaparral" and a later Dortort series, "The Cowboys," and William Lava, whose credits included numerous B Westerns and the theme for the series "Cheyenne." Fred Steiner, "Star Trek's" main composer, also made contributions.

Interestingly, none of these gentlemen had anything to do with the music heard in the "Bonanza" pilot. To save on the production costs of an unknown quantity, NBC had the soundtrack of the first episode recorded in Germany, a practice not uncommon in television during that period. However, back in the States, some guitar accompaniment was added by Joe Maphis, a session musician whose picking can also be heard in "The Deputy "and" Riverboat," two other Westerns that debuted in 1959, and the film "God's Little Acre," featuring a young Michael Landon.

Due to his close association with Hollywood's writing community, David Dortort was gradually able to recruit a wide assortment of scribes, some of whom had never before written for television, and he was not adverse to giving many novice writers their first (and sometimes only) break. Serious followers of the medium will no doubt recognize the names of Gene L. Coon, Ward Hawkins, Cy Chermak, B.W. Sandefur and Robert Pirosh, to name only a very few. And Western enthusiasts know well such old hands as Borden Chase, Clair Huffaker, Harold Shumate and the prolific Thomas Thompson.

In its fourteen seasons, "Bonanza" employed more than seventy-five directors whose careers ranged from Hollywood's past (Christian Nyby, Joseph Kane, Lewis Allen, William Witney, Jacques Tourneur, Tay Garnett, Paul Henreid), through reliable television stalwarts (Bernard McEveety, Joseph Sargent, Leo Penn, Harry Harris and Alf Kjellin) to Hollywood's future (Robert Altman, Michael Landon).

To this day there are loyal viewers who assume that all exteriors for "Bonanza" were filmed at Lake Tahoe's Incline Village. In reality, the majority of location work was done at numerous sites in California, including such famous Western settings as Vasquez Rocks, Bronson Canyon, Lone Pine, Red Rock Canyon, Iverson's Movie Location Ranch, Corriganville, Big Sky Ranch, Death Valley, Golden Oak Ranch and Simi Valley.

Incline Village, located on the northeast corner of Lake Tahoe, was named for the inclined sluice and railroad which carried timber over the mountains to Virginia City's silver mines. In 1959, the same year "Bonanza" began production, some Oklahoma investors started an expensive residential development in the area. Consequently, possibilities for location filming grew more restrictive as the years progressed, necessitating a search for similar looking surroundings in California. Often mistaken for Incline Village are Inyo National Forest, Cedar Lake, Toiyabe National Forest, Big Bear, Los Padres National Forest, Franklin Lake, Stanislaus National Forest and, after "Bonanza" moved from Paramount, the pine-dotted backlot of the Burbank Studios.

And supervising virtually every facet of this ground-breaking television monument, no matter where the location, was a pioneer named David "The Guide" Dortort. After the show was cancelled, one reporter remarked that Dortort had "clucked over 'Bonanza' like a mother hen." While that was true enough, a more appropriate analogy was made in 1965 by writer Dwight Whitney: "Because he enjoys that rarest of all TV commodities, autonomy, his show represents the taste, judgement and creative ability of one man. It is not too much to say that 'Bonanza' is David Dortort, right down to the last psychological nuance."

21

"They can handle anything," David Dortort told *TV Guide* in late 1959. "Comedy, drama, action, anything. I think the results are going to be sensational."

"They" were the four fairly unknown actors Dortort had personally cast in the lead roles of "Bonanza," prevailing over NBC's insistence that he use more familiar faces. And he was right: "The Boys", as he came to refer to them, displayed an admirably wide range of thespian skills, and yes, the results were sensational.

"I purposely developed the show to have more than one star," Dortort disclosed later. "I wanted to free myself from being totally dependent on one actor and his whims, as I had been with John Payne during 'The Restless Gun.'" The producer also confessed that he had based each character on a different aspect of his own personality.

Although not yet household names, the four Cartwrights had between them made guest appearances on several prime time shows, including nearly every major Western series, and each had a certain measure of stage experience.

Ben

History of a sort was made when Dortort gave the role of the Ponderosa patriarch, whom he had named after his own father, to Canadian actor Lorne Greene. Long before "Bonanza" left the air, the character of Ben Cartwright had become the most well-known and respected father figure on television, and Greene was even voted Father of the Year in 1965.

Choosing the right actor to portray Ben was crucial to Dortort's intention to "reinstate" the father as an authority figure on television after years of being reduced to "a boob" on domestic situation comedies. "Ben Cartwright as played by Lorne Greene is *not* a congenital idiot," Dortort declared. "He is not led around by the nose by anybody."

Greene, the son of a Russian-Jewish immigrant who made orthopedic boots and shoes, was born in Ottawa, Ontario, on February 12, 1915, and

Publicity shot for the 1964-65 season

CHAPTER TWO

The Cast

The Cartwrights in 1961.

named for his father's first customer.

"I don't know whether I could match my father as a person," Greene once revealed, "but as an actor I try to be like him." He said he based seventy five percent of Ben Cartwright on his father. "He never spanked. Just gave me one of those looks." And when one of Greene's television sons would act up: "I'd give him the same look."

BONANZA

Greene's father, Daniel, died in 1956, three years before "Bonanza." "But he will always be alive somewhere when the show is aired," Greene said.

Both his father and mother had an interest in the theater, and it was in high school that Greene first gave acting a try, encouraged by a teacher impressed with his "big voice". He played one of two deaf characters who spent the performance shouting at each other. "I kind of dug it," he recalled in a 1964 interview. "It was a big hit and we got tremendous applause."

He entered Queens University in Toronto to study chemical engineering at his father's request, but could not shake the acting bug. After serving as an actor and director in the school's drama guild, he won a fellowship to New York's prestigious Neighborhood Playhouse where he had the opportunity to study under the highly regarded Sanford Meisner for two years. Upon returning to Canada, the only job he could land was that of a program supervisor at an advertising agency at a lowly salary of ten dollars a week. There was a dearth of professional theater in Canada, but Greene was eventually able to find the next best thing: radio. He became an announcer with the Canadian Broadcasting Corporation and, thanks to his deep, richly textured tone, was soon known as "The Voice of Canada". One critic described that voice as "surely one of the finest ever wrought by nature." It is little wonder, then, that Greene was asked to do voice-overs for several episodes of "Bonanza," recorded a half dozen albums, and narrated numerous television specials throughout his career. Shortly after John F. Kennedy was assassinated, Greene was given the honor of presiding over a televised tribute to the late president.

During the Second World War, Greene, in addition to participating in programs broadcast to Nazi-occupied countries, served as a flying officer in the Royal Canadian Air Force.

Following the war, Greene, by then a married father of twins, resumed his radio work, both in Canada and the United States. He cofounded the Jupiter Theatre in Toronto, opened the Academy of Radio Arts, and became the only Canadian to win a broadcasting award from NBC.

Greene invented a watch which ran in reverse, enabling announcers to determine how much time remained in a broadcast, and went to New York to market his device. While there, producer Fletcher Markle offered him the role of Big Brother in a presentation of "1984" on "Studio One," a CBS television anthology. Greene accepted and was rewarded with excellent reviews. Jack Gould of the New York Times called his performance "superb, alternately friendly, understanding and deadly sinister."

More work on television led to major roles in three Broadway plays, including the lead in "The Prescott Proposals," and appearances at the Stratford Shakespeare Festival in Canada.

Actors with Lorne Greene's ability do not always come to Hollywood's attention, and even when they do, not all of them fare especially well. In Greene's case, Hollywood became, as he once put it, "the hand that feeds me." Beginning in 1954, he appeared in films with such stars as Paul Newman ("The Silver Chalice"), Edward G. Robinson ("Tight Spot"), Joan Crawford ("Autumn Leaves"), Lana Turner ("Peyton Place"), Charlton Heston ("The Buccaneer"), Lauren Bacall ("The Gift of Love"), and Lee J. Cobb ("The Trap"). He was also cast in two Westerns, "The Hard Man" (1957) with Guy Madison, and "The Last of the Fast Guns" (1958) with Jock Mahoney, Gilbert Roland and Linda Cristal. Roland and Cristal would later be among the hundreds of actors who guest starred on "Bonanza."

In Canada, Greene starred as a sea captain in a short-lived series called "Sailor of Fortune," and a widower with three sons in "The Vivian Carter Story," an episode of "Wagon Train." Ironically, David Dortort was seeking an actor who was both a former sailor *and* a widower with three sons. By further coincidence, "Wagon Train" and "The Restless Gun" were filmed on the same lot, and Dortort chanced to observe Greene holding his own in an argument with the blustery star of "Wagon Train," Ward Bond. As Dortort recalled, dominating Bond was not an easy task, but "Lorne not only dominated Bond, he made him look, by contrast, a weak, indecisive man." Regrettably, Greene and Bond shared no scenes in the episode.

Lorne Greene in 1966.

BONANZA

Had Greene valued money over exposure, he would not have been on the Universal lot that day. Earlier, he had been given a choice of doing either a segment of "Omnibus" for $4,000 or "Wagon Train" for $1,000. Although his agent thought he was crazy, Greene opted for the latter, reasoning that his being seen on what was then the Number Two show in the country would lead to more opportunities.

Three days after first seeing him, Dortort ran into Greene at a party. The producer said to his wife, Rose, "I think I've found my Ben Cartwright." In 1978, Greene told reporter Frank Swertlow that he was first approached about doing a series by an NBC lawyer who had seen "The Vivian Carter Story" before it aired. "I told him yes," recalled Greene, "but on three conditions: It had to be successful, I had to be the star and I had to make a lot of money." Obviously, there was no way to guarantee "Bonanza" would be successful

and make Greene a wealthy man, but he could have one of the four leading roles. While Greene had no objection to sharing the spotlight with three equals, he did have some reservations about his part.

In 1988, actor/director Lawrence Dobkin told author Allan Asherman of a conversation he and Greene had shortly before "Bonanza" began production: "He said, 'Next week I'm supposed to be testing to play the father of three grown men in some western...' and I asked who the producer was, and I said, 'That's all you have to go on. If the producer has some presence, and can be depended on to exercise taste and judgement, and this man can, then have a shot at it.' At the time they made the initial test, Lorne was probably between 45 and 50, and he was worried about whether or not he could photograph old enough to make the audience believe he was the father of those kids. That would have meant he fathered those kids when he

This RCA Victor record presented the Cartwright family at a surprise birthday party for Ben. With singing, fiddling, banjo picking and guitar strumming, the four "Bonanza" stars entertain with many musical favorites.

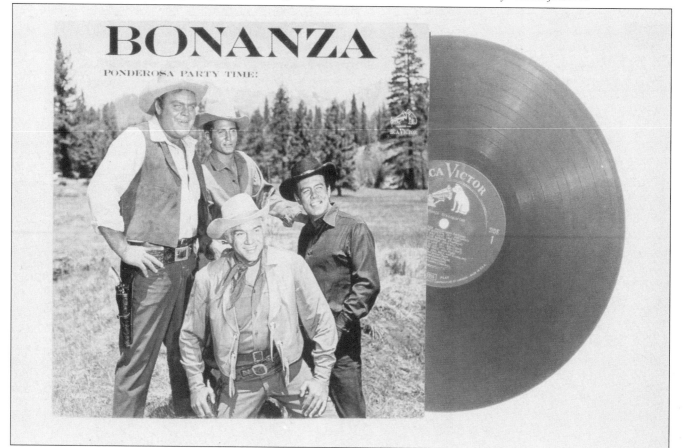

was between 18 and 25, which is reasonable."

Dobkin was not far off, as Greene had just turned 44, and it was certainly true that David Dortort's choice for Ben Cartwright was an example of perfect casting. What is *not* true is the belief still held by many viewers that Greene was first offered the role of the oldest son and turned it down. After filming an episode of "Cheyenne," Lorne Greene became Ben Cartwright.

Creatively, Greene was attracted to "Bonanza" because, as he explained during the show's early years, "it was a love story of four men. A true story of mankind. It showed the difference between good and bad." More than a decade after the series ended, he remarked: "'Bonanza' was an Eastern Western because we weren't cowboys roaming, but settled. It was a show about love—-of the land, of family, of one's country."

The role of Ben Cartwright fit Lorne Greene like a proverbial glove. As Greene himself declared in 1963, "I know Ben Cartwright inside and out." David Dortort was justifiably lavish in his praise, calling Greene "the perfect 'Bonanza' image." And in early 1961, as the show was concluding its second season, writer Dwight Whitney said Greene "is perhaps the most exciting and certainly most convincing 'father' ever to appear in regular series TV."

The other cast members, particularly Michael Landon, came to regard Greene as something of a father figure off-camera as well. "I've seen it happen time and time again," one of the show's technicians told a visitor to the set. "Without thinking, they'll seek Lorne's advice."

"I never stopped seeing Lorne as my dad," Landon admitted shortly after Greene's death. "Lorne was a solid pillar for both me and Dan Blocker. I'd known him for more than half my life, and he'd been my father for fourteen years on 'Bonanza.' You just don't quit being a son or a father. I'll always consider him my Pa."

Millions never stopped seeing Greene as Ben Cartwright, a notion he did little to discourage. In addition to making numerous personal appearances dressed in his television costume, Greene started his nightclub performances as Ben, not Lorne. Interviewed in 1965 during an engagement at the Nugget, a "family-type club" in East Reno, Nevada, Greene said, "When they come to see me,

"I never stopped seeing Lorne as my dad," Landon admitted shortly after Greene's death. "Lorne was a solid pillar for both me and Dan Blocker," (This photo was shot at Lake Tahoe for "Showdown at Tahoe" in 1967.)

they expect to see me as they do on TV. So I allow them to, then transform myself subtly." Several years after "Bonanza," he did a walk-on for an episode of "Happy Days" in his old Ben Cartwright garb, and his first scene when guesting on "The Hardy Boys" was accompanied by a brief but obvious musical reference to the "Bonanza" theme.

Greene did only one dramatic project outside "Bonanza" while the show was still in production, playing a Russian agent in "Destiny of a Spy," a 1969 made-for-TV movie. Critic Judith Crist accurately pegged it as "just another collection of cliches."

"It was the best and the worst thing that ever happened to him," Greene's manager, Charlotte Dial, said of her client's inseparable link with his most famous role. "It was very difficult for Lorne

27

to break out of that mold."

Greene's only public complaint was against the hearing aid he was forced to wear in later life. "I think the hearing loss started with 'Bonanza,'" he reflected in 1985. "Sometimes the director would put us in a box canyon and have us fire our guns. The sound would really reverberate in a box canyon."

That aside, Greene was grateful for his fourteen years as Ben Cartwright. "What 'Bonanza' has given me is freedom without fear," he told reporters after NBC announced the show's cancellation. "Actually, I never was fearful. I gave up a $70,000-a-year job as a newscaster to go into acting. But today I have a firm financial base to work from. I can only wish it for every actor."

An astute businessman, Greene made several lucrative investments–including some with Dan Blocker and Michael Landon–and for his second wife and their daughter was able to maintain homes in Los Angeles, Lake Tahoe and Mesa, Arizona, the latter a replica of the Ponderosa ranch house. At the same time, he was also a generous and socially conscious individual who devoted both time and money to the causes he believed in, including an Indian scholarship fund which was also supported by Greene's one-time oldest TV son, Pernell Roberts.

Greene and his second wife, Nancy, whom he married in 1961. She's holding their daughter, Gillian.

Left: As Col. Adama in "Galactica 1980" Green offers advice to young Barry VanDyke.
Right: Greene was Detective Wade Griffin in the short-lived "Griff," (1973-74).

Adam

It is strictly a matter of personal opinion, but some viewers continue to argue whether Lorne Greene or Pernell Roberts was the best actor of the "Bonanza" cast. The debate would doubtlessly be of absolutely no interest to Roberts, who always considered the show beneath his dignity as an actor, and questioned the "psychological motives" of people who developed a fanatical devotion to actors. He was courteous if he encountered admirers on a one-to-one basis, but mass adulation struck him as totally bizarre behavior, especially when it was inspired by "pap" like "Bonanza."

The part of Adam Cartwright, Ben's eldest son and the family intellectual, was the hardest to cast because, according to David Dortort, "it was the least appealing of the four roles. He was to be the independent-minded one of the quartet."

In that respect, Pernell Roberts was ideal for Adam. Critical of scripts, seldom inclined to socialize with the cast and crew between takes, and unwilling to make any personal appearances in connection with the show after the first season, he became known as the "dark presence" of "Bonanza," a characterization to which he remained completely indifferent. Tales of Roberts' difficulties relating to the other Cartwrights (mainly with Michael Landon) have been exaggerated, but it is true he often kept to himself when the cameras were not rolling.

Born the son of a Dr. Pepper distributor in Waycross, Georgia, in either 1928 or 1930

(depending on which source one consults), Roberts was, by his own admission, an undisciplined loner resentful of authority. He was still in his early teens when, disgusted by the hypocrisy of organized religion, he became a proponent for civil rights. "The preachers talked of the brotherhood of man," Roberts said in a rare 1964 interview, "and yet there were no Negroes allowed in our white church; and the Baptists, Methodists and Lutherans all kept apart from each other, too, and worshiped separately. What kind of brotherhood was that?" He realized he was risking both his career and his life by demonstrating against discrimination while "Bonanza" was at the peak of its popularity, but, predictably, did not care. The show and its sponsor, Chevrolet, were deluged with hate mail, most of it from Roberts' own Deep South. David Dortort, who shared Roberts' views, said, "I can only tell him what to do on a show. What he does off the show is his business."

Following high school, Roberts enrolled at Georgia Tech to study engineering. Bored by the subject and feeling restricted by the college regimen, he joined the Marine Corps in 1946. It was there, not in school, that he began cultivating a lifelong interest in philosophy and psychology, mostly as a result of discussions with men who had been prisoners of the Japanese. Years later, a member of the "Bonanza" crew quipped, "Pernell thinks too much." Nevertheless, Roberts had to be admired for sustaining his beliefs, especially in an environment like Hollywood, for which he did not have much respect. "I could understand him better if he were planning to stop being an actor," an exasperated Dortort said shortly before Roberts left the show. "But he isn't."

After two more failed attempts at college–both at the University of Maryland–Roberts took up acting to combat loneliness and meet people. While on the traditional "starving young actor" route, knocking on agency doors and going to auditions, he labored as a welder, butcher and forest ranger. Fortunately, he was also able to find some work in his chosen profession. In Washington, D.C., Roberts met his first wife, technical director of the Arena Stage, with whom he had his only child, a son.

Between 1952 and 1957, Roberts tried making a go of it in New York, and though he was cast in

only four Broadway plays, he did win a Drama Desk Award as the best off-Broadway actor of 1955 for his performance in "Macbeth." While appearing with Joanne Woodward in "The Lovers," he caught the attention of some Paramount talent scouts who offered him a supporting role in the film adaptation of Eugene O'Neill's "Desire Under the Elms."

Roberts moved to Hollywood in 1957 to make the film, which also starred Sophia Loren, Anthony Perkins and Burl Ives, and by the time it was released he had landed guest parts on such series as "Gunsmoke," "Have Gun–Will Travel" and "Cimarron City," the latter featuring a regular named Dan Blocker. In early 1959, he co-starred with Randolph Scott and no less than half a dozen future "Bonanza" guest stars (including James Coburn and Lee Marvin) in the exceptional Western, "Ride Lonesome," in which Roberts more than held his own.

One of those suitably impressed was David Dortort, who had also seen some of Roberts' other work and felt the actor possessed a quality necessary for being the "spoilsport" of the Ponderosa. What Dortort could not have predicted was Roberts' tendency to be the killjoy of the production as well.

"I had difficulties with Pernell right from the beginning," remembered Dortort. "On the second day of shooting, he came to my office and said he didn't want to wear his hairpiece. I didn't even know he was bald, and bald he looked fifteen years older. 'Wait a minute,' I said. 'When you and I shook hands on the deal, you had that on. You're going to keep it on as long as you're on the show.' And all through the years he'd ask me why he had to wear it. 'Because that's the basis on which I hired you,' I'd remind him. 'You can't take it off.'"

Dortort, one of the few producers who actually liked actors, believed it was essential for his cast to be involved in the show's progress and listened patiently to their various complaints. But in comparison with the others, Dortort at the time said, "Pernell is more aloof, rebellious, outspoken and analytical, a bit of his own man with his own ideas. I don't always agree. But I think his sounding off is good for his performance and for the show generally. So I say more power to him."

Roberts did not dispute his producer's views.

"We have honest fights. We all jump on David together. I speak my mind. I sound off. I'm always asking why. Maybe it's one of my failings as a human being."

As the second season got underway, he spouted: "'Bonanza' could be really good if the powers-that-be cared enough to make it that way. Everything in television is that monster, compromise. Nobody really cares. There isn't time."

"Pernell considers producers the enemy," said Lorne Greene. "I don't. I consider them sometimes to act in bad faith and bad taste, and I'll have it out with them–but usually to try to reach some kind of resolution. Pernell's way is to fight like hell and kick 'em in the balls."

Roberts lobbied for less sentiment and family togetherness, taking "a dim view" of Dortort's tendency to insist on stories written for all four characters. "I feel as if I'm playing one-fourth of a character. We need time to develop individuality in the given situation. As far as I'm concerned, the only question is: is an actor good or isn't he? After all, it's his face hanging out there."

"I can't disagree with Pernell," Greene reacted. "But I still feel that in the family kind of story, your own individuality should–and does–come through."

Roberts also felt the show needed an extra day for rehearsal "to learn a little bit about the material and about each other. Let's scream and shout at each other, but let's do it within the four walls of a room. Good things would come out of it." He may well have had a valid point, but the show, especially in the early years, often struggled to remain on schedule and within budget. Rehearsal time was an unaffordable luxury.

Regardless of how much the show improved during his six seasons as Adam Cartwright, it was never good enough to suit Roberts. At one point he even got Dortort to agree that he only had to call Ben "Pa" once or twice an episode. When asked why he was always so critical of the show, he claimed he had been misled: "It soon became evident to me that this wasn't what I had understood it to be. People can't appreciate what you mean when you talk about artistic integrity–we're taught to judge everything on the basis of economics. I would like to have approval of what I do. What we do here is just pap."

BONANZA

The Cartwrights were depicted more often than not as generous, socially responsible neighbors and citizens, yet Roberts was uncomfortable playing the member of a wealthy family. Nor was he happy about the way he said women characters were objectified. And then there was, he contended, the show's tendency to solve problems with violence rather than reason, though "Bonanza" relied less on gunplay than the majority of Westerns on the air.

Eventually, Roberts arrived at the conclusion that "Bonanza" did not, and never would, offer any challenges worthy of his acting ability. He told the press, in an oft-repeated quote, "Give the silly asses half of what the scene requires, and they think it's great."

In contrast, Lorne Greene commented: "If you accept a job here in Hollywood–in fact, if you accept any kind of job anywhere and accept money for doing it–you ought to have the good grace to do the very best you can and try to respect the work you are doing. To do less, I feel, is to demean yourself."

Needless to say, NBC was only too glad to grant Roberts' request to be interviewed less, and left the promotional duties to Greene and the others. As far as Dortort was concerned, "Pernell seems to have a hate on for Hollywood. I sometimes wonder whether he really belongs in the acting business. A very good actor, yes, but his performances tend to be erratic. An actor may not be enthralled with a part, but it is his responsibility always to do his best."

Pernell Roberts left "Bonanza" with hopes of joining a highly respected repertory group in Minneapolis. When that did not work out, he found himself back in Los Angeles and on horseback in such shows as "The Big Valley", "Gunsmoke," and "The Virginian." Despite his accusation in a 1978 interview that "the studios launched a campaign of vilification against me and it has never stopped", Roberts appeared in numerous made-for-TV movies (including "Desperado" with Dirk Blocker, though they shared no scenes) and series ranging from "The Odd Couple" and "The Six Million Dollar Man" to "Mission: Impossible," "Mannix," "The Rockford Files" and several others. In later years, he was reunited with Lorne Greene for an episode of "Vegas."

The January 18, 1964 issue of TV Guide *announced a bride for Adam. "Will pretty little Katie Brown bring peace and tranquility to the Ponderosa?" it asked. Actually, the wedding was a way to remove Roberts from the show at his request. TV Guide said, "David Dortort, the show's producer, is carefully assessing public reaction to the encounter before proceeding with any more scripts." Fans objected and Adam remained single.*

The Fall 1979 season found Roberts back in a series of his own (for financial security, he admitted), "Trapper John, M.D.," which ran for seven years and snared him his only Emmy nomination to date. Those who are under the impression that Roberts and Michael Landon had no use for one another may be interested to learn that when

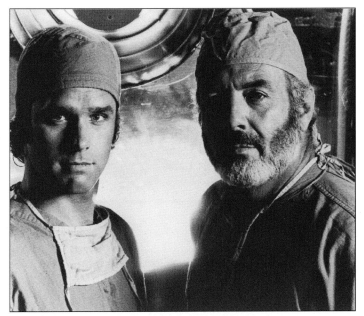

Roberts with Gregory Harrison (left) in "Trapper John, M.D." (1979-86). The role earned Roberts an Emmy nomination for 1980-81.

Roberts with Peter Graves in the background in an episode of "Mission Impossible."

Landon shot portions of a "Little House" episode on the 20th Century-Fox lot, where "Trapper John, M.D." was produced, he and Roberts took advantage of the opportunity to talk over old times. And according to E. Helene Sage, a former stunt rider, Roberts even stopped by the Incline Village location to say hello to his former co-stars during one of the final seasons of "Bonanza."

Today Pernell Roberts, the only surviving Cartwright, is semi-retired. His last Western was an episode of "The Young Riders," and he was seen most recently in a sequel to his 1973 "Mannix" appearance on "Diagnosis Murder" with Dick Van Dyke, Mike Connors and one-time "Bonanza" guest Julie Adams.

Off the set, Roberts had a reputation of being a loner, preferring to ride the countryside in solitude. This photo is from a 1964 issue of TV People.

33

Hoss

For David Dortort there was never any question who would fill the considerable boots of Ben Cartwright's second son, Hoss. "I created the part specifically for him. He was the only actor I ever had in mind."

"He" was Dan Blocker, a six-foot-four Texan who would portray one of the most beloved and memorable characters in the history of television for thirteen seasons. In a recent article, Mike Flanagan of the Chicago *Tribune* called him "big and humorous, perhaps television's most unlikely scene-stealer." Sometimes weighing as much as 350 pounds, Blocker could not help being the focal point of nearly every scene in which he appeared, but his ability to command attention so effortlessly went beyond his physical size. As Dortort has said, Blocker was also gifted with "enormous talent and humanity."

The conventional description of Hoss Cartwright as a naive soul with an appetite to match his size and strength has invited unfair and inaccurate comparisons to the mentally deficient and occasionally violent Lennie in John Steinbeck's "Of Mice and Men." Hoss is neither dull-witted nor brutal. The cliche "gentle giant" is appropriate, yet does not go far enough. More to the point, Hoss is as good natured and trusting as everyone ought to be, a student of life rather than books, and blessed with a capacity for love and forgiveness so large that he truly is a giant among his fellow mortals. It is not an exaggeration to call Hoss the most colorful cowboy to ever grace a television Western, with apologies to Chester Goode, Festus Haggen, Wishbone and Charlie Wooster.

Blocker saw his character as a simple, uncomplicated man of great compassion and kindness. "Such a man must be played accordingly," he told a reporter in 1966. "I see him epitomized in Stephen Grellet's prayer that we shall pass through this world but once, and if there be any kindness we can show or good thing we can do, let us do it now, since we won't pass this way again. That's Hoss all the way. And he has to be interpreted that way. To play him with all the drama stops out would be absurd. Who do my critics think Hoss is—King Lear?"

Regarding Dan Blocker, Dortort said: "The man

Unlike Hoss, Dan Blocker had a master's degree in drama. He was particularly fond of Shakespeare.

had range. I saw in him a great tenderness and sensibilities. Perhaps another Wallace Beery. I remember he was all ready, after the short run of 'Cimarron City,' to quit acting and go back to teaching school. I told him to stick around. He did."

The misconception exists that Blocker had virtually no experience when he was hired for "Bonanza," but it is far from true. He came to Hollywood in 1956 with a Master's degree in drama, intending to work on his doctorate at UCLA while holding down a teaching job at

Glendale High School. What really interested him, however, was getting work in television, and he had no trouble landing the role of an army lieutenant in "Alarm at Pleasant Valley," the last episode during the first season of "Gunsmoke." During the next few years he appeared on such shows as "Richard Diamond," "Maverick," "The Rifleman," "Jefferson Drum," "The Rebel" and even in a Three Stooges short. Blocker's sensitive portrayal of a deaf-mute on "The Restless Gun" affected Dortort to the extent of recommending him for a regular part on "Cimarron City." Dortort also made a mental note to keep the imposing actor in mind for future projects of his own.

"Cimarron City," starring George Montgomery (a future guest on "Bonanza"), premiered in October 1958, with Blocker playing a townsman named Tiny Budinger. The series lasted for only twenty-six episodes, and after it was cancelled by NBC, he decided to abandon show business.

"He was very discouraged," Dortort recalled. "He and his family were living in a motel, all set to pack up and leave. 'Wait a minute,' I told him. 'I'm getting ready to do a new series with a part I've written expressly for you.' When he thanked me he literally had tears in his eyes. Over the years, he gave me the least amount of trouble. We were actually a lot alike."

Dan, the son of Shack and Mary Blocker, was born in either 1929 or 1932. Sources vary, but no matter what the year, it is a fact that at fourteen pounds, he was the largest baby on record in Bowie County, Texas. When the Depression worsened, Shack, who was a farmer and blacksmith, moved the family from DeKalb to O'Donnell, where cotton was the main industry, and ran Blocker Grocery and Market.

Blocker's parents bought him a horse and saddle one Christmas, but the future Western hero was more interested in studying and reading, so the horse was sold. When not wrapped up in a book, Blocker enjoyed football and boxing, although, conscious of his size, he was careful not to hurt anyone. This trait was to find its way into more than a few Hoss stories on "Bonanza."

At the age of thirteen (and 200 pounds), Blocker enrolled at the Texas Military Institute in San Antonio, followed by Hardin-Simmons University in Abilene, where he played football. At

Blocker had a varied background before he was discovered by Dortort for his role in "Bonanza." (1960 photo)

Sul-Ross State College, he helped the football team rack up thirty-two wins and one tie game. His record as an amateur boxer was equally impressive, losing only one of 63 fights, and even that was a split decision. Academically, Blocker developed an interest in law and coaching. Though not a regular churchgoer, he was also curious about evangelism.

His real passion, however, was acting. After being recruited to carry the heavy "dead" in a student production of "Arsenic and Old Lace," he found he enjoyed the experience more than he ex-

35

Blocker, the gentle giant, was good natured and trusting as well as a good actor.

Christmas Eve 1951 found Blocker on Hill 255 in Korea, his squad hemmed in by enemy forces for ten hours. "I tasted real mortal fear," he admitted, "and realized for the first time that I was not indestructible." Although he had an interest in military history, the experience left him "with an abiding and active dislike of war." In a 1969 interview, he told a reporter, "I hate guns." Nor, viewers will note, was Hoss Cartwright especially trigger-happy.

After the war, Blocker returned to Texas to earn his degree and marry Dolphia. Rather than act, he decided to teach, first in Sonora, Texas, then in Carlsbad, New Mexico. By the time "Bonanza" ended his academic career, he had taught everything from government and biology to drama and football.

Everyone connected with "Bonanza" found Blocker to be the least "actorish" of the Cartwrights, as well as the most likeable. "Doing the show is a whale of a ball," he told a reporter. "My only problem is, I can't find anybody I don't like. In fact, things are so good, I'm afraid it's a frameup."

But as the show grew in popularity, Blocker found himself confronted by a real problem, namely his own popularity. When he and Dolphia would take their four children—twin girls and two boys—to a ballgame or out for ice cream, they were inevitably surrounded by fans of all ages. "A man never appreciates his privacy until he's lost it," he complained. "And it bugs me, it *really* bugs me. I try to keep the family normal, unaffected by Father's so-called celebrity. It's a losing battle."

Following a profile of the Blocker family in a 1962 issue of *Look*, a reader wrote the magazine asking to see another picture, preferably one including Mrs. Blocker.

Blocker explained that he was in the business to earn a living, not become famous. "I still can't believe that people are that interested in me. If they don't have anything more to concern them than Hoss Cartwright, then what hope is there? You know, if Dr. Salk walked down the street, nobody'd recognize him. I find that terrifying."

pected. "I did it reluctantly," he confessed years later, "and I hooked a pal into it, too. Much to my surprise, we had a ball. I came back for more." He enthusiastically rounded up the entire football team for a staging of "Mr. Roberts," which he also directed, then changed his major from physical education to drama. Specializing in Shakespeare, he gave a memorable performance as the title character in "Othello," and won an award as Best College Actor of 1949 for his portrayal of De Lawd in "Green Pastures." In the drama club's production of Noel Coward's "Fumed Oak," he was a despicable husband who abandons his wife, played by Dolphia Parker, the future Mrs. Dan Blocker.

Blocker received offers to play football professionally, but he opted to give acting a serious try, first in summer stock at Boston's Brattle Hall Theatre, followed by a stint on Broadway in "King Lear." Just as he was having doubts about his future in the theater, Uncle Sam interrupted.

Off the set Blocker was a strong family man. In this 1961 photo he relaxes with his sons, David and Dirk.

He was especially offended when "people grab me and say, 'You old slob, damn you, we love you.' They gotta put their hands on me. I hate to be pulled at and grasped and tugged."

Although Blocker never severed ties with his hometown, frequently telephoning old friends and making rodeo appearances for free, he considered it sad that he had to "lean over backwards for the folks back home. Oddly enough, they *want* to feel that you are above them. . .They become part of the adulation and that's heartbreaking."

O'Donnell once considered erecting a sign identifying the town as the former home of Dan Blocker, but then abandoned the plan. In the words of one citizen: "The more we thought about it, the more we felt Dan wouldn't care much for the idea. He's too regular a fella to care much about that sort of thing."

Dolphia Blocker confirmed that fame had definitely not gone to her husband's head, adding, "Dan .is the same. Only the conditions have changed."

"If I had it all to do over," Blocker reflected wearily while on the rodeo circuit in 1965, "I'd still be teaching sixth grade in Carlsbad, New Mexico. But I've saddled a bronc and I've gotta ride it." He had, in fact, approached the principal of the school with the idea as far back as 1961, only to be told: "Forget it. There's no place to hide in a classroom. You're not Dan Blocker any more. You're Hoss Cartwright."

Fortunately, Blocker was able to lead a satisfy-

Blocker on the Paramount lot with a sample from his Vinegaroon racing firm's "stable" (1964).

ing life outside his television character. A liberal Democrat, he, like Pernell Roberts, became involved with the Civil Rights movement. He was a partner in the Vinegaroon race car firm, and started the Bonanza chain of steakhouses. For children he recorded an album called "Tales For Young 'Uns," and did the narration for a 1964 folk album, "Our Land-Our Heritage," with singer/actor John Mitchum. Another turn at narration was a 1968 NBC news special about the vanishing lifestyle of rural America. (Blocker once remarked, "If I have any appeal, it is to the old farmer and his wife, not to the kind who write fan mail.")

Like Lorne Greene and Michael Landon, he did his share of variety specials and talk shows, although he did not enjoy the experience as much as his co-stars. "I'm an actor," he said. "If somebody gives me something that's written down, I can act it, but I can't go on these panel shows where you have to talk." Nonetheless, he once made a memorable appearance on "The Tonight Show," pretending to be drunk.

Most viewers are not aware that Blocker enjoyed writing, and in 1970 *Playboy* published his short-story entitled, appropriately, "The Best Kept Secret." His plan to develop it into a made-for-TV movie never got off the ground, however, nor did a script ("Star") he was said to be writing for "Bonanza" ever materialize.

As an actor, he did more work on the side than the other Cartwrights, including "Come Blow Your Horn" (1963) and "Lady in Cement" (1968), both with Frank Sinatra. Another film, 1970's "The Cockeyed Cowboys of Calico County," a minor comedy co-starring Mickey Rooney and such "Bonanza" guest stars as Jack Cassidy, Wally Cox, Noah Beery and Jack Elam, was originally produced for television but released theatrically instead. More deserving of feature film status was "Something For a Lonely Man," an outstanding drama with Susan Clark and past "Bonanza" guests John Dehner and Warren Oates. Critic Judith Crist said it was "one of the best tailored-for-television movies" she had seen, calling Blocker's performance "excellent."

Blocker may have felt his portrayal of Hoss was merely a job ("Television is to work in, not watch") and downplayed his popularity (telling his children that people watched "Bonanza" to see

Above: Blocker singing with Carol Channing. The Cartwrights appeared on several variety, talk and game shows. Below: Blocker with Susan Clark in the outstanding TV film, "Something for a Lonely Man" (1968).

the show, not him), but few who worked with him failed to be moved by his masterful acting ability. In a *TV Guide* story on Blocker, actress Gena Rowlands said she was amazed by his "sensitivity, the enormous natural talent, and the ease with which it flowed out." Marlo Thomas, who was then starting her career, told Dortort, "I have never had an actor give me so much in a scene."

Robert Altman, who directed many early episodes of "Bonanza" before going on to helm such classic films as "M*A*S*H" and "Nashville," became a good friend of Blocker's, and for years the two men were anxious to work together again. Altman, for example, wanted Blocker for one of the leads in "M*A*S*H," but was overruled by the producer. "The Long Goodbye," based on the Raymond Chandler novel of the same name, was to have featured Blocker as an alcoholic writer, but he died before production began. Altman dedicated the film, released in 1973, to his old friend.

According to a brief magazine piece in 1969, Blocker "admits he occasionally becomes bored being in a series for so long and wants no more when his present contract expires. He wants to concentrate on movies." Even if the story was true, it was not the only plan Blocker may have had that would never be realized. At the time of his unexpected death in 1972, he was making arrangements to move his family to Seattle, away from what he often criticized as the "snobbery" of Hollywood. A couple years before, the Blockers had leased a house in Lugano, Switzerland, where their children attended school and received an education broader than was possible in the United States. "My children," Blocker said, "are discovering that it takes all kinds to make up the world, that even though there are fundamental differences in appearance, in colors and shapes and sizes, human beings, under like circumstances, will do and act and react as all the others do."

Blocker's beliefs were shared by his television brother, Michael Landon, with whom he shared a sincere closeness that was just as real off camera as it was on. "For me, Dan's death was like losing a brother," Landon lamented more than once. Like Blocker, Landon had grown up without a brother, but the comparison ends there.

Blocker with Frank Sinatra in "Lady in Cement" (1968).

Little Joe

The Michael Landon story is so well known that going into any sort of detail about it seems unnecessarily redundant. He has been the subject of a television documentary and no less than five books, one written before his tragic death in 1991, and four since. None of these sources paints a definitive picture of the man, as they were produced either by family members and friends or tabloid-type writers out for a quick buck. Considered as a whole, however, they describe a highly imaginative and many-sided artist, undeniably one of the most creative people ever to work in television. He

was also human, with his own unique balance of gifts and shortcomings, as occasionally contradictory as anyone, neither a total saint nor sinner.

In 1990, Landon described himself as "fair, honest and aggressive." According to virtually everyone who knew him well, he felt he was a down-to-earth person whose ambition just happened to result in his becoming very, very lucky. On the other hand, few would argue that under the surface, he was quite complex, a driven individual who could be good natured and funloving one moment, yet impatient and irritable the next. Much of that temperament can, of course, be attributed to the pressures of working in television, particularly when an actor is also the writer, director, producer, or often in Landon's case, all four. It is not inaccurate to label him an emotional extremist, in his personal dealings as well as his work. For Landon there was no middle ground; one was for him or against him. On his shows, stories were very dramatic or very funny, characters were in their personal versions of Hell or Utopia. One might easily conclude that his background contained equal parts desperation and inspiration, and one would be correct.

The basics: Michael Landon was born Eugene Maurice Orowitz on Halloween, 1936 (not 1937, as some sources claim), in Forest Hills, New York, and raised in Collingswood, New Jersey. His mother, Peggy, was a former chorus girl in the Ziegfield Follies, inclined to suffer bouts of suicidal depression. Needless to say, her marriage to Eli Orowitz, a head of RKO publicity and once Gene Autry's press agent, was not a shining example of domestic bliss. Although Landon often confronted uncomfortable moments from his past in his work (sometimes with a sense of humor), he never could forget them. Even in his last year of life, he recalled the time spent under Peggy and Eli's roof as "wretched."

Their children, Eugene and his older sister Evelyn, endured a gloomy childhood during which the parents would clash over religious beliefs (Peggy was Catholic, Eli Jewish) and go for months without speaking to one another. While Peggy had grand notions of her daughter becoming a movie star, she offered no encouragement of any kind to Eugene. Eli worked incessantly and was rarely home when his son was awake.

As a child, Eugene was a good student but withdrawn and basically friendless, routinely escaping into a fantasy world populated by comic book and movie heroes. The pain of loneliness was compounded by the anti-Semitic attitude of bigoted classmates, and Eugene's problem with bed-wetting. (Landon would later deal with these issues in his work.) When he was older, he acquired a certain measure of popularity among his peers by becoming the class clown, the result of which was a drastic decline in his grades.

Eugene's salvation was his extraordinary ability to throw the javelin. As a senior he set a national high school record that stood for ten years and

Landon with his first wife, Dodie.

won him a track and field scholarship from USC. There, he decided to major in speech, remembering how much he had enjoyed participating in a community play at the age of fourteen.

Actually believing there was something to the myth of long hair being Samson's source of strength, Eugene wore his shaggier than was common in the ultraconservative Fifties. After a group of fellow athletes pinned him down and gave him a crewcut, he lost the psychological edge that contributed to his great skill with the javelin. Thanks to that–and a torn ligament–he also lost his scholarship.

Remaining in Los Angeles, he rented a small apartment and found a job unloading freight cars. One of his co-workers was an aspiring actor who asked him to come along and help at an audition. The reading was a more positive experience than Eugene had anticipated, and he was convinced he would do well as an actor. While working at a service station near Warner Bros. (where the last three seasons of "Bonanza" were filmed), he was advised by a studio executive to enroll in Warner's acting class. Upon doing so, he changed his name to Michael Landon after perusing the Los Angeles telephone directory for ideas.

In 1956, Landon married Dodie Fraser, a legal secretary, and began getting parts on such television anthologies as "GE Theater," "Studio One," "Playhouse 90," "Telephone Time," "Goodyear Theater," "DuPont Theater" and "Schlitz Playhouse of Stars." With veteran actor Lew Ayres (who would guest on Landon's "Highway to Heaven" series), he even made an unsold pilot called "Johnny Risk." In 1957 he starred as the title character in the cult film "I Was a Teenage Werewolf," which he later spoofed in an episode of "Highway to Heaven," and whose cast included "Bonanza" semi-regular Guy Williams. That little classic was followed by appearances in "Maracaibo" and "High School Confidential," both in 1958, as well as "God's Little Acre." In the latter, Landon portrayed a high-strung albino with the alleged ability to divine gold. The part was comparatively small, but his performance was a standout among such future "Bonanza" guests as Jack Lord, Tina Louise, Aldo Ray and Vic Morrow.

Fortunately for "Bonanza" fans, the single Landon recorded for Candlelight Records

Landon in 1972.

("Gimme A Little Kiss"/"Be Patient with Me"), and his subsequent participation in a package tour with Jerry Lee Lewis, posed no serious threat to Elvis and did not deprive the world of Little Joe Cartwright.

It was on television Westerns that Landon firmly established himself as an actor. While at least one source incorrectly states that he was on every Western series at least once, it is an understandable error, for he certainly made the rounds: "The Adventures of Jim Bowie," "The Texan," "Broken Arrow," "Tales of Wells Fargo," "Cheyenne," "Wanted: Dead or Alive," "The Rifleman," "Tombstone Territory," "The Restless Gun," and even a contemporary Western, "The Sheriff of Cochise."

Landon got top billing for the second–and last–time in "The Legend of Tom Dooley," a 1959 Western based on the Kingston Trio's hit song. During the filming of this Grade B "epic" (the cast of which included Richard Rust, Dee Pollock, Jack Hogan and Ken Lynch, all "Bonanza"-guests-to-be), his life took two significant turns.

While eating lunch in a Hollywood restaurant, Eli Orowitz died suddenly. Landon, who had recently become closer to his father, was devastated. Years later, he recalled: "I still use him in acting. All I have to do is think of him and I can cry. Or, if I want to portray fury, no problem. I just think of how people were dishonest with my dad." Landon was referring in particular to his father's humiliation at not being permitted to visit "friends" from the RKO days who were now working within the gates of Paramount. "They wouldn't even let him on the lot. The man had spent a lifetime working hard for people, worrying about whether he was doing all he could do. And they wouldn't talk to him. Just turned him away. He ended up carrying film cans up five flights of stairs to a projection room in a crummy L.A. theater." Unavoidably, Landon could not help but think of his father each time he reported for work at Paramount during the eleven seasons "Bonanza" was filmed there.

Only two days before Eli's death, Landon was signed to be Ben Cartwright's youngest son. David Dortort remembered his work on "The Restless Gun" and was actually surprised he was not yet in a regular series. "But I did not want just any handsome young actor," Dortort said. "It seemed to me that Mike had depth, certainly more than anybody the network wanted me to cast, and a great potential for growth." After "Bonanza" had been on the air for a couple of years, the producer told a reporter that Landon had "the most highly intuitive set of natural acting responses I've seen in a young actor." Dortort's own intuition proved correct, as Landon went on to first co-write five "Bonanza" scripts between 1962 and 1967, followed by fourteen of his own. In addition, he directed fourteen of the episodes broadcast from May 1968 to January 1973. Giving credit where it was due, Landon always referred to "Bonanza" as a better training ground than any film school.

Landon was ecstatic at landing steady work as an actor. No longer reliant on sympathetic producers to supply him with groceries between jobs, he celebrated his first "Bonanza" paycheck by eating all the egg rolls he could hold. But as is often the case, success proved to be a double-edged sword. Once the show was a hit, he grew suspicious of all the attention he received from the media, beautiful women and supposedly good buddies. "I didn't know who they really wanted to see, the star or me," said Landon. "And a lot of the people I could see, the ones all over you, wanted something from me. And they expected you to give it. Business people, the press, everybody. I wasn't going to fall into that. I remembered my father."

Resolving that he "wasn't going to take garbage from anybody," Landon became "a lot more private person." He grew moody and temperamental, depending on alcohol and tranquilizers for peace of mind. His marriage ended, though he and Dodie remained friendly, and like his father, he became a workaholic. Often he would leave the "Bonanza" set on Friday night and fly off to spend the weekend entertaining at rodeos and fairs all over the country. This non-stop schedule inevitably left him exhausted, sometimes causing him to suffer seizures. Eventually he calmed down, thanks in part to heart-to-heart talks with Lorne Greene,

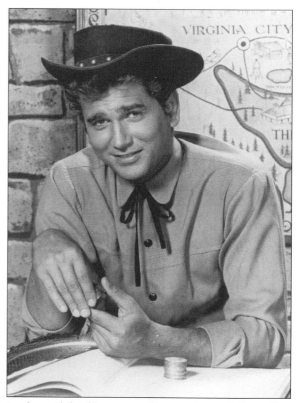

Landon said that his years on "Bonanza" were the best of his life—personally, creatively and financially.

Landon openly supported Dortort's concept of "Bonanza" when the Cartwrights' strong familial bond was being ridiculed in certain circles, saying, "The strongest attachments are between men–fathers, brothers." (1960 publicity shot)

who was one of only a handful of people in the entertainment industry Landon truly respected.

However, he remained generally distrustful of the press, and was especially annoyed at having to justify his success. On one occasion, when he was earning in excess of $10,000 per episode, he was asked if he was embarrassed at being so overpaid. Landon countered by asking the reporter's weekly salary. Upon learning it was $350, he acidly suggested that the reporter was also overpaid.

Landon took his work seriously, to the extent of doing many of his own stunts, and spared no effort in doing what he could to make "Bonanza" not only a success, but better. "The producers were often so busy they would send us scripts with scenes marked *interior saloon*. There would be no

dialogue. So I started writing dialogue for these two-minute scenes. I tried to inject some humor into them, like having Dan Blocker do something silly, like throw me out a window, at the end of a scene. It was fun, and it added something special to the show."

If Pernell Roberts was "giving a director fits," as David Dortort put it, Landon was frequently called on to reason with the uncooperative star. Though he does not dispute tales of Landon taking delight in needling Roberts now and then, Dortort said the two got along better than the public has been led to believe. "Pernell frustrated many people on a professional level," added the producer, "but the boys were fine with each other personally."

Nevertheless, the cast and crew breathed a collective sigh of relief when Roberts finally departed the series. "Pernell didn't like the show and would let you know it," Landon said. "But he rarely cared to do much about it. To say a show stinks doesn't make it better. I'd tell the director, 'This is a piece of crap.' But I wasn't like Pernell. His attitude was negative. I'd give reasons."

Landon was doubtlessly still stinging from Roberts' critical appraisal of his acting ability, a misunderstanding that went uncorrected for years. "I was trying to convey that he was not getting the fullest potential from his talent," Roberts said in regard to the incident. "I was attempting to say that he wasn't developing himself. Somehow he took it as a personal attack. He never forgot. I'm sorry."

"After he left we took one leaf out of the dining room table and we all made money because we split the take three ways instead of four," quipped Landon.

At one point, while Roberts was still with the show, NBC got on an economy kick and decided a good way to control costs would be to hold out on giving the Cartwrights a raise. Landon had the courage, not to mention nerve, to tell the network that if he did not get his raise, Little Joe would be riding off the Ponderosa permanently. NBC quickly reconsidered.

The remaining Cartwrights rode on together for another eight seasons, and the "Bonanza" set became legendary as one of the happiest in town. Greene, Blocker and Landon were forever pulling practical jokes on each other and participating in business deals, but as Landon recalled in 1980, "I loved Lorne and Dan, but I never socialized with them. Twelve hours a day for all those years? Who wants to go to a party and the minute you start a joke, the other guy's telling the punch line? Though if a series lasts long enough, you can start all over again. Jokes we told in the first year, we were telling again in the ninth." His years on "Bonanza" were, he said, the best of his life, satisfying personally, creatively and financially. After eight seasons, his investments included a potato packing plant in Oregon, a seat belt manufacturer, condominiums, an office building and a 10,000 acre ranch. With his co-stars, he acquired a half-mile stretch of beach in Malibu.

In 1962, Landon married Lynn Noe, a divorced model with acting ambitions of her own, and together they had four children in addition to her daughter and his two adopted sons. When watching "Bonanza," Landon reminded the younger kids that as Little Joe he was not really hurt or in danger.

Being remarried and gradually learning the technical aspects of the business had a mellowing effect on Landon, who during the show's early years could explode as easily as the television character he played. In 1969, Dortort observed, "Mike used to be the kid who lost his temper. Now, when guest stars get temperamental, it's Mike who calms them down."

Although they drifted apart as Landon became involved with his own projects, Dortort and his youngest star respected each other's talents. In the beginning, Landon openly supported the producer's concept of "Bonanza" when the Cartwrights' strong familial bond was being ridiculed in certain circles, saying, "The strongest attach-

Greene and Landon, seen here in 1985, remained close friends until Greene's death.

ments are between men–fathers, sons, brothers." In 1966, he told a reporter, "Dave develops the stories with his audience and their viewing interests always in mind. You can't minimize his guiding hand in all this. The stories are the best he can buy, and he's a great artist when it comes to production."

A few years later, shortly after Landon had started working behind the camera on a regular basis, Dortort commented, "The truth is that Mike is a very good director who knows how to handle actors with a firm rein. He's also a very good writer and a very good actor."

"People aren't just surprised that I write scripts," Landon said in a 1967 interview, "they're surprised I can even write my name." He revealed that other writers had called a "Bonanza" writer to ask who was really turning out Landon's scripts. "And that's part of it, the cowboy-actor stigma, the feeling in this town that we're all no smarter than our horses."

Initially Landon received guidance in the mechanics of screenwriting from Dortort and others, but aside from the stories he collaborated on, the ideas were his. "I'll think about the characters for weeks," he explained. "I may lie on the bed and stare at the ceiling for hours. Then, when it's all straight in my head, I work very fast, getting it down on paper in two days." His first "Bonanza" effort was indeed written over a single weekend.

Dortort sometimes considered Landon's scripts overly sentimental, and felt his true calling was directing. Unfortunately, the producer remembered, "It got bad because Landon developed very quickly as a good director. Then, as an actor, he began to criticize what he thought were errors being made by other 'Bonanza' directors. They'd come to me and say, 'We spend most of our time arguing.' It was the same with Mike Landon, the writer. He'd challenge nearly every line, every scene, every setup in other writers' scripts. Everything would halt for endless story conferences on the set, and I finally had to use Dan Blocker as an intermediary to say, 'Let's get on with the damned thing.' It got increasingly bitter toward the end."

"Mike is a very sweet guy," said Lorne Greene, "but extremely stubborn. He's too impulsive. Mike will do a thing one day that he'll regret eight days later."

In retrospect, it is not difficult to believe that Landon was compelled more by his admitted perfectionism than ego. Joe Cartwright was rarely the center of attention in his scripts, and the episodes he directed were consistently inventive, featuring unusual establishing shots, high angle views and panoramic sweeps. Ted Voigtlander, one of the show's directors of photography, was largely responsible for teaching Landon about the art of cinematography. "Many writers can 'see' things that maybe you can't photograph," said Voigtlander. "Well, after getting to know the camera and the lenses, Mike can write things that you can actually do."

Appreciative of Voigtlander's kindness, Landon made a point of using him for all his post-"Bonanza" productions. In fact, a majority of the "Bonanza" crew went with him into "Little House on the Prairie" and beyond. This included, among others, production manager Kent McCray, who clashed with Landon at their first meeting on a hot and dry location shoot in 1962. Sweaty and tired, Landon announced that he was done for the day and wanted a ride back to the studio. McCray held firm and told him if he wanted to leave before completing his scenes, he would have to walk. The two ultimately became close friends and business associates. "He's matured," McCray said several years later. "He's level-headed. He *gives* more of himself. The kid's okay." Before dying, Landon told his third wife, Cindy, that like Dan Blocker, "Kent was my brother."

After more than three decades in front of and behind the camera, Michael Landon had written 107 hours of television, directed another 208 and produced over 330. As an actor, he had logged well over 800 hours, becoming America's quintessential Family Man. "Little House on the Prairie" found him at the head of a Minnesota farming family. On "Highway to Heaven" he was something of a father to all mankind. And he began as the youngest member of a Western dynasty named Cartwright.

CHAPTER THREE

> **"In the old days, all you had to do was shoot any western in Technicolor and you had a box-office hit. But the novelty soon wore off, and as always it was learned that nothing ever takes the place of top entertainment values, no matter how you dress up the material."**
> –Louis B. Mayer, 1955

The Early Classics 1959-1967

It is not known if anyone at NBC ever heard the speech quoted above, but no sooner had David Dortort surmounted color and casting objections than the network decided to cancel "Bonanza," arguing that it would be too expensive to produce. In addition to the cost of renting Paramount's facilities, the crew required to produce the show was going to be considerably larger than average for television. And while the cast's salaries would not exceed $1,000 per episode until the first season was almost over, there were four lead actors to pay, not one or two.

Dortort persisted and was given permission to film thirteen episodes, but cost-conscious NBC was still nervous about the show's budget (well in excess of $120,000, high by 1959 standards) and wanted to pull the plug before even these were filmed.

Over the years, a number of former network executives have been only too glad to take credit for the success of "Bonanza" without mentioning the fact that it came close to never making its debut on Saturday, September 12. *TV Guide* described the show simply: "This hour-long filmed Western series, set in the mid-1880's, centers around the activities of three half brothers and their father, who run a timberland area near Virginia City, Nevada." The magazine was some

Left: David Dortort, in his office in 1961, when "Bonanza" moved to its famous Sunday night time slot. (Photo by Linda Palmer.)
Right: Lorne Greene in the 1959 pilot "A Rose for Lotta."

49

The cast prepares for the final shot of the pilot, "A Rose for Lotta" (1959).

twenty years off, as the show in the beginning took place shortly before the outbreak of the Civil War. Nor was there any special mention of "Bonanza" being broadcast in color.

In November, Dortort proudly declared: "'Bonanza' is a great living pageant. The Comstock Lode was an explosion of men completely disrupting a whole society. Ours is not the phony West, not one of those preposterous fables, but the West as it actually happened."

His optimism, however, was not supported by the initial ratings. The genre certainly had not lost its appeal: 1959 was the year of such theatrical classics as "Rio Bravo," "Last Train From Gun Hill," and "Warlock." On television, four of the Top 10 shows were Westerns, and seven more ranked in the Top 25, but "Bonanza" was scheduled opposite the immensely popular "Perry Mason" on CBS. (Ironically, "Perry Mason" starred

Raymond Burr, for whom David Dortort had written the 1955 TV adaptation of "The Ox-Bow Incident" and the 1956 film "A Cry in the Night.")

Nor were the first reviews very promising. At least one trade paper reported that "Bonanza" was "in mortal danger of being canceled", and had today's "instant hit" hunger prevailed at the networks in 1959, the ax surely would have fallen. David Levy, an NBC vice-president, did not help matters any by stating that he found the show "inept." It would not be his last criticism of the series.

On the positive side, "Bonanza" was beautifully photographed, memorably scored and more than competently acted, lending credence to Dortort's claim that it and other hour-long programs could "probably end up hitting movies in the mid-section with a sickening thud." And in comparison with much of what television was offering, watch-

50

ing "Bonanza" was the equivalent of seeing a feature on a small screen. Its production values and frequent "name" guest stars resulted in several episodes being just as good as the films currently being done by Randolph Scott and director Budd Boetticher, or those Anthony Mann had made with Jimmy Stewart.

But there was still a major problem: a shortage of scripts, specifically good ones. "Bonanza" had been rushed into production less than six months prior to its first airdate, ample time for a black-and-white half-hour program with one or two regulars, but nothing of this scope had ever been attempted. Veteran movie writers John Lee Mahin (who had just scripted "The Horse Soldiers" for John Wayne and William Holden) and Martin

Rackin were brought in to help, but they felt television was somehow beneath their abilities and did not contribute anything worthwhile.

The four stars were, to varying degrees, critical of the writing. Even Dan Blocker remarked that the scripts were "sometimes terrible." Seen today, the majority of the early episodes are no better or worse than other Westerns on the air at the time, and the worst one might point to is the scattering of stilted dialogue that was prevalent in virtually all television of the day. As for the plots, they were often a cut above the average sagebrush saga. The first season in particular included several historical references almost no other series (with the possible exception of "Bronco") would have bothered digging up, and the occasional inaccuracies

Between shots of "A Rose for Lotta" (1959).

can be attributed to creative license. While Dortort either wrote or co-wrote only four of the first season's thirty-two episodes, many of the scripts were based on his ideas. His practice of contributing significantly to the writing without taking credit would continue for the entire run of the series.

Generally unimpressed by the quality of the scripts, Lorne Greene actually hoped "Bonanza" would not last beyond the thirteen episodes NBC had ordered, but a steady improvement in the ratings convinced the network to allow the show to at least finish out the season. It was then that Greene decided something had to be done.

"It was January 1960," he recalled, "and we were getting ready to shoot the sixteenth episode. I told my agent that I wanted to see our producer to get a lot of things off my chest, because I was beginning to feel as though I had to get out of the show. The problem was that the scripts *had* to be improved. We had characters that people believed in, liked, and with whom they identified, but we lacked scriptwriters who could *write* for those characters."

In addition to the scripts, Greene had a problem with the Ponderosa's isolationist policy toward Virginia City and neighboring ranches. During the first season, the Cartwrights definitely suffered from a siege mentality, running off anyone who set foot on their land. As early as the second episode,

Ben and his two oldest sons (1959).

however, Ben Cartwright does tell a prospector and his family: "No one's going to starve while we have cattle to sell. Now, get yourself some men together and come over to the Ponderosa."

"We were always pointing guns at people," Greene continued, "always saying, 'What're you doing on the Ponderosa?' Well, my attitude was who *cares*? Let 'em be there. For one thing, the Ponderosa is a thousand square miles without a single sign that says 'Keep Out' or 'Private Property.' For another, I felt the Cartwrights should make nice-nice, say to people, 'Hey, you're on the Ponderosa, but that's all right. C'mon in. You hungry? You want to stay with us for a couple of weeks?' There were no radios or television, and I thought that would be a great way for the Cartwrights to find out what was happening in the world.

"I finished by telling the producer that if the only way you can keep a story moving is by pointing a gun at people and threatening to blow their heads off, there's *definitely* something wrong with the writing."

Changes were made, and shortly after, Greene confided to an interviewer: "There are times when I think we almost manage to transcend our constant lack of good scripts, proper rehearsal and all the other things that bug a man in this business."

Several years after "Bonanza" ended, Michael Landon called "A Rose For Lotta," the show's debut episode, "the worst pilot in the history of television." Not only was his charge inaccurate, it was unfair. True, the acting is melodramatic, but this was before a more subtle and sophisticated style emerged in the late Sixties. Concerning the story itself, the plot is, by necessity, a simple one, as it was more important to introduce the characters. Today a network would most likely allow two hours to launch a show with the scope of "Bonanza," but such a luxury did not exist in 1959. One must also remember that in addition to having very little time to write the pilot, David Dortort was heavily involved in other aspects of the production *and* still committed to finishing "The Restless Gun."

Pilots rarely resemble exactly what a show eventually becomes, and "Bonanza" was no exception. Actors must discover and develop their characters, as well as explore their relationships with one another. Producers and writers have to decide on the overall tone and direction of the show. The process can be frustrating, particularly in those rare instances where a television show attempts to achieve a vision approximating originality. For "Bonanza" this was especially difficult, considering the multitude of Westerns competing for viewers' attention.

The fast pace of television frequently thwarts creativity, yet the first season of "Bonanza" features 32 episodes that manage to avoid the majority of Western cliches. The Cartwrights are a refreshing change from typical cowboy heroes, a firmly-rooted family comprised of four sharply contrasting individuals. Each of them would evolve as the series progressed, but the basics for each character are present in the pilot.

"A Rose For Lotta" finds the silver barons of Virginia City up in arms over Ben Cartwright's unwillingness to supply them with timber for "deeper mines and richer veins of silver." Their ringleader complains, "To old Ben Cartwright, a tree is something sacred, something money can't buy." The mine owners offer entertainer Lotta Crabtree (Yvonne DeCarlo) $10,000 to lure Little Joe to town, but do not tell her they plan to hold him hostage until Ben gives in to their demands. Naturally, the scheme fails, but not before the Cartwrights tangle with what Adam calls "that Virginia City bunch," which includes, in the episode's only blatant concession to convention, a hired killer with twelve notches on his gun.

In the first scene, as they survey their empire, Ben says to Adam: "Look at it, Adam. Feast thine eyes on a sight that approacheth Heaven itself." Later, when he finds Adam and Little Joe brawling in the living room, he shouts, "Fire and brimstone!" Fortunately, Ben's Moses-like pretensions–not to mention Lorne Greene's florid style–quickly subsided as the character was refined.

The first impression one gets of Adam is that of a surly cynic, more Ben's "muscle" than eldest son. He tells Lotta, "We don't cotton to strangers, male or female" and later threatens to break her arm. When thrown by a horse he is attempting to break, he rejects his brothers' display of concern and, more alarmingly, refers to Little Joe's epee as a "New Orleans monkey pick handed down to you by your French Quarter mother." Hardly an example of brotherly love. Nor is their violent fight.

Demonstrating the hot-headed personality that would distinguish him from the rest of the Cartwrights, Little Joe responds–with a slight Southern accent never again heard after this episode–"If you weren't my brother, Adam, I'd kill you for that." For good measure, he adds, "I've never been able to see myself being kin to anything whelped out of a thin-nosed, blue blooded Boston Yankee." Even after Hoss has interceded, Joe says Adam has a "rock-bound New England head" and calls him a "Yankee granite head." In a later scene, he tells Lotta he has a hard time believing Ben's first wife was the daughter of a New England sea captain, "a Yankee."

When Lotta asks Joe why people refer to him as little even though he is "not that small," he replies it is because "brother Hoss is that big." He reveals that Hoss' mother was from Sweden, and that Hoss is not his real name. Little Joe's affection for his other older brother is obvious if unstated.

Not so obvious, judging by the pilot, is how hugely popular Hoss would become. In "A Rose For Lotta," he is used mainly for comic relief ("I've only had a couple three breakfasts since mornin'") and exhibitions of strength, tossing his brothers around like rag dolls and lifting a disabled stagecoach with one hand. Dan Blocker's instant appeal is as undeniable as Michael Landon's good looks and physical prowess. Dortort's prediction that the two of them would click, both together and with the public, was right on the money. It did not take long for Blocker and Landon to begin mirroring the pranks of their television characters: Requested to be on their best behavior for the first visit by the "suits" from NBC, they responded with a fake fistfight that trashed the set. The network brass, unsure of what they were witnessing, quickly scattered.

There are a few oversights in the pilot, the first of which really could not be considered one at the time. In one scene, Little Joe tells Lotta his mother's name was Felicia; it would later be changed to Marie. Coincidentally, the third Mrs. Cartwright was portrayed by Felicia Farr (Mrs. Jack Lemmon) in a fourth season flashback episode.

The depiction of Ponderosa caretaker Hop Sing, and his father Hop Ling, as little more than stereo-

typical Orientals is an error in judgement which was quickly corrected before the season ended. On "Bonanza" all foreigners and minorities, Indians included, were accorded more respect than they generally received on other Westerns. Though Ben calls Hop Sing a "celestial sky gazer" and mocks his accent, he is clearly fond of his domestic right hand. And Hop Sing is no whipping boy, protesting being shouted at all the time. Hoss, afraid he is going to quit, points out that Hop Sing is "the best cook this side of San Francisco."

Hop Sing was portrayed by the late Victor Sen Yung, who actually was from San Francisco, born there in 1915. An experienced character actor, he had worked in films with Humphrey Bogart, Bette Davis and Alan Ladd, to name only a few, co-starred in eighteen of the forty-seven Charlie Chan movies, as well as the Oscar-winning adaptation of Pearl Buck's "The Good Earth" (1937). Few people were aware that Sen Yung had a degree in economics, and had served as a captain with air force intelligence during World War Two. Because he was used in only fourteen to eighteen episodes each season, he was able to accept roles on such shows as "The Rifleman" and "Bachelor Father," and in the films "Flower Drum Song" (1961), "Confessions of an Opium Eater" (1962) and "A Flea in Her Ear" (1968). Despite having worked in over 300 movies and television programs, he considered show business "too insecure, too tough."

The final flaw of the episode is one of historical chronology: Lotta Crabtree did exist, and was indeed a popular entertainer not only in this country but abroad. However, she was only twelve years old in 1859, the approximate year of the show's first season. A slightly more accurate representation of the character would occur in an episode of the eleventh season.

"A Rose For Lotta" was directed by Edward Ludwig, a veteran of primarily B movies, and filmed in and around Los Angeles, not Lake Tahoe, as many viewers have mistakenly assumed. The opening credits show the Cartwrights riding down a dirt road rather than across the more familiar Stateline meadow in Tahoe. This scene is used for eight other first season episodes, but only in the

Blocker in "A Rose for Lotta" (1959).

pilot are the horses' hooves audible. If one watches closely, Pernell Roberts can be seen laughing and saying something to Dan Blocker. Perhaps he was making a remark about their comparative lack of riding ability, for none of the actors was an accomplished horseman. In an interview, Michael Landon once joked about Lorne Greene's inexperience at riding, and told of how they all lost control of their mounts during a Rose Bowl Parade.

He added that in the beginning Blocker was probably the best rider. However, Dortort sent both Blocker and Landon to riding school following an incident in which Blocker was thrown, injuring his shoulder. The horses, incidentally, were rented from Fat Jones, owner of an eleven-acre ranch in North Hollywood which regularly supplied the film industry with everything from longhorn steers to buckboards. On the show, Ben called his mount Buck, Joe's was Cochise and Hoss' was, appropriately, Chub. Landon swore that Chub would have a look of dread in his eyes whenever he noticed Blocker preparing to saddle up. As for what Adam named his horse, who knows?

At the end of the first episode, the credits scroll past the Ponderosa map; the brilliant watercolor portraits do not appear until later in the season. Significantly, no doubt due to Wally Westmore's low regard for television, Frank Westmore's makeup contribution is not acknowledged.

One final note: Ben, Hoss and Joe do not sing the lyrics of the theme at the conclusion of the pilot, although a scene in which they do has been shown in several television documentaries. Their serenading was wisely cut.

A few weeks before it aired, "The Newcomers" was previewed for the public at the Granada Theater in Reno, Nevada, with the cast, local dignitaries and assorted network people in attendance. The showing was such a success that it and one other episode had to be rerun more than once.

The third show to be actually broadcast, "The Newcomers," was an early landmark in the history of "Bonanza" and the career of Dan Blocker, who was not given much to do in the first two installments. For the first time, Blocker was allowed to portray more than an amiable giant, and it can be safely said that "The Newcomers" made him a star, one of television's immortals. The story, by

Thomas Thompson, can be viewed as a variation of "Beauty and the Beast," yet more poignant. Hoss falls in love with a dying young woman (Inger Stevens) who at first refers to him as an "ugly brute." Good naturedly, he replies, "Ma'am, I can't hardly help bein' ugly, can I?"

She softens while observing him tending to some horses. "They like for you to talk to them," he explains. "Makes 'em feel good. I like all animals. You can trust 'em. Some folks have a natural mean streak animals don't know nothin' about, I guess." Later, when she apologizes for calling him ugly, Hoss shrugs it off with, "Oh, that's all right. I've heard it before."

In a beautiful scene toward the end of the episode, she gently touches his face and says, "I love you, Hoss." Dazed, and still unaware she is fatally ill, he humbly removes his hat as David Rose's music swells and the viewer becomes more a participant than an observer. "Bonanza"'s power to move is fully demonstrated, and it is not sugarcoated. When Joe wants to console Hoss, Ben stops him, explaining that because he has had to bury three wives he knows "for awhile it's a hurt you have to bear alone."

A few weeks later, in "The Julia Bulette Story," Michael Landon amazed both cast and crew by effortlessly providing Joe with tears for an emotional death scene with guest star Jane Greer.

"We are not afraid to show our feelings," David Dortort admitted in 1962. "We have made more people cry than anyone in the business." A proud but odd statement for a producer of Westerns. Yet it was clear from the start that "Bonanza" was not going to be a run-of-the-mill horse opera.

More tears punctuated "Feet of Clay," in which Hoss is forced to kill a young boy's father.

But there were lighter moments as well, such as "Enter Mark Twain," with Howard Duff the first of three actors who would portray the famous writer during the series' run. "The Gunmen," featuring Blocker and Landon in dual roles, and "San Francisco" (the first episode to take place entirely off the Ponderosa) were played mainly for laughs, but the most significant of these was "Mr. Henry Comstock," written by David Dortort and guest starring Jack Carson in a performance worthy of W.C. Fields.

"Mr. Henry Comstock" flashes back to the

origin of Virginia City and features references to the "Bonanza" credo ("Don't cut unless you plant," Ben tells Hoss. "That's why we're here. Not just to take from the land, but to give."), particularly when Ben rages at the memory of what happened to his friend in Sacramento. "Is it any wonder John Sutter sits on his porch now, staring into the sun by the hour, recognizing no one, seeing nothing?"

Based on "Mr. Henry Comstock," it is a pity Dortort did not write more for "Bonanza" than he did, though his poetic style manages to pervade many of the series' best moments.

Other highlights of the first season included "The Truckee Strip" (Romeo and Juliet out West), "Vendetta" (a respectable nod to "High Noon"), and "The Paiute War" (a mini-epic for television).

The Cartwrights' family history was detailed to a greater extent than "A Rose For Lotta" in "A House Divided" and "The Stranger," both of which related to Ben's third wife. In the latter, Ben tells Joe: "I've told you a great deal about your mother. You never really knew her. She was a wonderful woman–beautiful, slender, delicate, gentle. Treated Adam and Hoss like they were her own. She was like an angel to everyone who ever came into contact with her." Such recollections of the past by regular characters were not exactly uncommon in series television, but no show employed the device quite as effectively as "Bonanza." While watching the series, the audience gradually became aware that they were watching a family closely linked to its past, not merely living in the moment.

In addition to the talent already mentioned, "Bonanza" was nurtured through its troubled genesis by such guests as Barry Sullivan, Jack Warden, Ida Lupino, Ruth Roman, James Coburn, Jack Lord, Cameron Mitchell, Henry Hull, Ellen Corby, Everett Sloane, Lloyd Nolan, Vic Morrow, Buddy Ebsen and Robert Middleton. Among the TV Western regulars making appearances were Leo Gordon, R.G. Armstrong, Mort Mills, Gene Evans and Claude Akins. "Bonanza" was soon regarded as something of a prestige gig in the acting community, and it was not unusual for a well-known personality to request a part without having to be asked. Although it may seem as if the show employed everyone in the Screen Actors Guild at one time or another, there were several luminaries who expressed interest in visiting the Ponderosa but

On location for "The Paiute War" (1959).

never made the trip, including Carl Reiner, Sammy Davis, Jr., Joan Crawford, Dorothy Lamour and even the inimitable Mae West.

Behind the camera, the first season benefited from top drawer writers Gene L. Coon, Clair Huffaker, Harold Shumate and Carey Wilber, and veteran directors Joseph Kane (a major force behind the careers of Roy Rogers and Gene Autry), Christian Nyby (who eventually directed 26 episodes, 12 in the first season alone), and Lewis Allen (director of an astounding 43).

As the season was winding down, *TV Guide*, attempting to explain the show's growing popularity with viewers both young and old, commented: "It's undeniable that this togetherness has a potent appeal in a Nation obsessed with the idea of security." Had the network cancelled the show, it would have been remembered, perhaps as a noble failure, but remembered nonetheless.

Thanks to an increase in ratings, not to mention

57

sales of color sets, NBC renewed "Bonanza" for 1960-61, still on Saturday night. By the end of the season it was, at #17, the fifth highest-rated Western on the air. Western Publishing Company issued the first of 37 Dell/Gold Key "Bonanza" comic books, and Popular Library released a paperback novel based on the show by Noel Loomis, a winner of the Golden Spur Award from the Western Writers of America. David Rose released his soundtrack album, and Al Caiola's instrumental version of the theme was a 1961 hit. At the May 16, 1961 Emmy Awards ceremony, Lorne Greene and Dan Blocker humorously aped what the show looked like on Japanese television. That same month, "Bonanza" made the first of fourteen appearances on the cover of *TV Guide* with a story about Greene. In June, Blocker and Landon posed with their sons for a brief Father's Day story in the magazine called "Sons of Guns."

One of the few sour notes was sounded by outgoing NBC executive David Levy, who was sensitive to violence on the network's shows and openly critical of "Bonanza" from the start. A report from the A.C. Nielsen Company, the main source of television ratings, found that 35% of the show's viewers during the second season had been seventeen or younger, prompting Levy to respond: "If Adam Cartwright kills two men in his first show, by the end of the year the combined slaughter of the four Cartwrights would be pretty impressive." He was particularly concerned with the violence in Westerns and did not hesitate to express his views to several producers, including David Dortort.

Levy could have singled out guiltier targets than "Bonanza", which during its second season actually contained less fighting and killing than its first, and was frequently downright tame in comparison with other Westerns. Overall, the 34 episodes of 1960-61 are more varied and stronger than those of the previous year. Especially noteworthy were stories about an ill-fated romance - between Hoss and a compulsive gambler ("The Courtship"), Ben's attraction to the wife of an embittered cripple ("The Mill"), Joe's attempts to

Lorne Greene slugs Dan O'Herlihy's stunt double in "The Artist" (1962).

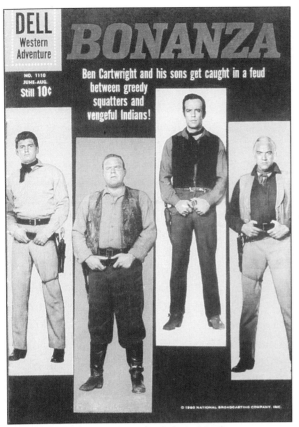

Dell's first "Bonanza" comic book (June 1960).

open up the world for a deaf and mute girl ("Silent Thunder"), Adam's problems dealing with a mentally ill friend ("The Dark Gate"), and Hoss' relationship with a feeble-minded ox of a man ("The Ape").

Other episodes of significance were "The Last Viking," in which Hoss discovers his uncle (played by familiar heavy Neville Brand) is the leader of marauding outlaws, "Elizabeth, My Love," in which the story of Ben's first wife is detailed, and the introduction of Ray Teal as Sheriff Roy Coffee in the season opener, "Showdown."

Teal, who would be with the show until the end of the 1971-72 season, made his acting debut in 1938 (Gene Autry's "Western Jamboree") and was usually cast as a villain or some unsavory sort in Westerns and other types of films. On television he appeared in both major and minor Western series, including "Cheyenne," "Maverick," "The Restless Gun," "Klondike," and "The Alaskans."

The second season featured terrific performances by Dan Duryea ("Badge Without Honor"), Ricardo Montalban ("Day of Reckoning"), Robert Lansing ("Cut Throat Junction"), Leif Erickson ("The Rescue"), Henry Hull ("The Mission"), and Martin Landau ("The Gift"). The parade of TV Western icons continued: Jack Lambert, Peter Whitney, Harry Carey, Jr., Edgar Buchanan, Robert J. Wilke, Lee Van Cleef, Jack Elam and Ford Rainey.

Prolific action expert William Witney began working for the series by directing three of his eventual two dozen episodes, and Robert Altman, whom David Dortort said "had a large share in the strength and popularity of the show" directed seven, most among the season's strongest: "Silent Thunder," "Bank Run," "The Duke," "The Rival," "The Secret," "The Dream Riders" and "Sam Hill," the latter a Dortort story for a never-realized spin-off series.

Altman's originality as a filmmaker is evident in his work for "Bonanza," in particular his penchant for shooting familiar settings, such as the yard of the Ponderosa, from unfamiliar angles. Dortort told Altman biographer Patrick McGilligan that Altman's use of the camera "was consistently brilliant" and gave the show "an extremely professional look."

In the fall of 1961, "Bonanza" replaced "The Dinah Shore Chevy Show" on Sunday night, and the results were astounding. The Cartwrights, finally outfitted in the costumes they would wear for the duration of the series, charged across the home screen (in the series' third and most famous opening sequence) for a ten-season run in the Top 10. "Bonanza" sailed upward in the new time slot, becoming the #2 show, behind "Wagon Train" and ahead of "Gunsmoke." With the exception of "Rawhide," they were the only Westerns remaining in the Top 25. Though the genre had obviously run its course, "Bonanza" was unaffected by this change in public taste because Dortort had been savvy enough to see beyond the limitations of the traditional Western.

Which is not to say that "Bonanza" had forsaken the format. The third season, in fact, featured a number of solid Western stories, including Michael Landon's first attempt at writing, "The Gamble," in which the Cartwrights are framed for robbery and murder. When production was on the verge of ceasing for lack of a ready script, Landon decided to dash one off over the weekend. The

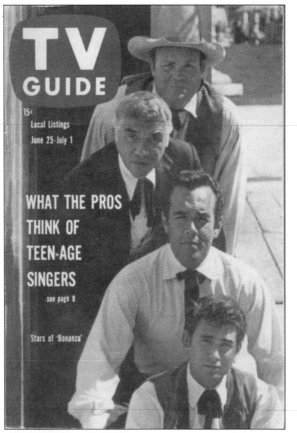

TV Guide, *June 25, 1960.*

first version was rough and not long enough, but Dortort judged it suitable for filming once he and regular contributor Frank Chase helped Landon polish it up.

It is rare when quantity equals quality, but "Bonanza" rewarded its growing audience with an abundance of memorable episodes during its third year. In addition to adventures such as "The Honor of Cochise" (written by Western pro Borden Chase and directed by Don McDougall, who would go on to do 30 more episodes by 1965), "Land Grab" and "The Ride" (both by future Landon associate Ward Hawkins), there was the first of two flashbacks to Ben's relationship with his second bride ("Inger, My Love"), the death of Joe's bride-to-be ("The Storm") a sad story involving the tragic fate of Hoss' unrequited love interest ("The Tall Stranger"), and the Cartwright boys' alternately touching and amusing attempts to handle the business affairs of a wealthy old man they have accidentally injured ("Springtime").

Even funnier was Robert Altman's final effort,

"The Many Faces of Gideon Flinch" and the Cyrano-like farce "The Wooing of Abagail Jones" with big band crooner Vaughn Monroe. The latter gives Pernell Roberts one of his few opportunities to demonstrate his own vocal talent, which he would later showcase on an album of his own.

Roberts' acting ability, however, is the focal point of "The Crucible," reported to be his favorite episode. It is certainly the most widely known segment of the 1961-62 season, and for good reason. Stranded in the desert, Adam must contend with a psychopathic prospector, expertly played by Lee Marvin. Marvin, incidentally, was attempting to concentrate solely on his film career but did the episode as a favor to David Dortort, who once helped him with a script for his series "M Squad."

No examination of the 1961-62 season can be complete without making note of Ben Cartwright's still-timely speech to the citizens of Virginia City in "Look to the Stars": "There's a little prejudice hidden in every one of us whether we like to admit it or not. It isn't enough just to be against bigotry. It takes some doing to reach down deep inside yourself, admit it and face it down."

While "Bonanza" had been spoofed in a Bob Hope/Bing Crosby sketch filmed in the Ponderosa living room and broadcast as part of an NBC special, the most high-profile evidence of the show's increased notoriety came when it was satirized in an episode of ABC's "Maverick" on November 11, 1961. Entitled "Three Queens Full," it featured Jim Backus as Joe Wheelwright of the Subrosa Ranch and his three sons, Henry, Moose and Small Paul. A month after the third season ended, *TV Guide* critic Gilbert Seldes gave the show one of its better reviews: "Maybe it is by contrast with other programs that this one gets ahead. It is always on the verge of being believable; and when you don't believe it, that doesn't matter much either. At least two-thirds of the time it isn't violent, and it is never vulgar. If this spells success, even in a negative way, it might well be a lesson to some other productions." Even so, Seldes admitted he could not fully explain why "Bonanza" was such a huge hit, prompting a reader to respond with some answers: "A reasonable proportion of good scripts, a few actors who can handle their lines as expertly as their guns, and a basic format which makes possible a wide variety of story lines."

Greene recorded six albums.

At the same time that exchange was taking place, the four Cartwrights were gathered in RCA's Hollywood studio to record "Ponderosa Party Time," a variety album meant to take advantage of the cast's burgeoning fame. Of the four, only Dan Blocker does not fare particularly well in carrying a tune, but as on the show, he gets by on charm alone. "We'd like to know if you're as excited about our four new singing stars as we are," RCA executive Steve Sholes wrote in the liner notes. "Please let us hear from you." There would be one more cast album, and Lorne Greene went on to record six of his own. In early 1962, Greene recorded a duet with Johnny Cash, "The Shifting Whispering Sands," but it was not released until 1965.

As the fourth season got underway, the show was satirized as "Bananaz" in the September 1962 issue of "Mad." This time the cast was dubbed the Cartwheels: Pa, Yves, Ox and Short Mort of the Pawnderosa.

More important was a *TV Guide* story which revealed that Paramount was seriously considering making blueprints of the ranch house available to the many people who were requesting them. In addition, librarians across the country were reporting an increased interest in the history of the Comstock, more than 450 "Bonanza Booster" clubs had been established, and James Arness, Matt Dillon on "Gunsmoke," confessed he was an admirer of the show.

Predictably, Pernell Roberts (who did not pose for the cover of the magazine, nor join the rest of the cast in celebrating the 103rd anniversary of the Comstock) griped: "Togetherness—who needs it? It usually just gets in the way of all the good stories crying to be told." When asking the script girl for his next line, he said: "What little gem do I have here?"

Roberts doubtlessly found recording his own album, "Come All Ye Fair and Tender Ladies," a far more fulfilling experience. Ordinarily, such vanity projects by celebrities are ridiculed, but this collection of folk songs ("The Water is Wide," "Shady Grove," etc.) was, for anyone who had not heard Roberts sing on the show, a pleasant surprise. Its most outstanding cut, "Alberta," could rightfully be considered a standard of the early Sixties folk movement.

Lorne Greene, on the other hand, chose the easy listening route for his first solo recording, "Young at Heart," which featured such chestnuts as "September Song" and "As Time Goes By."

Despite a slight drop in the ratings (#4 at season's end), "Bonanza" became the most watched Western on television in its fourth year, due in part to an unusually high number of compelling stories, both serious and otherwise.

Joining the show as Deputy Clem Foster was Bing Russell, who had played a badman in "The Long Night" the previous season. His numerous Western series credits included, among others,

"Gunsmoke," "Maverick," "Laramie," "Rawhide" and "Have Gun-Will Travel." Clem and Roy Coffee rarely appeared in the same episode, and by the final season, Clem was Virginia City's sole lawman. The character of Clem had been portrayed in earlier episodes by Robert Foulk, who later took on the role of a general store owner.

Some of the more prominent moments of the 1962-63 season were "The First Born" (Joe meets a half-brother he did not know existed), "Marie, My Love" (Ben's third wife), "The Quest" (Joe is determined to have the "little" removed from his name), "A Stranger Passed This Way" (Hoss suffers from amnesia and nearly leaves for Min-

nesota), "The Way of Aaron" (Adam comes to the rescue of a Jewish peddler and his daughter), "My Brother's Keeper" (Adam accidentally shoots Joe and announces his disgust of Western life), "Knight Errant" (a mail-order bride falls for Hoss instead of the man who has sent for her) and "The Last Haircut" (Joe takes unusual revenge on a killer who has managed to get away with murder).

Two comic Hoss episodes, "Half a Rogue" (with Slim Pickens) and "Any Friend of Walter's" (with Arthur Hunnicutt), came off so successfully that Pickens and Hunnicutt repeated their roles the following season.

Carroll O'Connor, the future Archie Bunker,

"Broken Ballad" (1961).

"Santa's Little Girl"

Porcelain Christmas Doll™

For only $5?

New

Genuine Porcelain!

©1992, Masterhand USA, Inc. Styles and colors may vary. We reserve the right to substitute similar merchandise of equal or greater value.

Special Pre-Christmas Offer!

Baxter & Smythe, Ltd. proudly presents *"Santa's Little Girl"* Porcelain Christmas Doll—a magnificent portrait of *little girl loveliness* designed especially for this glorious Christmas Holiday Season! Each doll is authentically crafted in creamy hand-painted porcelain bisque and lavishly costumed in her finest Christmas best with rich velvety berry red jumper trimmed with layer upon layer of fine snowy-white imported lace. And with frilly bloomers, lacy complementing bonnet and satiny ribbons too! Each *"Santa's Little Girl"* Porcelain Christmas Doll™ has all porcelain hands, feet, face and eyes, generously stuffed cottony-soft body and combable life-like golden blond hair. Just think what a wonderful and cherished gift she'll make for that very special Christmas *"little girl"* in your life!

Money-back Guarantee! Each *"Santa's Little Girl"* Porcelain Christmas Doll™ is covered by the company's full-one-year money-back guarantee. Please Note! At this special promotional price, there is a limit of four (4) *"Santa's Little Girl"* Porcelain Christmas Dolls™ per address, but if you send in your request early enough (before November 30, 1993) you may request up to eight (8) dolls. (No exceptions, please!)

Order NOW! To request your *"Santa's Little Girl"* Porcelain Christmas Doll,™ send in your name and address and $5 for each. Add just $3 shipping and handling no matter how many dolls you are requesting. Please allow 4-8 weeks for shipment. New York State residents, please add sales tax.

Mail to: **Baxter & Smythe, Ltd.**
Santa's Girl Doll Offer, Dept. SLG-45
P O Box 9000, Westhampton, NY 11977-9000

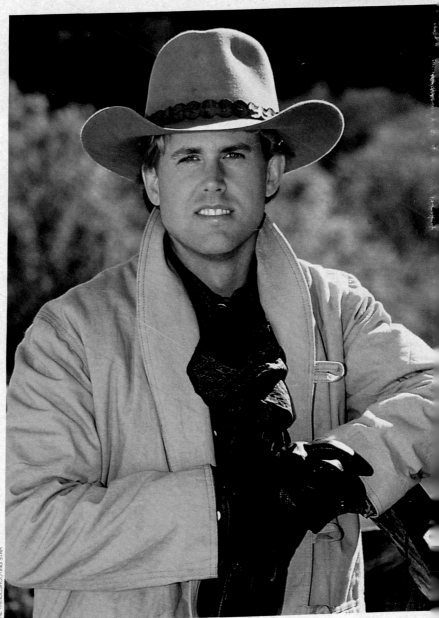

GENE TRINDL/SHOOTING STAR

played a crooked town merchant who ultimately repents in "The Boss." To this day, O'Connor calls David Dortort "Boss" whenever they happen to meet.

Also starring with the Cartwrights during the fourth season were Robert Vaughn, DeForest Kelley, Denver Pyle, William Demarest, Aneta Corsaut, Dabbs Greer, Simon Oakland, Ross Martin and many other television favorites.

The 1963 Christmas album.

In the 1962 episode, "The Quest," Little Joe seeks to change his name.

Only nine directors handled all 34 episodes, including, for the first time, the late William F. Claxton, who did four and went on to do 57 in all, making him "Bonanza"'s busiest director. Somehow he also found time to help David Dortort produce "The High Chaparral" from 1967 to 1971, and when "Bonanza" was over, he worked extensively on Michael Landon's "Little House on the Prairie," "Father Murphy" and "Highway to Heaven."

Before starting work on the 1963-64 season, the cast recorded a Christmas album, "Christmas on the Ponderosa." Evidently wanting to continue distancing himself from "Bonanza," Pernell Roberts joined in on only one track.

If a series is fortunate to last into a fifth season, its creative engine is usually running on fumes. "Bonanza"'s fifth year, however, was its strongest yet, and arguably the best of the six seasons Pernell Roberts was with the show. While it was kept out of the top slot in the seasonal ratings by

"The Beverly Hillbillies" (the Sixties, after all, has been described as the era of the "idiot sitcom"), its audience was the largest ever for "Bonanza", an astounding 36.9 share. No show after 1963 has matched those numbers. As far as competing Westerns went, the only ones remaining in the Top 25 were "The Virginian" and "Gunsmoke." Theatrically, no classic Westerns were released.

From such an exceptional season it is very difficult to single out the "best" episodes because, in a television rarity, there were no "bad" ones. To be sure there were a couple not quite as good in comparison to the rest ("The Lila Conrad Story" and "The Companeros"), but that opinion is entirely subjective.

"She Walks in Beauty," in which Hoss gives Adam a beating, began the year with a definite jolt. The following 33 episodes offered an incredible variety of stories: Ben nearly marries ("My Son, My Son") and again thinks back to his second wife ("Journey Remembered"), Adam lends support to

"Hoss and the Leprechauns" (1963).

Hoss. "Hoss and the Leprechauns" is justifiably remembered as one of the classic Hoss shows of all time, but "The Pure Truth," in which Hoss tries to help Roy Coffee and fouls everything up, turned out to be the highest-rated "Bonanza" ever. In the first edition of "The Book of Lists," this episode ranked #4 of the Top 13 TV episodes broadcast between 1960 and 1977.

Without question, the two serious landmarks of the 1963-64 season were "The Legacy" and "Enter Thomas Bowers." In the first, the Cartwright boys believe Ben has been killed and split up to track the men responsible. Ben, who of course has only been injured, is aided by a passing peddler, with whom he shares his feelings toward his sons. Adam, he says, has deep thoughts, Hoss deep feelings. As for Joe, Ben admits he is not certain he knows his youngest all that well, and agonizes over the prospect that Joe may kill the man he believes to be a murderer. Later, after all the Cartwrights but Joe have been reunited, Hoss tells Ben not to worry: "He's hot-tempered, but he's still one of your sons." Joe, like his brothers, does catch up with his man, who happens to be carrying Ben's rifle, but leaves matters to the law. The peddler, touched by the family's obvious affection for one another, refuses the money Ben has promised for causing him to lose business. "I've been paid," he assures Ben.

"Enter Thomas Bowers" dealt with the bigotry faced by a black opera singer who has come to Virginia City to perform. General Motors, the show's sponsor, feared the episode would anger pro-segregation viewers in the South and asked NBC to refrain from showing it. Earlier, Greene, Blocker and Landon had offended the governor of Mississippi by refusing to make an appearance before a segregated audience, prompting the narrow-minded politician to call for a boycott of the show. Deciding that airing "Enter Thomas Bowers" was more important than a decrease in the sale of Chevrolets, the network backed David Dortort.

"When NBC asked me which episodes I wanted them to rerun during the summer months, I told them to make sure they included 'Enter Thomas Bowers,'" Dortort recalled.

Drama of another sort was being played out behind-the-scenes, specifically the fate of Adam

a drunken artist ("The Toy Soldier") and Sheriff Coffee ("No Less a Man"), Hoss becomes involved with nuns ("A Question of Strength") and a mail order bride from China ("A Pink Cloud Comes From Old Cathay"), Joe grapples with ghosts ("Twilight Town") and the issue of mercy killing ("The Quality of Mercy"), the family is visited by not one but two relatives ("Return to Honor" and "The Saga of Muley Jones") and Virginia City plays host to Charles Dickens ("A Passion For Justice") and Jean Lafitte ("The Gentleman From New Orleans").

Michael Landon once told Johnny Carson that NBC hated it when "Bonanza" did comedy, but considering the show's great success, the network was no doubt keeping quiet by the time of funny installments like "Calamity Over the Comstock," "Ponderosa Matador," "Hoss and the Leprechauns", "King of the Mountain," "Walter and the Outlaws," and "The Pure Truth," most featuring

Greene with Inga Swenson in "Journey Remembered" (1963).

Greene with Ilka Windish in "A Question of Strength" (1963).

Cartwright. In December of 1963, Kathie Browne, who had been in two earlier episodes as different characters, was introduced as Laura Dayton, a young mother who is widowed when her husband is killed in a riding accident ("The Waiting Game"). Adam is attracted to her, steps in to help run her ranch ("The Cheating Game"), finds their relationship complicated by Laura's Aunt Lil ("The Pressure Game") and ultimately loses her to his cousin Will ("Triangle") by May.

Over the years it has been assumed that Guy Williams (previously television's Zorro) was brought in as the Cartwrights' cousin in case Pernell Roberts made good on his threats to break his contract with the network and walk off the show, which is only partially true. In truth, since NBC had no intention of letting Roberts go (some sources claim the network threatened to blacklist him), the main concern was whether or not viewers would accept a married Cartwright. Dortort's ideal scenario had all three actors remaining with the show: Adam and Laura are married, and Will stays on at the Ponderosa. The producer hoped "the new dimension in his role" would make Roberts more content, a sentiment which was shared by Kathie Browne. And although it was

announced in January that Guy Williams would be joining "Bonanza" on a regular basis, when Will rode off into the sunset with Laura at the conclusion of "Triangle," so did Williams. According to Dortort, the rest of the cast, Landon in particular, did not feel the character (originally intended to be Ben's younger brother) was necessary. "And, of course, whatever Mike wanted, Lorne went along with," said Dortort.

Strangely, Pernell Roberts wrote a letter to NBC, suggesting that if Adam was to take a wife, Mrs. Cartwright ought to be an Indian, played by a black actress. Roberts considered his idea "an unparalleled opportunity which might help toward the rebuilding of our national image and integrity. This would be one of the most progressive and constructive statements in television drama, as both the Negro and the American Indian have constantly been exploited 'second class citizens'." The network passed. In response, Dortort said even if NBC agreed, it was too late to recast the role and rewrite the scripts. He called Roberts' notion "well meaning, but confused. To ask a Negro to play an Indian doesn't solve anything. It is an empty gesture toward civil rights."

Roberts reacted to the general situation by say-

65

Roberts with Kathie Browne in "The Waiting Game" (1963).

Kathie Browne and Guy Williams in "Triangle" (1964).

ing, "I'm resigned to staying another year and a half. I'll go to rehearsal and give an intelligent reading, but that's all. No more suggestions for script changes. I'll wait it out. And after all, the money isn't bad." By then the four leads were earning in the area of $10,000 per episode.

All the debate involving a wedding and Cousin Will proved immaterial. In January, Dortort was said to be "carefully assessing public reaction to the encounter" between Adam and Laura "before proceeding with many more scripts." By March, responding to thousands of letters from "Bonanza" fans, Dortort told reporters, "The viewers made it very clear they not only want all the Cartwrights–they want 'em unmarried." Browne and Williams were originally scheduled to leave the show March 22, but their exit was postponed until May 17.

In a February 1964 issue of *TV Guide*, feminist Betty Friedan wondered: "If housewives control the dial, why, with no women at all, are Westerns perennially so popular? 'Beefcake' of course. 'Bonanza,' for instance, really gives the panting women a choice of sizes and ages– four unmarried men: Daddy and his three sons. According to reports, the producer has been toying with idea of

letting one of the four get married but, evidently out of consideration for all those women 'out there', hasn't had the nerve to let it happen yet."

That same month, "The Cheating Game" and "Bullet For a Bride" were the highest-rated episodes of the series to date. Apparently viewers of both sexes (as well as sizes and ages) were satisfied with the way "Bonanza" was progressing.

In its sixth year, long after most shows have worn out their welcome, "Bonanza" became the Number One series on television. This achievement seems even more fantastic when considering that Westerns in general were no longer the general public's preferred bill of fare. "The Virginian", trailing at #22, was the only other Western in television's Top 25 for 1964-65, and though the big screen offered John Ford's "Cheyenne Autumn" and Sergio Leone's "A Fistful of Dollars" (Clint Eastwood's first "Spaghetti Western"), neither was a smashing success.

President Lyndon Johnson, not wishing to incur the nation's wrath, admitted to avoiding "Bonanza'"'s time slot when he had an announcement to make. In an unusual move, NBC aired the season's second episode, "The Hostage," without interruption, placing an extended commercial for the 1965 Chevrolets at the end. The experiment, which had been tried the previous year, met with favor but, unfortunately, was never repeated. (Viewers who recall this as being a regular practice on "Bonanza" are mistaken.)

"Bonanza" merchandise–toys, board games, coloring books, lunch boxes, etc.–was popular with younger viewers, and in spite of the Beatles, Lorne Greene managed to have a hit album ("Welcome to the Ponderosa") and single ("Ringo"). Michael Landon did not do as well with an RCA single, "Without You"/"Linda is Lonesome," which few "Bonanza" fans realize he recorded.

Almost as rare is "Our Land– Our Heritage," the patriotic flavored album by actor/singer Jim Mitchum for which Dan Blocker recorded narration. The Cartwrights were even made honorary citizens of Nevada, then celebrating its centennial year. Pernell Roberts did not attend the ceremony.

The charge that Roberts was merely going through the motions during his final year on the show is one he has never disputed. "I don't even read the scripts," he confessed to a magazine writer early in the season. "I just ask the script girl what my line is before I go into each scene."

"You can imagine how it is for an actor to be delivering his lines and get nothing but a blank stare from the person he is talking to," Michael Landon complained.

"The only time I could get a good performance out of Pernell was when the show was centered around his character," said David Dortort. "But we couldn't suddenly be the Adam Cartwright Show."

The sixth season episodes featuring Adam are, in retrospect, many of the year's best, including "Thanks For Everything, Friend," "The Flannel Mouth Gun," "Right is the Fourth R" and "Dead and Gone." Otherwise, he does indeed appear to be coasting, delivering his lines without much conviction, disappearing into the scenery and seeming curiously amused in serious situations. Only in "Woman of Fire," the first episode by Suzanne Clauser (one of the show's best writers), does he look like he is having a genuinely good time.

Depending on who is talking, the Emmy

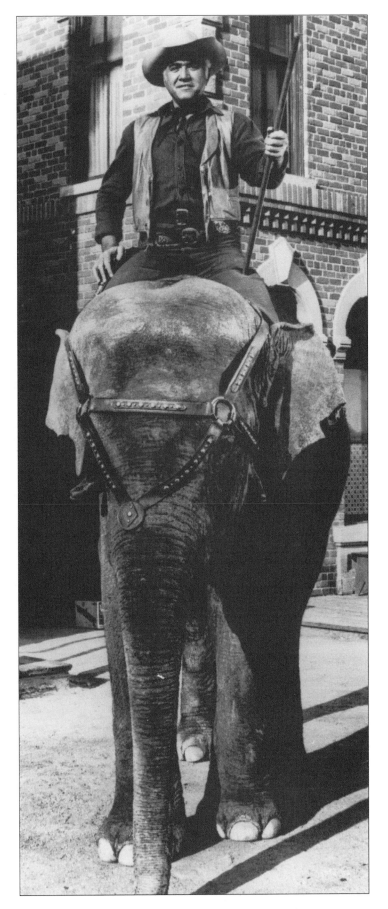

Greene in "Old Sheba" (1964).

Awards are either a popularity contest or a sincere recognition of achievement. Regardless of one's sentiments, even those not enamored of "Bonanza" had to agree that Edward Ancona's award as color consultant for the season was well deserved and overdue.

Among the highlights of 1964-65 were "The Hostage" (Ben held for ransom in an abandoned mine), "Between Heaven and Earth" (inspired in part by Landon and Dortort's shared aversion to heights), "The Saga of Squaw Charlie" (the usually villainous Anthony Caruso as a sympathetic Indian), "The Trap" (Joe gunned down in the season's highest-rated episode), "The Underdog" (Charles Bronson as a rustler who, in a twist, is not reformed by the Cartwrights' kindness) and "To Own the World" (Telly Savalas attempts to acquire the Ponderosa).

One episode, "A Man to Admire," contained a rare chronological inconsistency: Though the Civil War had broken out by the fourth season's "The War Comes to Washoe," and Abraham Lincoln was president of the Union, viewers are told he is still an Illinois lawyer in this sixth season segment.

As always, the guest stars were a collection of Hollywood's past, present and future, including Guy Stockwell, Harold J. Stone, Aldo Ray, Rory Calhoun, Dan Duryea, George Kennedy, Bruce Cabot, William Demarest, Earl Holliman, Ed Wynn, Cesar Romero, Mariette Hartley and several others. For the first time, the names of the characters played by supporting players were listed in the closing credits.

Also for the first time, there was a plethora of comedies: "The Scapegoat," "Old Sheba," "A Knight to Remember," "The Flapjack Contest," "The Ponderosa Birdman," "A Good Night's Rest," "Lothario Larkin" and "Hound Dog," the latter featuring the return of cousin Muley Jones. Fortunately, the Cartwrights were as capable of clowning as dispensing heroics.

Not so funny was the impending departure of Pernell Roberts, who did not hesitate to let the press know he felt his six years with "Bonanza" had been a waste of his time. Whereas a year before he had admitted the money was good, he now

Blocker in "The Ponderosa Birdman" (1965).

claimed it was not important to him. "If you're locked into a philosophy of nickels and dimes, then you have a pretty limited approach to life. I don't need a lot of money to live with dignity." Nor was he worried about his future: "I was always able to do the kind of work I wanted to do before 'Bonanza,' and I expect to be able to do it after I leave."

"He felt time was rushing by," Lorne Greene explained. "I said, 'Look, Pernell, if you stay with 'Bonanza' you'll make so much money you'll be able to build your own theater and get Tennessee Williams to write a play for you.'"

But Roberts had made up his mind long before Adam Cartwright's final season began. There are more than a few conflicting accounts of exactly how he left the show, all of which may contain an element of truth, yet the fact remains that David Dortort did what he could to satisfy his star. "You've got to keep an actor happy if you want a great performance from him," the producer said. "We offered him more money, allowed him time off to do plays, everything."

Perhaps only Roberts knows the whole story behind rumors that range from NBC rejecting his outrageous financial demands to stay with the show, to his actually being fired, but it is a subject he has always been reluctant to discuss. In 1978, thirteen years after leaving "Bonanza" in the dust, he told a reporter, "The studio launched a campaign of vilification against me and it has never stopped. I didn't reply then and I won't now. I'm disappointed anyone would bring it up." The comment is at odds with the abundance of guest roles Roberts landed after his days as Adam Cartwright, but again, only he knows the personal details.

Shortly before Roberts left, Dortort said, "The problems, all his rudeness, his impossible conduct and lack of professionalism–I would forgive him all that if he would come back. He is that good." And the door was indeed left open in the event Roberts changed his mind. Though they decreased in frequency as the years went by, there were references made to Adam as late as 1970.

More than a year after moving on, Roberts was asked if he would consider returning to "Bonanza," and his response was predictably blunt as well as bitter: "No. It's amazing how I managed to survive six years of utter frustration. It really was a

crusher for me, mentally. I even went to a doctor for help. I had to get out..." He added that he happened to see part of an episode recently and found it "funnier'n than hell" even though it was not a comedy.

Roberts' contention that television "can't produce anything of real merit if it has to be cranked out on a weekly basis" was not entirely wrong, as

Roberts with Joan Hackett at Golden Oak Ranch in "Woman of Fire" (1965).

even an above average series will have its lesser moments, but it was still unfair. Even Roberts' own "Trapper John, M.D." turned out segments far superior to the general run of televised entertainment.

"He was a deep-thinking person who constantly wanted to see 'Bonanza' more socially oriented," said Bill Kiley, a press agent for the show, "but it was a hit action Western and nobody paid him much mind."

Actually, "Bonanza" already had explored several timely issues not normally associated with traditional Westerns before Roberts left, and in

The U.S. Postal Service shows its appreciation of "Ride the Wind" (1966).

later seasons there were numerous storylines that doubtlessly would have met with his approval.

The departure of Roberts was regrettable, and while it was strange (and maybe a little sad) to see only three Cartwrights galloping up to the camera on September 12, 1965, the seventh season of "Bonanza" was another triumph. Total viewership decreased somewhat, but the show remained Number One when the year-end ratings were tallied. There was substantially more shooting done at Incline Village, as well as other locations, and some episodes ("The Other Son," "Five Sundowns to Sunup," "Ride the Wind") were filmed and cut more like movies than television shows. Not surprising, then, were the Emmy Awards given to "Bonanza"'s chief editors (Marvin Coil, Everett Douglas, Ellsworth Hoagland) at the end of the season. The show itself received its only nomination–the first for any Western since 1958–as Best Dramatic Series, but lost to "The Fugitive."

It mattered little that most of the stories involved the Cartwrights rather than being specifically about them, for the scripts were of a high order. Especially memorable episodes were "The Lonely Runner" (with a marvelous performance by Gilbert Roland), "*The* Meredith Smith" (typically hilarious job by Strother Martin), "All Ye His Saints" (Clint Howard proving some child stars can be refreshingly natural as opposed to irritating automatons), "Peace Officer" (Eric Fleming in his first post-"Rawhide" role), "Home From the Sea" (with the subject of Adam coming up so many times one expects him to appear), and two with characters who would return in subsequent seasons ("The Unwritten Commandment" and "Big Shadow on the Land").

"Ride the Wind" deserves special mention as being the first two-part installment of "Bonanza," directed by Western veteran William Witney and filmed at such classic locations as Red Rock Canyon and Vasquez Rocks. A mini-epic in tribute to the Pony Express, the episode was honored with a citation from the United States Postal Service, and released theatrically to foreign markets in 1967. While the Cartwrights share the screen almost equally with the guest cast (including Victor Jory, Rod Cameron and DeForest Kelley), one of the most affecting scenes (criminally cut from the syndicated print) involves Ben and Hop Sing, alone after Joe and Hoss have left to help the new mail service. The camera pans from Ben's vacant spot at the dining room table to other empty chairs. Hop Sing emerges from the kitchen to find his employer standing in the center of the room. "Listen to this house, Hop Sing," says Ben.

"Listen to the silence of it." He puts his arm around the cook. "Do you remember when we built this house, Hop Sing? This room was filled with so much happiness. Mrs. Cartwright, Little Joe's mother, Adam, Hoss, Little Joe? They filled this house. That's what it was built for: happiness, love, family. Where's it all gone?"

Although "Ride the Wind" was released on home video in 1984, the entire 1965-66 season, incredibly enough, was not put into syndication until 1988. With the exception of "The Virginian," barely squeezing into the Top 25, the only other Western among the year's most-watched shows was "The Wild, Wild West," which managed to distinguish itself by cashing in on the popularity of James Bond rather than the Cartwrights.

There was, however, an obvious attempt at duplicating the successful "Bonanza" format that fall, namely ABC's "The Big Valley," on which Pernell Roberts made one of his first post-Adam appearances. In this version, the head of the wealthy ranching family was a woman (Barbara Stanwyck), and in addition to her sons was a daughter. Comparisons between the two shows invariably put Stanwyck–who told reporters that her TV sons were more manly than Lorne Greene's–on the defensive. She went so far as to label Greene "the Loretta Young of Western Soap Operas." On another occasion, she made a point of criticizing Dan Blocker for complaining about his salary: "What so-called artist is this who feels he is wasting his talent for $10,000 a week? He seems to feel the public loves him for himself as an actor. But what was he before playing Hoss? The love the

Blocker in "A Real Nice, Friendly Little Town" (1966).

public has given him is due to the role, the script, the actions of the person he is employed to portray. If he is now a multimillionaire, as he says is–and from this part–what a shame he should continue to fool the public and to accept the love they give him." Ms. Stanwyck, who never hesitated to complain when she found her own professional situation unsatisfactory, neglected to mention that her salary was higher than Blocker's.

Though never a big hit, "The Big Valley" lasted four seasons and turned out over a hundred episodes using some of the same writers, directors and guests as "Bonanza."

Judging by accounts of the day, the "Bonanza" clan was unruffled by the barbs of Stanwyck or anyone else. Visitors to the set discovered the atmosphere to be, if anything, even happier than in the past. The three stars continued to attract huge crowds at personal appearances, and in addition to his club act, Greene had another album ("The Man") out and recorded two more, "Lorne Greene's American West" and "Have a Happy Holiday."

"A Bride for Buford" with Lola Albright (1967).

After passing the "test" of a season with a three-member cast, "Bonanza" returned for an eighth year that was nearly as consistent as its exceptional fifth. And though its ratings took a dip in a bi-weekly poll taken during March 1967, the show finished at Number One for the third time in a row. Once again, a majority of the scripts found the Cartwrights' problems not as personally focused as in earlier seasons, yet the stories (three co-written by Michael Landon) managed to be both fresh and absorbing. Hoss' latest romantic disappointment ("To Bloom For Thee"), for instance, was considerably more "adult" than those of "The Newcomers," "The Courtship" or "The Tall Stranger." And the circumstances surrounding the fate of Joe's intended ("Justice") were downright grim. In fact, many of the season's episodes are characterized by a vaguely ominous mood, particularly "A Woman in the House" (spousal abuse), "Tommy" (an outlaw father with no redeeming qualities), "The Unseen Wound" (post-combat stress), "The Wormwood Cup" (a price put on Joe's head) and "Something Hurt, Something Wild" (mental illness) to name only a handful.

There were, of course, lighter moments such as

"A Christmas Story," "Ponderosa Explosion," "A Bride For Buford," "Maestro Hoss" and "Joe Cartwright, Detective," yet even some of these had dark shadings. If the season had a low point, it was probably "Napoleon's Children," an unintentionally amusing attempt to deal with juvenile delinquency in Virginia City.

At the other end of the spectrum was "The Pursued," unquestionably a milestone in the history "Bonanza." A two-part saga shot at and around Lone Pine's legendary Anchor Ranch, it features, in the words of David Dortort, "some of the finest shots of riders in action we ever filmed, with the great Mount Whitney in the background." Going on location at Lone Pine was a journey to the past for director William Witney, who had done the first Lone Ranger serial for Republic there in 1938.

In "The Pursued," the Cartwrights travel to Beehive, Nevada to purchase horses from Heber Clauson (Eric Fleming, who drowned while filming a segment for another series only one month before "The Pursued" aired), a Mormon rancher with two wives. The Cartwrights, true to their nature, are tolerant of the Clausons' beliefs, Ben explaining to his sons that all ancient religions

72

practiced polygamy, and because the Mormons have always been so persecuted, they have adopted the practice of taking more than one wife in order to avoid extinction. The local "Christian" population, inflamed by the fanatical provocations of its self-appointed preacher, frowns on the Clausons' presence, and the situation is further inflamed by the town boss' infatuation with Susannah (Dina Merrill), one of Heber's wives. When the narrow-minded citizens of Beehive come to burn them out, Joe helps the Clausons escape into the desert. Complicating matters is the fact that Heber's other wife, Elizabeth Ann (Lois Nettleton), is about to give birth and in no shape for a torturous wagon ride filmed in the rugged Alabama Hills. The persecuted party has little choice but to take cover and wait for the return of Hoss and Ben, who are rounding up horses at another ranch. The other Cartwrights come to the rescue, but in a shockingly unexpected turn of events, the town boss, Carbo, shoots Heber in the back from ambush, killing him immediately.

Joe's shooting of Carbo conflicts with the Cartwrights' customary practice of letting the law take its course, but only the most rigid liberal could argue the villain did not have it coming. Nor does the tragedy end there. After Carbo's gang loses its taste for violence and rides off, leaving the preacher futilely beseeching them to not turn their backs on their mission, Hoss brings back a true minister and his wife to see if anything can be done about Elizabeth Ann's precarious condition.

Blocker with Zsa Zsa Gabor in the 1967 episode, "Maestro Hoss." Note script pages on table.

Viveca Lindfors and Greene in "The Spotlight" (1965).

As a whole, the season featured outstanding performances by guest stars such as Ed Begley, Henry Darrow, Diane Baker and Beau Bridges, striking new musical motifs by David Rose, and a visit from Ben's cousin ("Clarissa") which demonstrated perfectly how a female could upset the dynamic of the Ponderosa. Though David Dortort has been quoted as considering his mother "a saint", he maintained as early as 1960, "we do not have any Moms built into our show—or, for that matter, any women. We are, as it were, anti Momism." Female viewers obviously did not object, one even writing to say, "I like your show because it's the only Western I know where the girl rides off into the sunset."

"Bonanza" itself was hardly ready to ride off into the sunset at the end of the season. Greene

A 1966 novel by Thomas Thompson.

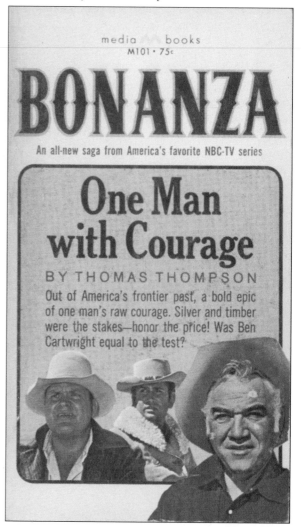

A baby boy is delivered, but there is no hope for its mother. "If only Heber could have known," she tells Susannah just before she dies. "He knows," Susannah reassures her. The minister and his wife announce they have no intention of judging another's religion, and tell Susannah their home is hers and the baby's for as long as she wishes. As the four of them ride away, Joe says he hopes the world is a better place by the time Heber's son is old enough to find his place in it.

The script for "The Pursued" was by the prolific Thomas Thompson, who had by this time written or co-written a dozen episodes and was listed in the show's credits as executive consultant. The basic story, by Thompson and Mark Michaels, had the approval of the Mormon church, whose history had provided the episode's inspiration. Yet more than thirty years later, "The Pursued" itself is a victim of religious prejudice, as Pat Robertson, the Family Channel's conservative extremist, refuses to air it. Until the cable network's right to the episode expires, viewers will have to be content with their memories of the show, or seek out the few collectors who are fortunate enough to own prints.

recorded yet another album, "Portrait of the West," and Thomas Thompson began what was intended as a series of original "Bonanza" novels, with "One Man with Courage," complete with a foreword penned by Greene. The book seemed to have "feature film" written all over it, but such was not the case. A second novel, "Black Silver" (1967) by William R. Cox, was the second and final book of the short-lived literary experiment.

"Bonanza"'s competitors were routinely trampled in the ratings, including its former foe, "Perry Mason," which CBS had moved to Sunday in 1965. Amusingly, on the final episode of that classic series, a show business attorney actually tells another that any network pitting a program against "Bonanza" was fighting a losing battle. Even Judy Garland, whose variety show was defeated by the Cartwrights before the 1963-64 season was over, said she did not blame viewers for watching "Bonanza"; she was a fan herself.

In February of 1967, however, a serious challenger arrived in the form of "The Smother Brothers Comedy Hour." Tom and Dick Smothers were comic folk singers who wasted no time in upsetting their network, CBS, with subversive political satire while at the same time exciting younger viewers with appearances by the day's biggest rock bands. Within a month, "Bonanza"'s ratings showed a troubling decline.

Michael Landon, for one, was not worried, telling a reporter that after eight years, the "game" was making him restless, though he admitted he had no complaints about the money. In addition to $13,000 per-episode, he was collecting separate checks for writing and executing his own stunts. The rodeo circuit was bringing in another $175,000 a year. Dan Blocker (who had no real love of appearing in public) commented, "Mike knows he can't sing. He's flat. He's off-key. Michael's not kidding himself. But if those jerks'll pay for it, he'll sing." Landon had also started itching to direct.

In late July, it was announced that the Cartwrights would be hiring a regular hired hand during the upcoming season, presumably in an effort to fill the void left by Pernell Roberts, and hopefully inject new life into the series. "Bonanza" may have finished the year at the top of the ratings heap, but "The Smothers Brothers Comedy Hour" managed to place at #16 after only three months on the air. It was clear that an era had most likely come to an end, not only for "Bonanza" but for Westerns in general. During the 1966-67 season, there had been fourteen of them in prime time, but aside from "The Virginian" (#10), none made it into the Top 25. Younger viewers apparently determined what shows were most popular, as sitcoms, variety shows and movies held all but half a dozen of the top positions. With Vietnam and race riots dominating headlines, viewers obviously preferred their escapism light rather than dramatic.

Movies, on the other hand, were becoming more realistic and tougher, including such Westerns as "Duel at Diablo," "The Good, the Bad and the Ugly," "The Professionals" and Jack Nicholson's underrated "The Shooting." How the small screen would present the genre–"Bonanza" in particular–would be interesting.

In its ninth season, "Bonanza" became a Western, as outlandish as that sounds. To be sure, it had always been a Western, but in a larger sense, it was a multifaceted drama which just happened to take place in the Old West, more character-driven than dependent on traditional frontier plots. While other series had long ago ridden the latter into the ground, it remained relatively fresh territory for "Bonanza." Most of these adventures took place away from the familiar surroundings of the Ponderosa and involved all manner of crooked lawmen, corrupt politicians, murder trials and wayward acquaintances from the Cartwrights' past. The majority of these episodes were done with former "Combat" line producer Robert Blees, David Dortort (now listed as series creator and executive producer) having to divide his time between "Bonanza" and his new series, "The High Chaparral." Virtually every installment credited to longtime associate producer James W. Lane ("The Sure Thing" and "The Gentle Ones" for example) are a bit lighter in tone and seem to belong to another, earlier season.

The increase in location filming meant more trips to Incline Village, where that summer a replica of the Ponderosa ranch house had been built under the supervision of one Bill Anderson, with the financial participation of the network, Greene, Blocker and Landon. Anderson, who worked with the Crystal Bay Development Company (given occasional screen credit during the early years of the show), also ran a riding stable on the side and tended to the production's livestock when "Bonanza" made its annual trek to the Sierras. Contrary to common belief, the original series did no interior filming at Incline Village, and exterior photography of the house was limited to a brief establishing stock shot taken from an overlooking ridge. In order to reach Lake Tahoe for a week or more of filming, as many as fifteen trucks had to leave Paramount Studios Saturday morning, with the rest of the crew flying into the Reno airport early on Monday.

As NBC announced prior to the start of produc-

Left: David Dortort as the "father" of the cast (1961).
Right: David Canary's performance in "Hombre" (1967) earned him the role of Candy..

CHAPTER FOUR

RANGING WIDE (1967-70)

tion on the 1967-68 season, a new regular character was added to the cast of "Bonanza," and Michael Landon satisfied his creative urges by co-writing a script ("Six Black Horses"), writing his own for the first time ("A Dream to Dream") and, most significantly, both writing and directing one of the year's best episodes, "To Die in Darkness."

Despite these fresh developments, "Bonanza" fell out of the Top Five in the seasonal ratings for the first time since 1960, coming in at #6, behind four sitcoms and, surprisingly, "Gunsmoke." By coincidence, "Gunsmoke" had disappeared from the Top 25 the same three years "Bonanza" was Number One, and during the previous season had dropped to #34. In reality, CBS had given the citizens of Dodge City their walking papers, but in an unusual move, network chief William S. Paley strongly suggested the show be given another chance on a different night. By switching to Monday and concentrating on more currently topical themes, "Gunsmoke" attracted a whole new audience and continued until 1975, setting a twenty season record no dramatic series has yet equalled. Ironically, some critics felt the show's renewed success was due to its borrowing a bit of the domesticity "Bonanza" was in the process of at least partially abandoning.

For the record, the Smothers Brothers mixture of controversial humor and music, which has not aged well, began to flame out rather quickly. At the end of the season, it ranked #18, behind even "The Virginian" at #14, and the following year, its last, did not appear in the Top 25 at all.

A survey conducted in late 1967 determined "Bonanza" to be the third most-watched program in the country, and that its largest audience was comprised of adults over the age of 34 who lived in the South and held down blue collar jobs. While such studies are neither scientific nor definitive, it did indicate that watching "Bonanza" was not the family activity it had been earlier in the decade.

At the box office, Westerns were enjoying a small comeback. It was the year of "El Dorado," "The War Wagon," "Hang 'Em High," "Hour of the Gun," "Will Penny," "Welcome to Hard Times" and a solid Paul Newman feature, "Hombre," whose cast included an obscure but dynamic actor by the name of David Canary.

David Dortort, in Arizona for pre-production

work on "The High Chaparral," first observed Canary playing out a tense barroom scene with Newman. "I realized immediately I had found the new foreman of the Ponderosa," said the producer. "He's the kind of kid who comes on and suddenly there's no one else on the screen."

Canary, the son of a J.C. Penney store manager, was born in Ohio. While playing football for the University of Cincinnati, he broke his nose, an injury which later led him to describe his face as "a bowl of oatmeal thrown against the kitchen wall." His appearance made no difference to the Denver Broncos, who offered him a position playing left end, but Canary turned them down. What really interested him were music and theater, so he took off for New York and got a job singing in the chorus of an off-Broadway show. He also enrolled in acting class, and before being drafted, landed the lead in "The Fantasticks." By the time his military stint was over, he had directed "the army version" of the play.

Arriving in Hollywood, he spent six months as Dr. Russ Gehring on ABC's prime time soap opera "Peyton Place," followed by a small role in the film "The St. Valentine's Day Massacre" with Jason Robards and George Segal. He nearly had the distinction of being the final major guest star on "Gunsmoke," as the episode he appeared in (a two-parter entitled "Nitro!") was the last one filmed before the show's brief cancellation. Prior to being chosen to portray Candy on "Bonanza," he did a segment of CBS's ambitious but short-lived "Cimarron Strip" with Stuart Whitman.

"Candy is a loner, a stray," David Dortort said when describing Canary's character. "He is not a Cartwright, so he is not necessarily bound by family ties. He has no Ben Cartwright to fall back upon in solving his problems."

Line producer Robert Blees was more specific: "Canary is the sand in the gears. He's there to shake up the Cartwright establishment, put a bomb under all those cliché little morality plays. While Papa Ben is yelling for a fair trial, Candy is capable of something a little more underhanded, and human."

The new cast at Incline Village for the episode "Kingdom of Fear" (1967).

Opinions vary as to whether or not the cast initially welcomed Canary with open arms, but Dortort said "he held his own."

"I'm the new kid on the block," Canary explained at the start of his association with the show. "They don't know me. I can't expect to be accepted right away. They have too many memories, confidences."

Dan Blocker had no problem with the Ponderosa's new resident, and later introduced Canary to the person responsible for arranging personal appearances. "We're all so damn goody-goody we can't get involved anymore," grumbled Blocker. "The kid is great. The show needs him."

Even so, Canary admitted it took a while before he felt completely comfortable with the rest of the cast. "It's hardest when they're cutting up, telling stories on the set. I'm not there–like when you first walk into a party. I may never catch up. Maybe it's not necessary that I do."

Before long, however, Canary was smoothly integrated both off and on camera. Lorne Greene publicly praised his acting, and Michael Landon (who in particular had been against Guy Williams joining the show) was kind enough to provide a heating pad when he pinched a nerve during a fight scene.

Upon returning to the show in 1972, after a two-season absence, Canary said he discovered that "Bonanza" had "a really tremendous following, which you only begin to get an idea of when you do public appearances. I was amazed that everybody I met knew who I was."

Canary need not have been surprised. Widespread recognition is an inevitable result when one's face flashes on the screen in 81 episodes of a show which spends most of its time in television's Top 10.

Candy, a former army brat who now simply drifts along when the mood strikes, is introduced in the season's second episode, "Sense of Duty."

His name, he explains, is short for Canaday, and that is nearly all he ever reveals about his possibly shady past. In a later story, Joe refers to him as "Candy Canaday", but his actual first name is never learned. When Ben offers him a steady job on the Ponderosa, he accepts with the understanding that he can leave whenever he wants, and in "Trouble Town" he does just that, but not for long.

Canary as Candy, Ponderosa foreman and honorary Cartwright (1967).

The 21 episodes Canary did during "Bonanza's" ninth year were more often than not among the best, and by the end of the season it was clear Blocker knew what he was talking about: the "kid" was good, and added an exciting new dimension to the show. He is the primary focus of Thomas Thompson's "Star Crossed," a tragic love story which gives him the perfect opportunity to do more than play cowboy, and his talent is striking. In "Showdown at Tahoe," also written by Thompson, Candy goes undercover as the pilot of Ben's riverboat and helps foil the plans of murderous thieves.

Director Leon Benson also joined "Bonanza" in 1967 and directed almost half of the season's episodes, including several regarded as classics by many of the show's fans: "Night of Reckoning" (with Richard Jaeckel riveting as a sadistic outlaw), "Desperate Passage" (a bang-up wilderness adventure with Steve Forrest), a pair of good mysteries ("A Girl Named George" and "The Thirteenth Man") and "The Late Ben Cartwright," which could very well have been fashioned into a solid two-part entry.

Johnnie Whitaker and Michele Tobin with Blocker in "A Dream to Dream" (1968).

"A Dream to Dream," written by Michael Landon, gave Dan Blocker another chance to shine in a dramatic story, as Hoss becomes involved with the wife and children of an alcoholic rancher. Lending more than competent support were Julie Harris, Steve Inhat and one of the better child actors of the day, Johnny Whitaker.

More important was "To Die in Darkness," which was both written and directed by Landon. He had been pressuring David Dortort to allow him to direct, and during a press conference introducing David Canary, the youngest Cartwright enlisted the aid of reporters to make the producer consent. With suggestions from William Claxton, Landon turned out one of the best episodes in the series' history, not only in terms of story but visually as well. Ben and Candy are confined to a deep pit by an embittered ex-con for practically the entire show, but Landon's imagination was undoubtedly expansive.

The second episode written and directed by Landon, "Kingdom of Fear," was but one of several network shows voluntarily delayed due to governmental concern about television violence follow-

ing the assassinations of Martin Luther King, Jr., and Robert Kennedy. By the time it finally aired (April 4, 1971), David Canary was no longer with the series, but viewers assumed he had suddenly returned.

Shortly before the next season started, "Bonanza's" main sponsor, Chevrolet, asked famed artist Norman Rockwell if he would be interested in painting portraits of the show's cast. Regrettably, NBC would not help meet Rockwell's asking price, and the idea died.

"Bonanza," however, was very much alive, and on September 15, 1968, began its tenth year. "The Big Valley" began its last. Of the twenty-seven Westerns which shared the prime time schedule with "Bonanza" in 1959, only "Gunsmoke" remained on the air. The rookie Western that fall was "Lancer," a CBS variation of "Bonanza," complete with a widowed rancher (the late Andrew Duggan), two half-brothers (James Stacy and Wayne Maunder), and in its second season, a colorfully cantankerous cook ("Rawhide's" Paul Brinegar). To make the Lancer family just a bit different from the Cartwrights, the producers added

81

Greene and Canary in "To Die in Darkness" (1968), Landon's directorial debut.

a regular female character to the mix. "Lancer" was a modest success, lasting for 51 episodes but always losing its time slot to ABC's "The Mod Squad."

As for "Bonanza," viewership was up (#3 for the season), perhaps because, in the words of David Dortort's newest assistant, producer Richard Collins: "We're going back more to what made the show big in the beginning–the relationship between the father and his sons." Although the close family relationship to which Collins referred was not fully revived for another two seasons, the Cartwrights were, of course, as loyal to each other as ever.

Once again, many of the stories take place off the Ponderosa, including "The Real People of Muddy Creek" (with future regular Mitch Vogel), in which Joe reluctantly leaves Ben to almost single-handedly defend a town from outlaws, and "Catch as Catch Can," which finds the Cartwrights up against a community of strangers and a plot to destroy their good name.

Candy appears in all but six of the year's thirty episodes, and in one,"Salute to Yesterday," it is revealed that he was once married. In "Company of

Forgotten Men," he becomes unwillingly involved in an old acquaintance's scheme to rob the Carson City mint, and "Mrs. Wharton and the Lesser Breeds" finds him lending frustrating assistance to a British widow determined to explore the West.

In "Mark of Guilt," a clever story in which Hoss defends Joe against a murder charge, Victor Sen Yung is given a rare opportunity to share the spotlight as he comes to the rescue with the ancient Chinese art of fingerprinting. The guilty party, incidentally, is played by Lou Frizzell, who would be introduced as semi-regular Dusty Rhoades the following season.

Until recently, Hollywood has always been notorious for its generally inaccurate and unfair depiction of Native Americans, on screens both large and small. During the 1950's, however, a few filmmakers adopted a more enlightened attitude, and it can be argued that Indians were shown to be something other than anonymous savages more often on television than in motion pictures. There

Blocker and Victor Sen Yung engage in the Chinese art of fingerprinting in "Mark of Guilt" (1968).

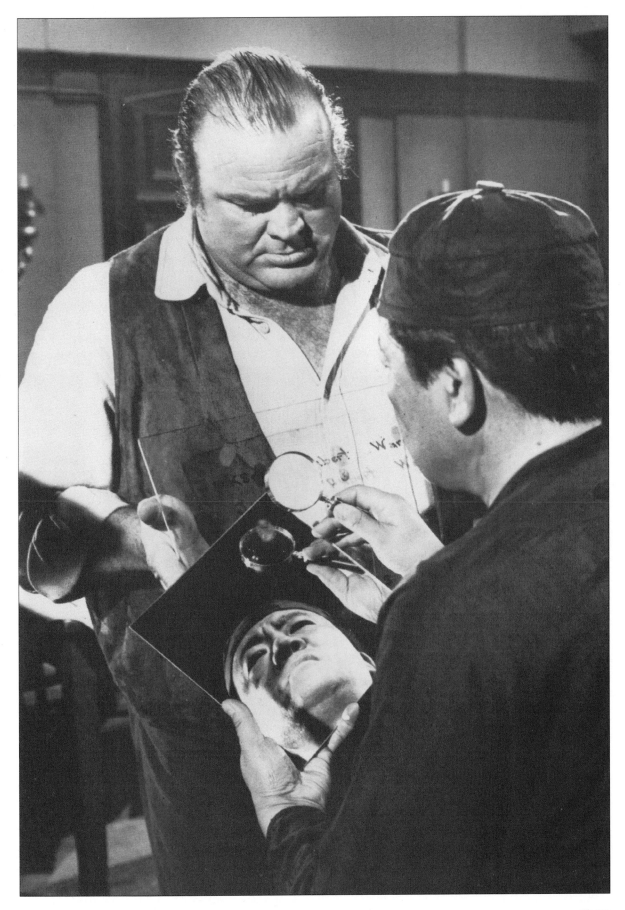

were, of course, several lapses of good taste, but it is equally true that some shows were better than others regarding the treatment of this country's original citizens. "Bonanza's" approach to the subject was usually well-balanced, portraying Indians as neither all savage nor totally noble. In other words, human. As the series progressed, so did its awareness and authenticity, good examples of which were this season's "The Survivors," "My Friend, My Enemy" and "Sound of Drums." In the latter (third in a trilogy with Jack Kruschen as Italian immigrant Giorgio Rossi), Indians prove to have more common sense when it is necessary to remind white men that corn cannot grow in sand.

Perhaps the most noteworthy moment of 1968-69 was "The Wish," a powerful story written and directed by Landon, and the episode of which he was proudest. In it, a well-meaning Hoss fumbles while attempting to help a black widower (Ossie Davis) and his three children. "Mainly I wanted to get across the idea to whites just why black people are angry and frustrated," said Landon, "and I wanted to cool some of the backlash. One black writer saw the show and he said to me, 'You've gotten so close to what it's like to be black, I could hardly believe it was written by a white man.' For me that was my Emmy." In an interview conducted shortly after Landon's death, Ossie Davis said the script "was ahead of its time."

Not every show could be of that high caliber, however. "The Last Vote," a comedy with Tom Bosley and Wally Cox, seemed like a throwback to the series' simpler days, "The Lady and the Mountain Lion" was one of the few boring installments in the show's history, and "Little Girl Lost" featured a child actress who appeared perpetually on the verge of breaking into laughter.

But the few low spots were more than compensated for by such substantial dramas as "A World Full of Cannibals," (written and directed by "Gunsmoke" veterans) "The Deserter" (with the late, great Ben Johnson), "Five Candles" (Ben is trapped when the floor of the Virginia City courthouse collapses) and "A Ride in the Sun" (Joe crosses the desert in pursuit of cunning bank robbers who have shot Ben). "Erin," about a white

"Showdown at Tahoe" (1967).

woman who lives with the Indians, was another doomed romance for Hoss, and one of the year's best. "I was afraid she was going to run off and leave me," he tells Ben and Candy as he cradles his love's limp body. "Now I wish to God she had."

"The Unwanted" guest-starred Bonnie Bedelia, who as another character would have gone on to play Hoss' bride in 1972 had Dan Blocker not died. In light of that, it is interesting to watch them together and imagine what might have been.

An otherwise fine episode, "My Friend, My Enemy," contains one of the series' few chronological errors. Hoss mentions the fate of General Custer, who died at the Little Big Horn in 1876, whereas in "A Man to Admire," only a little over four years before, it was supposed to be 1861. The Cartwrights certainly did not look like they had aged fifteen years in that short span of time.

The Western was restored to a position of some prominence in 1969, the year of "Bonanza's" eleventh season, thanks primarily to the films "Butch Cassidy and the Sundance Kid" with Paul Newman and Robert Redford, Sam Peckinpah's controversial epic "The Wild Bunch," and "True Grit," for which John Wayne finally received an Oscar.

On television there were but six Western series, and the only two in the Top 25 at the conclusion

George Spell and Blocker in "The Wish" (1969).

John Anderson and Greene at Big Bear in "The Fence" (1969).

of the season were the old reliables, "Gunsmoke" (#2) and "Bonanza" (again #3).

By the time the 1969-70 season began, Landon's hair, which had been getting longer over the previous two seasons, was even shaggier. Greene had lost some weight, and Blocker had gained more than a few pounds. As for less immediate changes, only three episodes revolved around Candy, though he appeared in 25, and the intriguing premise of his becoming involved with a widow and her young son ("The Stalker") was not pursued. Sheriff Coffee was no longer seen as often as in years past, and judging by the startling way a mob roughs him up in "Anatomy of a Lynching," the writing is on the proverbial wall regarding his future as Virginia City's leading constable.

Unlike the preceding season, there were no substandard moments and a good number of outstanding ones. The show's past was recalled in "Return Engagement," with Sally Kellerman as Lotta Crabtree, and "Is There Any Man Here...?," which surprises viewers with an unexpected mention of Adam, five years after he left the ranch.

Michael Landon continued to establish himself as a talent to be reckoned with by writing and directing three quite different episodes, the first a

comedy with the delightful Arthur Hunnicutt (and some of Landon's wife's relatives among the extras) called "Dead Wrong." True to its title, Hoss is almost buried alive.

In "It's a Small World," Landon grabs the audience from the start by having a little person in clown makeup (Michael Dunn) burst in on Ben and Clem's card game, only this story is not played for laughs. Alternately sad and uplifting, Ben tries to help the man make a go of it without relying on the circus.

Landon's final show of the season, "Decision at Los Robles," is a suspenseful effort in which Ben is backshot, and Joe attempts to rally a town against gunmen led by the son of the man Ben was forced to kill. Filmed on some of the same Paramount sets used by Dortort's somewhat grittier "The High Chaparral," this grim episode demonstrates perfectly that not everything Landon did was sweet and light.

Sweet and light, however, are apt descriptions of "Meena," with Dub Taylor and Ann Prentiss as a prospector and his loony but lonely daughter. Carrying on a tradition of bringing back characters deserving of another look, there was a sequel, "The Horse Traders" (which introduced semi-regular Lou Frizzel as Dusty Rhoades) before the season was out.

The funniest episode of the year, however, was "Caution: Easter Bunny Crossing," which could have been merely silly but was instead a riotous live-action cartoon. The spectacle of Dan Blocker running around Iverson Movie Location Ranch, along with comics Art Metrano, Len Lesser and Vic Tayback, is not easily forgotten.

In an entirely different vein was "The Trouble with Amy," highlighted by Jo Van Fleet's remarkable performance as an eccentric widow with more animals in her house than in her barn. Although there are several humorous touches, the story is a gentle drama focusing on Ben's fight to prevent Amy from being institutionalized.

Unbelievably, none of the Cartwrights ever received an Emmy nomination. Perhaps it was because, as "Gunsmoke" producer John Mantley claimed, the television industry no longer paid much attention to Westerns. Or maybe it had something to do with what Michael Landon termed "the cowboy-actor stigma, the feeling in this town that we're all no smarter than our horses." Whatever the reason, Landon should have been recognized for "A Matter of Circumstance," the one-man tour de force that closed the 1969-70 season. Alone at the ranch, Joe is seriously trampled by a horse and not discovered until on the verge of amputating his own arm. Also ignored was William Claxton's superb direction.

Possibilities for developing the character of Candy were almost unlimited, given his purposely hazy background. In addition to "The Stalker," this potential is glimpsed in "The Big Jackpot," which finds him under the mistaken impression he is about to become a wealthy land baron. The merchants of Virginia City have no trouble imagining Candy as more than the Ponderosa's foreman, nor does the viewing audience. Unfortunately, David Canary, anxious to exercise his creative muscle as a writer and director, decided to quit the show. Although not happy about it, David Dortort understood and wished him well. Candy's disappearance from the ranch was never explained.

In retrospect, Candy's time on the Ponderosa (1967-70) was a more sharply defined period of transition than the two previous years without him, or Adam. Most critics, and even some fans, consider the Canary era to be strictly secondary in relation to 1959-67, but that is an extreme opinion informed more by nostalgia than objectivity. To debate who is the better actor, Pernell Roberts or David Canary, is pointless, as there is no correct answer. Personal preference is entirely subjective, absolute only for the individual making the decision.

In all fairness, David Dortort and his people were wise and creative enough to keep "Bonanza" refreshingly vital without altering its foundation. As one of the very few shows in the history of television to actually improve with age, it is not surprising to realize that no two seasons are alike. Each of them has its own subtle color and tone beneath the obvious. Again, which seasons a viewer regards as "best" is no accurate reflection of the series' overall quality. The styles of acting and writing grew more sophisticated as time went on, but only the most jaded viewer would fail to appreciate the simple charm of the early years.

Irene Tedrow and Landon in "Different Pines, Same Wind" (1968).

To say "Bonanza" in the late Sixties was not as good or as memorable as before David Canary joined the series is to dismiss such superior moments as "The Wish," "The Trouble with Amy" and "The Survivors"–to name only a few–as nothing more than routine, which is far from true. "Bonanza" may have gotten closer to its Western roots on a fairly regular basis during these years, but even when the show was not completely authentic, it offered an original vision of the Old West unmatched by any of its contemporaries.

And the well was far from dry.

T he final 69 episodes of "Bonanza" have never been given the recognition they deserve, largely because the majority of them were broadcast only once and not seen again until the Family Channel began airing them in the fall of 1988. In fact, not a single episode from the last season was ever rerun by NBC; by the time of their cable debut in early 1989, the series had been off the air for sixteen years.

When "Bonanza" returned for its twelfth season on September 13, 1970, viewers were greeted by new opening credits, a new theme song and a new Virginia City.

Replacing the familiar riding scene revealed by the blazing Ponderosa map were individual action shots of each Cartwright, eventually including new regular Mitch Vogel as Jamie. For the next two seasons, Ben was shown in four different poses, Joe in five, Hoss in six and Jamie in four.

Composer David Rose, who had left all musical scoring chores to Harry Sukman the previous year, was invited by David Dortort to write his own theme. The result, called "The Big Bonanza," captured perfectly both the show's vast scope and its frequently wistful nature.

After eleven seasons of rising production costs at Paramount Studios in downtown Hollywood, "Bonanza" arranged a more economically favorable deal with Warner Bros. in Burbank. Ironically, the Cartwrights would be walking the same streets on which they were spoofed by "Maverick" nine years before. To explain why Virginia City no longer looked the same, associate producer/writer John Hawkins simply wrote a story in which much of the town is destroyed by an arsonist. The episode, "The Night Virginia City Died," was not the first to be filmed for the new year, but was by necessity used as the season opener. Cleverly, most of the action takes place at night, making possible a dramatically revealing daytime shot of the new Virginia City at the show's conclusion. In another inventive twist, the arsonist (Deputy Clem's fiancee) dies in the last fire she sets, with no one but the audience ever knowing the truth.

The following episode, "A Matter of Faith,"

Left: Landon, Greene and Blocker and Mitch Vogel begin the twelfth season of "Bonanza."
Right: Greene in "Long Way to Ogden" (1970).

CHAPTER 5

BACK AT THE RANCH (1970-73)

introduced new regular Mitch Vogel as Jamie Hunter, the orphan son of a rainmaker. Vogel, not yet fifteen years-old when he joined "Bonanza," began acting at the age of ten, appearing twice on "The Wonderful World of Disney" and in such high profile films as Steve McQueen's "The Reivers" and with Henry Fonda, Lucille Ball and future "Bonanza" regular Tim Matheson in "Yours, Mine and Ours." As noted earlier, he had a small part in "The Real People of Muddy Creek," the fourth episode of "Bonanza's" tenth season, and was seen on "Gunsmoke" three months after his arrival on the Ponderosa.

A self-described rock collector, swimmer and horseback rider, Vogel was schooled between scenes by a private tutor. David Dortort, who early in the show's history vowed he would cast no "little Einsteins", was pleased to find the young professional "surprisingly normal."

"I think I would like to be an actor all my life," Vogel declared in early 1971. "But maybe by the time I turn 16, there won't be any parts for me. So I'm figuring on going to college. When I get older, I don't want to be broke." ("Bonanza's" final episode was broadcast the night before Vogel's seventeenth birthday.)

Lorne Greene in particular was impressed by the thespian skills of the Ponderosa's new resident: "It takes a pretty bright kid to change hats as he does and handle a script with such ease. Just for the fun of it, I decided to test him one day. I wanted to find out what kind of actor he was. Playing a scene with him in rehearsal, I made departures from the script, changing lines and movements. This would rattle most kids, who wouldn't be prepared for anything that didn't appear on paper. But Mitch was concentrating on me, not merely on the words he had learned, and he responded to my changes perfectly. I realized that this was no ordinary kid, but a boy with unusual talent."

Dortort created Jamie Hunter as a way of restoring some of the warmth he felt "Bonanza" had lost as Ben Cartwright's sons grew older, and the producer's creative instincts once again proved correct. The addition of Mitch Vogel's character, complete with a teenager's concerns and occasional nervous laughter around adults, only strengthened the show's durability.

Asked during the twelfth season to explain "Bonanza's" longevity, Lorne Greene responded: "Basically five things. First, the show has good writing. Second, it has good characters, the kind with whom viewers readily identify. Third, it offers the big outdoors, good for color. Fourth, it is set in America's most romantic period; Western expansion is close to the hearts of the people. And, finally, the history of dramaturgy shows strong appeal of father-son relationships. This angle probably made 'Hamlet' a success."

It is interesting to recall that Greene initially did not want "Bonanza" to last even a full season, and when it became a success hoped it would run for at least three. Several years after the show ended, he remarked that five would have been enough, perhaps because, as many viewers feel, the fifth season was the best with the original cast.

As for the twelfth, it was, like 1967-68, a time of major transition. In place of Candy were Jamie and Dusty Rhoades (Lou Frizzel), introduced at the end of previous season. And after three years spent roaming the range, the Cartwrights seldom strayed from their stately ranch house, which was, in the opinion of David Dortort and millions of viewers, another member of the cast.

Generally unknown is the fact that the "Bonanza" cast would have had another member in addition to Vogel and Frizzel had NBC let the show's executive producer have his way. In "The Weary Willies," a story about peace time difficulties experienced by veterans of the Civil War, the main guest star was Richard Thomas, whose outstanding performance convinced David Dortort there was room on the Ponderosa for one more permanent character. The network did not agree. "They told me it wasn't in the budget," Dortort lamented.

Fortunately, the production budget was able to cover the cost of filming some of the season's most memorable episodes at several scenic locales far from Hollywood, including, for the first time, Old Tucson, Arizona (home of Dortort's "The High Chaparral," then in its final year), Los Padres National Forest, Big Sky Ranch and, of course, Incline Village.

A number of old friends showed up during 1970-71: Neville Brand ("The Luck of Pepper Shannon," in which Jamie befriends an aging

Marlene Clark and Blocker in "The Desperado" (1971), which was shot in Arizona.

outlaw), Jack Elam ("Honest John," an amusing episode that takes a sad, unexpected turn), Jeff Corey ("A Single Pilgrim"), Vera Miles ("A Time to Die"), Ben Johnson ("Top Hand," featuring the unofficial debut of David Rose's theme for "Little House on the Prairie"), and Jo Van Fleet ("The Stillness Within").

Prejudice was again confronted in "The Power of Life and Death" (with the late, underrated Rupert Crosse), "The Desperado" (Lou Gossett), "Shadow of a Hero" (Dean Jagger) and "Terror at 2:00" (a suspenseful story of attempted assassination written and directed by Landon).

The warmth Dortort feared "Bonanza" had been lacking in recent years returned in stories driven more by character than plot, including "Thornton's Account" (Joe works desperately to rescue a badly injured Ben), "The Gold Plated Rifle" (Jamie struggles to adapt to his new life) and especially "The Stillness Within," an unforgettable episode about Joe's battle to accept blindness, written by Suzanne Clauser and directed by Landon, with the cooperation of the Braille Institute of America, Inc. This "Bonanza" landmark did not but should have garnered Emmy nominations for Clauser, Landon, Greene, Jo Van Fleet and David Rose.

Rose, however, actually won the Best Music for a Series Emmy in 1971 for "The Love Child," another segment written and directed by Landon.

91

BONANZA

The story, in which a father (Will Geer) rejects a daughter who has had a son out of wedlock, is no doubt one of the episodes Dortort had in mind when he said Landon's scripts were sometimes "mawkish". Nonetheless, Landon was well on his way to becoming the Steven Spielberg of television, an effective emotional manipulator of the highest order. Even in stories such as "Kingdom of Fear" (filmed in 1967 but finally shown on April 4, 1971), Landon wove a thread of sadness that was to characterize the majority of his work and even foreshadow his own fate.

Unfortunately, David Rose's award did not result in a follow-up to his 1961 "Bonanza" soundtrack. Instead, an outfit calling themselves the Xanadu Pleasure Dome (Xanadu was the name of Dortort's production company) recorded a double-album titled "Music From Bonanza and The High Chaparral," a misguided attempt which bludgeoned familiar themes into something approximating rock and roll. David Rose and Harry Sukman deserved better.

Susan Tyrrell and Blocker in "Fallen Woman" (1971).

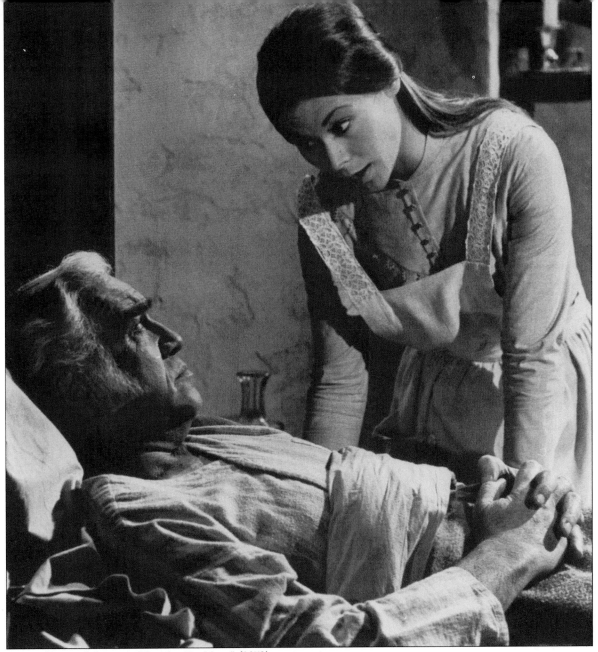

Kate Jackson and Greene in "One Ace Too Many" (1972).

During the season, RCA released "Five Card Stud," a compilation of songs from the albums Lorne Greene had recorded for the label, and in November the Cartwrights received a tremendous ovation when they walked onstage in costume for a John Wayne television special. Four months later, they turned up in a less likely setting, "Sesame Street."

Although the point is debatable, many "Bonanza" enthusiasts regard 1970-71 as the last consistently exceptional year of the series. The twelfth season was indeed the Cartwrights' last in the Top 10 (#9), but ratings have always been a better gauge of popularity than quality, which in large part accounts for the significant drop suffered by the show in its unlucky thirteenth year.

By the end of the 1971-72 season, "Bonanza" was #20 in the Top 25, its lowest ranking since 1960. Competing with major films receiving their first network airing, on both ABC and CBS, was tough on any night in the days before VCRs. Producer Richard Collins was philosophical about the situation when interviewed prior to the start of what would be the final year for the series: "My belief is that nothing can do well against those big movies," he said. "But when the shows were rerun this past summer, they were back in the Top 10 again–our audience came back to see the ones they'd missed."

And they had missed seeing a season in which Jamie Hunter became Jamie Cartwright ("A Home For Jamie"), Hop Sing got an entire episode to himself at long last ("A Lonely Man"), Ben went undercover on his own ranch to catch rustlers ("Saddle Stiff"), Hoss nearly adopts a son ("Fallen Woman"), and Joe is shot and left for dead in the most surreal episode ever ("Bushwhacked!").

There were some merely average stories ("Warbonnet," "Customs of the Country," "A Place to Hide") but not enough to signal a decline in overall vitality. Examples to the contrary include the season opener, "The Grand Swing" (Ben takes Jamie on an extended tour of the Ponderosa), "The Rattlesnake Brigade" (Jamie abducted in one of the series' most hard-edged moments), "He Was Only Seven" (Joe and Jamie help a crippled man track the killers of his grandson) and "Rock-A-Bye Hoss" (Hoss judges a baby contest in a story not played entirely for laughs).

In a humorous vein, though, were "The Younger Brothers' Younger Brother," (a Landon written/directed-show with the hilarious Strother Martin), "Easy Come, Easy Go" (the third and final appearance of Ann Prentiss as Meena) and "One Ace Too Many" (with Greene as Ben and Ben's crooked double, a sequel to the previous year's "A Deck of Aces," but funnier). The latter episode was the last with Ray Teal as Sheriff Roy Coffee.

More significant was the last misadventure of Hoss and Joe, "A Visit to Upright," in which the Cartwright brothers' ownership of a rundown saloon jeopardizes a big cattle deal Ben has pending with a woman who happens to be a teetotaler. Unfortunately for "Bonanza" viewers, the Family Channel refuses to show this episode. Evidently, "A Visit to Upright," like "The Pursued," does not conform to their narrow guidelines of what constitutes quality television, presumably because the plot revolves around the traditional barroom painting of a nude woman. In the story, Hoss objects to Jamie seeing the undraped figure until it is determined to be a stolen masterpiece. "Why couldn't I look at the naked lady when she was just a naked lady, but now I can because she's a great work of art?" asks Jamie. No one can come up with a straight answer, and neither can the Family Channel.

On February 13, 1972, NBC broadcast "Shanklin," in which Hoss is critically wounded and nearly dies. Ironically, exactly twelve weeks

later, May 13, Dan Blocker died unexpectedly at the age of only forty-three. Official reports stated his death was "due to complications following routine gall bladder surgery." Specifically, a blood clot that had formed in Blocker's lung burst as soon as he returned home, and by the time he was brought back to the hospital, nothing could be done to save him.

The loss of Blocker, television's most cherubic cowboy, stunned the millions of fans who had come to consider him a member of the family, and dealt a major blow to "Bonanza."

"After Dan's death I didn't see how the show could continue," Lorne Greene admitted several months later. "I said to my wife, 'That's it–it's finished. I know Michael Landon felt the same way.'"

"We never thought we could die," said Landon. "We'd been shot, stabbed, kicked, run over by wagons. You begin to believe all that–then someone tells you your brother's dead..."

Blocker's death was not the only challenge facing "Bonanza," due to begin production on its fourteenth season in early June. Chevrolet abandoned the Ponderosa for what they perceived as the more youthful demographic of "The Men," a collection of three different adventure series. (Dortort branded the sponsor's judgement "hasty, unwise.") And NBC, discontent with the previous season's ratings, demonstrated perfectly how television is strictly a numbers game by deciding to banish the Cartwrights to Tuesday even before Blocker died. To prepare viewers for the change, early episodes of "Bonanza" were rerun on Tuesday night as "Ponderosa" from May through August.

"I begged the network not to move us," Dortort said, "that people were used to seeing us on Sunday after so many years. But NBC told me there were too many other shows anxious for our time slot." That fall, four rotating detective series known as the "NBC Mystery Movie" took over "Bonanza's" old stomping ground. "Gunsmoke" had made an amazing recovery in the ratings when CBS switched the Saturday night staple to Monday. Perhaps, Dortort reasoned optimistically, "Bonanza" would experience the same good fortune.

Dan Blocker's death at age 43 left a huge void.

"Rock-a-Bye Hoss" (1971).

Dortort circled the wagons by first inviting David Canary to return as Candy. A proposed NBC show with Canary ("The Young Prosecutors") was not given the green light, nor was he having any luck locating financial backers for his own projects, so he rejoined "Bonanza," hoping to eventually write and direct episodes as Landon had done.

Next, Dortort shelved David Rose's relatively new theme and brought back the more familiar Livingston-Evans classic used from 1959 to 1970. The opening credits were similarly replaced by scenes closely resembling those to which viewers were most accustomed, with individual shots of the stars riding through a mountain meadow.

Finally, hoping to appeal to Tuesday night's potentially younger viewership, Dortort hired Tim Matheson to play "a new character more in line with that audience." Matheson, just shy of twenty-five, had been acting for ten years, including a regular role for one season of "The Virginian."

Ungraciously, in an interview with "TV Guide,"

he commented: "I don't think 'Gunsmoke' or 'Bonanza' can last much longer; their formats are outdated, new concepts are coming up to take their place."

Producer Richard Collins, who with Dortort had conceived Matheson's character, Griff King, did not agree. "We've got lots of contemporary, nontraditional stories. We can't do conventional Westerns any longer; since NBC owns the show, they apply the nonviolence thing especially strictly, and we're not very interested in doing shows like that anyway. So we have to move farther afield, into unexplored areas. All of which could help us get a whole new audience."

Everyone's chief concern, naturally, was the absence of Hoss. "I know at the beginning it was Ben Cartwright who was the central character," said Dortort, "but you know, after a few years Hoss became the foundation for the show, the central character, and you just don't find another Hoss. Of course Dan is irreplaceable. How could a man with his enormous talent and humanity be replaced?"

Collins wondered aloud if the fans of "Bonanza" would remain loyal. "Whether they'll do what families do—what we've done—which is to close ranks and go on, remains to be seen. Obviously, this year is a crucial one, and there's nobody who isn't curious to see if we can make it."

Due to the show's widespread popularity, David Canary was confident it would run for at least three or four more years, a sentiment shared by David Dortort, whose exclusive production contract with NBC was expiring. Nevertheless, contrary to reports he was leaving the series in the hands of others, the veteran producer confirmed he was "still tremendously committed to 'Bonanza'–it's my baby, my creation, and I'll continue to give it my closest supervision."

To begin the pivotal fourteenth year, Dortort wanted to grab the audience right away with an episode so important anyone who had ever liked "Bonanza" would be sure to tune in. He gave the assignment to Landon, who wrote "Forever," in which Hoss finally makes it to the altar. Blocker's death, of course, necessitated a major revision of the script, and although the delay caused the episode to be the third one filmed, it began the new season. Ironically, the date was September 12, the same as the series' debut in 1959.

Landon and Bonnie Bedelia as Alice Cartwright in "Forever" (1972).

In "Forever," the only two-hour segment of "Bonanza" to be broadcast on a single night, Joe becomes the first Cartwright son to marry, but his joy is short-lived. When outlaws show up to collect gambling debts from Joe's shiftless brother-in-law, the new Mrs. Cartwright and her unborn child are murdered. Accompanied by Candy, Joe tracks the killers down.

"What I wanted to do with it was try to make it a catharsis for everyone," Landon explained, "not just the audience but for us, too–to try to incorporate a sense of loss. We mention Hoss's death very simply, in passing, the way it happens in real life; there's no discussion of how or when because everyone knows how and when. I'm sure that some people would rather have a whole hour memorial to Dan, but we just couldn't do that. We tried to do what we thought he would have wanted us to do."

However, many who saw "Forever" objected. *TV Guide* reported that "droves of viewers resented" the death of Joe's bride, although regular

readers of the magazine should not have been surprised: In an article published four months earlier, it was revealed that Hoss would have been widowed as well.

Regardless of how one feels about the decision to kill off the character, "Forever" is unquestionably the most affecting episode of "Bonanza." Two scenes in particular are the most emotionally devastating in the series' history. In the first, Joe and Ben tearfully embrace in the burned out ruins of Joe's house. The second, during which Joe departs on his quest, concludes with a long shot of Ben gently touching an object before leaving the room. As David Rose's music (a mournful version of "The Big Bonanza" theme) swells, the camera slowly moves in to reveal framed portraits of Hoss and Joe.

This landmark in the history of series television, the first to confront the loss of a major character, was not seen again until February, 1989.

Michael Landon may have considered "The Wish" his favorite of all the episodes he wrote and/or directed for the series, but "Forever" represents his peak contribution to "Bonanza." All the hallmarks of what by then was his distinctive directorial style (high angle views, unusual establishing shots, panoramic sweeps) are evident, and the story itself is characterized by a dark undercurrent more common in Landon's work than is generally acknowledged.

After experiencing the generally mournful atmosphere of "Forever," one cannot help but arrive at the unavoidable conclusion that things are no longer the same on the Ponderosa, and never will be again. The last fifteen episodes are set apart from the others of the series by a somber mood due largely to the knowledge that Hoss and the man who played him are gone. Although brief, references to the character (in "The Initiation" and "Ambush at Rio Lobo") are, in a way, comforting. Otherwise, the season is almost completely unrelieved by comic relief, and even the more light-hearted stories ("The Twenty-Sixth Grave" and "The Bucket Dog") have their shadowy corners. This is merely an observation rather than a criticism, as under the circumstances, the atmosphere was quite appropriate.

"The first day we went back to work was just incredible, it was so bad," Landon confessed.

The Cartwrights Carry On

How 'Bonanza,' now in its 14th year, plans to get along without Hoss

By Dick Adler

Sometimes, it's hard *not* to find symbols everywhere you look. For instance: in front of the sound stage at the Burbank Studios, where *Bonanza* is shooting a saloon scene, stands a big red truck full of lights and props. On it is painted the legend "BONANZA—NBC SUNDAY 9 P.M." The truck is a Ford.

It doesn't mean much until you remember that this season *Bonanza* has been pried out of its traditional niche on Sunday night and moved to Tuesday at 8 (ET)—and that its long-time sponsor, Chevrolet, has switched its brand from *Bonanza*'s burning map over to ABC's new anthology series, *The Men*.

Neither of these changes would have stirred up much industry gossip had they not been followed by an authentic tragedy—the death this past May of Dan Blocker, that vast and gentle man who in 13 years as Hoss Cartwright worked his way up from a former Texas schoolteacher to one of the best-loved television actors in the world. Around Hollywood, where spite often counts for as much as sentiment, the word was out: *Bonanza*, which last year had occasionally slipped out of the Top 10 shows in the ratings, was on its last legs. The giant was about to topple.

"After Dan's death I didn't see how the show could continue," admits Lorne Greene now. "I said to my wife, 'That's it; it's finished.' I know Michael

Left: Tim Matheson (foreground) is a new Ponderosa resident, and David Canary a returnee. Right: The two remaining original-cast regulars are Lorne Greene (left) and Michael Landon.

TV GUIDE OCTOBER 7, 1972

Landon felt the same way. But that's the way it is in any family when a death occurs. The family feels that something so radical has happened that life can't go on, that everything has changed. Nevertheless, you do go on. Things *are* changed, but not as much as you first thought. You don't go out and hire somebody else to take the place of the member who died; what happens is that the character of the family unit changes to include other people."

Who those other people would be became the immediate problem of *Bonanza*'s executive producer, David Dortort, a literate and sensitive man who has just ended a lengthy exclusive contract with NBC but insists that "I'm still tremendously committed to *Bonanza*—it's my baby, my creation, and I'll continue to give it my closest supervision." His first decision was to bring back Candy, a rowdy and rambunctious ranch hand played for three years (from 1967 to 1970) by David Canary. Then he and producer Richard Collins sat down with their associates to come up with a new character.

"Of course Dan is irreplaceable," says Dortort. "How could a man with his enormous talent and humanity be replaced? So, how does the show go on? The answer is that we have to find new directions. We've had an intensely close family situation which began with

a father and his three sons; then Pernell Roberts left and we had two sons. There was Candy, of course, and we had Ben Cartwright adopt a boy, Jamie, played by Mitch Vogel. Now, we're introducing another new character, a young man who brings his own set of problems that are unique to him, to his background and experiences—it opens up new avenues for dramatic exploration." Shortly before shooting began, Dortort hired Tim Matheson—who was a regular on *The Virginian* for the 1969-70 season—to play Griff King, an ex-convict who comes to work on the Ponderosa against his will.

If you note in all this a shifting emphasis to youth, you are correct. At least part of the reason for the Chevrolet decision to transfer its corporate backing was the fear that after 13 years the *Bonanza* audience was getting too old, wasn't buying that ideal new car every two years. "It was a hasty, unwise decision," Dortort comments, quickly adding (lest anyone accuse him of sour grapes) that the show is "100 per-cent sponsored" this year. As for the shift to a new night and an earlier hour, he is full of optimism. "It's a very healthy change; it opens us up to an entirely new audience—in some respects a younger audience—which is why we've brought in a new character more in line with that audience."

Michael Landon, who as Little Joe Cartwright—the youngest brother—has matured from a fresh-faced newcomer to a rugged, slightly graying, highly talented writer and director as well as an actor during his *Bonanza* stint, feels the absence of Dan Blocker perhaps more deeply than anyone. He tried to write about his memories of the man who played his older brother for so many years but found that his thoughts were too intensely personal to be put on paper.

"The first day we went back to work was just incredible, it was so bad," he remembers. "Everybody was trying to →

39

TV Guide, *October 7, 1972.*

15¢ Local Programs Oct. 7-13

TV GUIDE

Bonanza: How They'll Carry On
Page 38

"Everybody was trying to force good humor, because here we were, back in the same place again. Fortunately, we stayed out of the dining room that day. We've had so many laughs in that dining room after the last thirteen years; they were always the deadly scenes–they were so terrible because they were exposition scenes so you could find out what was going to happen in the next act–and that's where Dan and Lorne and I did most of our horsing around."

Tim Matheson may have felt Griff King was "not very well delineated yet" at the start of the season, but the character develops smoothly through the nine stories to include him. In "Riot" and "New Man," which can be considered as one extended episode (the latter opens with the final scene of the former), Griff is paroled in Ben's custody and must adapt to life as a ranch hand. By "The Sound of Sadness," concerning the fate of two orphans, he is no longer thinking solely of his problems, and "The Marriage of Theodora Duffy"

Tim Matheson, Ponderosa short-timer.

gives him an adventure all his own. Griff seemed content with his lot on the Ponderosa, but after "Bonanza" was cancelled, Matheson's only comment was, "It's not easy to move into an established television series, especially when you have to move into it under the circumstances in which I did. It's like moving into a new neighborhood where no one wants to talk to you."

While he was not able to write or direct as he had hoped, David Canary returned as though he had never been gone. Nor was there any explanation given as to where Candy had been the past two seasons. He simply appears on the main street of Virginia City with Joe in "Forever," and in his ten episodes of the final season comes across as more an equal of the Cartwrights than ever before. The story spotlighting him ("The Witness") emphasizes how much his presence has been missed, and it is indeed a shame Canary's feeling the show would go on another few seasons was not accurate.

Mitch Vogel was aging nicely as Jamie, and his last ten appearances (of thirty-nine) in the series include the delightful "The Bucket Dog" and "First Love." The first concerns Jamie's attachment to a supposedly misfit purebred Irish setter, a boy-and-his-dog tale which is touching on a realistic instead of saccharine level. In "First Love," written by producer Richard Collins, Jamie forms a differ-

ent kind of emotional bond when he befriends the young wife of a rigid teacher. After Jamie realizes there can be no future with her, Ben dispenses the series' last bit of fatherly wisdom. It is a quietly beautiful scene demonstrating once again that "Bonanza" did not hesitate to put its heart on the proverbial sleeve whenever the occasion demanded.

Ben, as always, extends his hand to those outside the Cartwright circle who need it. In addition to Griff, he aids another ex-con (played to perfection by Robert Lansing) in "Heritage of Anger," and in "Ambush at Rio Lobo" he comforts an expectant mother and, after they have been abducted by outlaws, delivers her child.

Following the death of his wife, Joe does not exhibit much of his charm and good humor in a season where there is little opportunity to display either. He is forced to ride a beloved horse to death in "Stallion," and in the very last "Bonanza" to air ("The Hunter") he is stalked through the desert by a psychopathic soldier.

By the time "The Hunter" was shown on January 16, 1973, "Bonanza" had been out of production for over two months. Although the first few episodes of the season had finished in the Top 15, viewer interest began to decline during October, and when the show sank to #52 during the first week of November, victim of "Hawaii Five-O" (#3) and producer Norman Lear's new sitcom, "Maude" (#4), NBC did not hesitate to swing the ax. The network allegedly toyed with the notion of moving "Bonanza" back to its 1959-61 time slot of Saturday where, opposite Lear's "All in the Family" (#1), the inevitable cancellation would possibly seem more justified. Instead, the plug was pulled virtually without warning.

NBC's behavior greatly offended Lorne Greene. "They told us on Monday that we would quit shooting on Wednesday. After you've been on the air for fourteen years, even if you're a caretaker, you should get a month's notice. They felt they didn't have to do that because our contract said we got paid for that year, whether we did any shows or not. But that wasn't the point. The point was: Wind up the show in the nicest way possible. There was a lack of dignity."

"When it ended it was very painful for everybody," Michael Landon remembered. "It really was." Several years later, he disclosed that NBC's insensitive treatment of "Bonanza" was one of the main reasons he was determined to retain as close to total control of his productions as possible. He would personally decide a series' fate, whether that meant ending it or moving to another network.

Publicly, David Dortort was stoic. "We've had a very long and beautiful run," he told reporters. "I broke the tradition of the Western hero as a rootless, homeless wanderer with no family who went out with the sunset. I said this wasn't true at all. So we started the tradition of a group of people in one place."

In private, however, Dortort felt extremely bitter about the network's lack of respect for his creation. "I was suddenly called over to Burbank one day and given the news," he recalled. "Needless to say, I was shocked. Locations were being scouted, scripts were being prepared. I pleaded with this young guy from New York to please allow us to at least finish out the season, but he said it was too late, that the decision was final."

Innumerable shows of lesser longevity and merit had been given a better chance, but networks are mainly concerned with the bottom line, and in 1972 Westerns were all but extinct in prime time, a rarity as well as a liability. If one counts Richard Boone's "Hec Ramsey," which was shown approximately once a month as part of the "NBC Sunday Mystery Movie," there were but three Westerns left besides "Bonanza," the others being "Alias Smith and Jones" (who left the air three days before the Cartwrights) and the apparently invincible "Gunsmoke."

A few months later, the late Amanda Blake, "Gunsmoke's" Kitty Russell, told TV Guide's Joseph Finnigan: "We're all by ourselves now, don't have a stablemate. That's too bad. I particularly felt bad about 'Bonanza.' It was a household word and a living legend, kind of like 'Gunsmoke.'"

At a press conference on "Bonanza's" last day of filming, Michael Landon made a few remarks, then, as part of a prearranged gimmick, went flying backward in a stuntman's harness after a blank was fired.

"I thought he was acting a little peculiar that day, not very upset," said Dortort. "What I didn't know was that he'd already signed his own production deal with NBC, so he must have been looking forward to that."

As for his thoughts about the end of his epic vision, Dortort reflected, "I guess when you really get down to it, we just didn't have enough time to find a substitute for Dan. But the show may very well have continued anyway had we been allowed to remain on Sundays."

Performing on a weekly series for fourteen years can be an exhausting routine, even if the show does not rely solely on one actor. In 1977, when asked if he missed portraying Ben Cartwright, Lorne Greene admitted it was "nice to be free. I loved 'Bonanza.' It was a good show, and it provided me with a platform around the world. But do I miss it? No. We had become slaves to 'Bonanza.' Once we got on the treadmill, we had to keep going."

Precisely how long Greene felt like a "slave" one can only speculate, but it is safe to say he would not have disputed that to varying degrees, "Bonanza" had been a once-in-a-lifetime experience for him and millions of others. A television series is fortunate to be remembered for one or two outstanding episodes, if it is remembered at all, and Greene could look back with pride on an extraordinary number of memorable moments from every season: "The Newcomers," "Silent Thunder," "The Crucible," "The Last Haircut," "Hoss and the Leprechauns," "Between Heaven and Earth," "Ride the Wind," "The Pursued," "To Die in Darkness," "The Wish," "A Matter of Circumstance," "The Stillness Within," "Bushwhacked," "Forever" and at least that many more unforgettable stories which viewers have recalled vividly for years.

Critics have attributed the decline of the Western on television to everything from dwindling patriotism and political scandal to racial injustice and sexism. And these arguments are not without a certain measure of validity. The United States never has been a country providing equal prosperity and justice for all, except in the estimation of revisionist flagwavers, and frontier shows perpetuating that myth were already beginning to vanish by the time "Bonanza" debuted. As stated previously, "Bonanza" was more than a Western. Its balance of the real and the ideal was actually a reflection of life's complexities rather than simply the Old West. Anything less would have made it as anachronistic as the programs it outlived. "Bonanza's" decline in popularity most likely was due more to the loss of Dan Blocker, the scheduling change and, perhaps, a median audience not as attractive to youth-oriented advertisers. And in that order.

In reality, the television Western may well have been an early victim of an increasingly cynical public. The clear-cut black or white, good or evil world depicted on a majority of network dramas conflicts with what intelligent people know to be true: Heroes do not always triumph. Villains are not always punished. This is usually acknowledged on the big screen, where Westerns continue to flourish in justly acclaimed films such as "Dances with Wolves" and "The Unforgiven."

A socially relevant, humanistic (and even epic) Western like "Gunsmoke" or "Bonanza" could very well succeed with the right cast and the support of a network willing to both wait for an audience to build and refrain from interfering with the creative process. That scenario is highly unlikely, but there is hope: Infrequent surveys indicate viewers would enjoy seeing more Westerns. The success of the "Lonesome Dove" mini-series, the fact that "Paradise" and "The Young Riders" each lasted three seasons, and the ongoing popularity of "Dr. Quinn, Medicine Woman" all prove a potential audience is there.

Now all that remains is for a magical mixture of timing and talent to occur, as happened in 1959. The Cartwrights of the Ponderosa are gone forever, but their legend continues.

"Blessed Are They" (1962).

CHAPTER SIX

Lorne Greene once told an interviewer that "Bonanza" was a show about love, love of the land, for one's family and between people. It was an opinion evidently shared by Michael Landon, who was inspired to make a career out of accenting the positive. His initial post-"Bonanza" project was, in fact, directing a segment of NBC's anthology series "Love Story." (Coincidentally, one of the leads was Bonnie Bedelia, Joe Cartwright's unfortunate bride in "Forever.") Following that, Landon directed "It's Good To Be Alive," a television film based on the life of baseball catcher Roy Campanella, whose career was ended by a paralyzing car wreck. The subject was tailor-made for the former Eugene Orowitz, who knew a thing or two about triumphing over life's setbacks, and one to which he would return regularly in his work.

Slightly more than a year after "Bonanza" left the air, Landon was back on NBC as pioneer/family man Charles Ingalls in a movie based on the "Little House on the Prairie" books by Laura Ingalls Wilder. That fall, "Little House" debuted as a series, with Landon in charge and using a crew made up chiefly of people who had worked on "Bonanza." The large cast included several former "Bonanza" guest stars, including Karl Swenson, Richard Bull, Kevin Hagen, Dabbs Greer, Charlotte Stewart, Ted Gehring and Victor French. Nor was Landon hesitant about recycling several of the scripts he had written for "Bonanza" as "Little House" stories, although the best episode was probably "Remember Me," a two-part installment with Patricia Neal. The show remained on the air well into 1984, never threatened by the network guillotine, and actually running longer than Landon thought it should. During those years he also produced (but did not appear in) another series, "Father Murphy," and "The Loneliest Runner," a film based on his childhood. In 1983 he starred in a true story, "Love is Forever," which for once found him in a contemporary setting as a journalist who rescues his girlfriend from Laos. Originally intended as a theatrical release, it aired on NBC instead. A second film about Landon's youth, "Sam's Son," was released to theaters the

THE LEGACY

Left: 1960 publicity shot.
Right: Michael Landon

Dirk Blocker with Landon for "School Mom," a 1974 episode of "Little House on the Prairie."

following year but was more widely seen on video.

Although never out of work, Lorne Greene did not fare as well as his television son. Within weeks of "Bonanza's" cancellation, he signed to play private detective Wade Griffin in a new ABC series, "Griff." Shortly after production began, he told a reporter: "Compared to this, Westerns are easy to do. You get on a horse and it takes you there. Here, you run. You get into a car and hope the ignition works. You climb buildings. You get on ships in San Pedro Harbor at four o'clock in the morning. You get into fights." This regimen did not last long, as "Griff" was cancelled less than four months after it premiered.

A 1971 television film of John Steinbeck's "The Harness" had demonstrated Greene's ability to be effective away from the character of Ben Cartwright, but of the few theatrical features he was offered following "Bonanza," only "Earthquake" is worth mentioning. (Not surprisingly, he was chosen to host a special about earth-

quake preparation in connection with the film.) Without a doubt, his most significant role in a "movie" produced for television was slave owner John Reynolds in the historical mini-series "Roots."

Greene also hosted two syndicated nature series, "Lorne Greene's Last of the Wild" (1974-79) and "Lorne Greene's New Wilderness" (1982-86), narrated a documentary on the famous showdown at the OK Corral, and made commercials for Alpo dog food, some with "Little House's" Melissa Gilbert.

In 1978 he returned to network television as Commander Adama in the science-fiction series "Battlestar Galactica," which he described as a "Ponderosa in outer space." And there was, he said, another difference: "On 'Bonanza' I gave orders and then went out to help implement them. Here I just give orders. I don't get to leave the ship." Produced by ABC to cash in on the phenomenal success of the film "Star Wars," the show

104

(later renamed "Galactica 1980") was impressive in only a visual sense and was gone by August of 1980.

For one season (1981-82), Greene was Joe Rorchek, a battalion chief in the Los Angeles City Fire Department, on the now-forgotten "Code Red." Joe was, of course, a widower with three children, one a daughter.

Greene was reunited with Pernell Roberts on an episode of "Vegas," and for years many viewers waited for him to turn up on an episode of "Little House on the Prairie," as Mitch Vogel had, not once but twice. It never happened, though in 1975 Landon did tell his television father there was a part on the show for which he would be perfect. Unfortunately, Landon could not let him have it.

"Michael called and said if we worked together, people would ask, 'Why doesn't he recognize his own father?'," Greene reported. "He said he wanted me to know he was thinking of me."

Ten years later, however, the former Cartwrights once again shared the screen in an episode of Landon's then-current series, "Highway to Heaven," and NBC advertised the November 20, 1985 episode ("The Smile in the Third Row") as "A Bonanza of a Reunion!"

"When Michael started 'Highway to Heaven,' I knew he would call me if the right thing came up, and he did," said Greene. "He sent me this strange, different and wonderful script. I read it and said, 'Yeah, I think it's the one.'"

Because the "Highway to Heaven" crew in-

Greene in the TV film "The Harness" (1971).

cluded so many "Bonanza" veterans, Greene described working on the show as "old home week." Toward the end of their days on the Ponderosa, Greene said of Landon, "No finer director exists in this business," and his opinion was unchanged in 1985: "Michael has a wonderful imagination and he knows how to touch people."

What millions yearned to see–a real "Bonanza" reunion–was destined never to be, even if David Dortort was among those millions. Since the show's demise, the producer had remained busy, first with a thirteen-week series in early 1974 based on the John Wayne film "The Cowboys." More ambitious was the 1979 mini-series, "The Chisholms," which evolved into a short-lived series the following year.

The announcement "Bonanza" fans had been waiting for since January 1973 came during the summer of 1987: David Dortort had written a re-union movie to be syndicated to stations before year's end. Rumors circulated that Michael Landon would be included in the cast, but in truth only Lorne Greene had agreed to return to the Ponderosa. Fate had other plans.

On August 19, Greene underwent abdominal surgery for a perforated ulcer. Within two weeks pneumonia developed, and though doctors felt he was responding to treatment, his recovery was slow. Fans around the world sent cards and flowers to the hospital in Santa Monica as Dortort revised the reunion script to lessen Ben Cartwright's workload.

"Our prayers are for Lorne's full recovery," associate producer Steve Syatt told the press. "Not for the sake of the project, but for him. He's been looking forward to going back on the ranch for a long time now, and we hope to hell he can."

Sadly, on Friday afternoon, September 11, Lorne Greene succumbed to "respiratory arrest followed by cardiac arrest", his wife and three children in attendance. The next day was the twenty-eighth anniversary of "Bonanza."

"He was Ben Cartwright to the end," said an emotional Michael Landon, who had visited Greene only two days earlier. "I took his hand in

Lorne Greene died of complications following surgery on September 11, 1987.

mine and held it. He looked at me and slowly started to arm wrestle like we used to. Then he broke into a smile and nodded. And everything was okay. I think he wanted me to know everything was okay."

Production of "Bonanza: The Next Generation" commenced in Lake Tahoe on October 24. Starring as Ben Cartwright's brother Aaron was John Ireland, who had a guest role in a 1967 episode of the original series ("Judgement at Red Creek"). Also in the cast were Robert Fuller (a regular on both "Laramie" and "Wagon Train") as the Ponderosa foreman, John Amos ("Good Times") as the cook, and Barbara Anderson ("Ironside") as Joe Cartwright's wife, Annabelle. Dortort denied reports that Michael Landon was going to appear but had changed his mind when Lorne Greene died. "That was more than likely just wishful thinking on the part of hopeful viewers," he said.

Michael Landon, Jr., however, was introduced as Joe's son, Benjamin, complete with a pinto as his mount of choice. The younger Landon's previous acting work had been limited to brief appearances as an extra on "Little House on the Prairie," and his lack of experience was obvious. Nor were thespian skills all he had not inherited from his father. A good-looking kid, he nevertheless resembled a blonde Jerry Seinfeld more than Michael Landon. To be fair, his true passion was working behind the camera, and the documentary he later produced about his father was excellent.

Gillian Greene, Lorne's daughter, had a small part as the granddaughter of Virginia City's banker ("Bonanza" and "Little House" vet Dabbs Greer), and did a capable job during her few moments of screen time. In addition to Greer, other guests from "Bonanza's" past included Peter Mark Richman and Kevin Hagen, familiar to "Little House" fans as Doc Baker.

Some purists were not exactly pleased to learn Hoss had a bastard son, Josh (Brian A. Smith), and the revelation that Hoss had been best man at the wedding of Joe and Annabelle conflicted totally with the storyline of "Forever," which had Joe marrying for the first time after Hoss' death.

Not as confusing was the character of Aaron Cartwright, a former sailor who had spent most of his life in the South Seas. In the series, Ben had said his brother's name was John, and that he lived

in Ohio. One can only presume Ben's sons had more than one paternal uncle.

With a story by Dortort, script by Paul Savage (a writer for the classic series), and "Bonanza's" most prolific director, William F. Claxton, in command, one might logically have expected "Bonanza: The Next Generation" to be a nostalgic trip through Tahoe's towering pines, but the experience was a decidedly bittersweet one. Thematically, the movie was pure "Bonanza," as the Cartwright heirs battled to save the Ponderosa, circa 1905, from the ravages of hydraulic mining. But the original cast members were sorely missed, their absence emphasized by an oil portrait of Ben, a photograph of Hoss, and a visit to their graves. The return of David Canary as Candy, had it been possible, could have helped fill the void considerably.

In early December a brief news item stated, "Production has been completed for 'Bonanza: The Next Generation,' a syndicated TV-movie pilot that will air between March 7 and 31 in at least 90 percent of the United States." The story went on to say that the character of Joe Cartwright "is missing in the Spanish-American War. If the new 'Bonanza' becomes a series, Joe's whereabouts will be determined according to Landon Sr.'s interest in the project."

Michael Landon, deeply involved in the production of "Highway to Heaven," was not interested, nor apparently were very many others, as interest in reviving the series cooled for the next few years. Following its run in syndication, "Bonanza: The Next Generation" was shown on The Disney Channel, then released on home video.

In the meantime, "Highway to Heaven" ended after Landon's longtime friend and co-star, Victor French, died of cancer in 1989. French was also a regular on "Little House" and had six episodes of "Bonanza" to his credit.

Landon next produced, directed and co-starred with Art Carney in a beautiful 1990 made-for-TV movie, "Where Pigeons Go To Die." The film was a hit with viewers and critics alike, but lack of recognition from the NBC brass convinced Landon it was time to become affiliated with a dif-

ferent network. Before the year was over, he had done a two-hour series pilot called "Us" for CBS.

The following spring, while preparing the third of his "Gambler" movies, singer/actor Kenny Rogers informed the press he was rounding up as many former TV cowboys as possible for cameo roles, and that he really hoped the cast might include Michael Landon as Little Joe.

Whether or not Landon would have accepted was of no consequence: On April 8, 1991, he invited the press to his Malibu home and announced that he had inoperable cancer of the liver and pancreas. He was only 54. Ever the fighter, he vowed to do all he could to beat the disease despite serious odds. At best, three percent of pancreatic cancer victims and five percent of those with liver cancer last beyond five years.

In less than a week, Landon was flooded with literally thousands of letters from well-wishers and fellow cancer sufferers, many offering suggestions for treatment. One dose of traditional chemotherapy was all it took for him to switch to an enzyme treatment that included vitamins and a strictly regimented diet. A month later, doctors discovered the cancer had spread to his colon. Undaunted, he went ahead with plans to appear on longtime friend Johnny Carson's "Tonight Show." According to Harry Flynn, Landon's publicist, "He wanted to go somewhere where he could show people he isn't all that sick."

When Landon made his entrance May 9, dressed in the familiar denim of Jonathan Smith, the everyman angel he had portrayed on "Highway to Heaven," the "Tonight Show" audience erupted in a standing ovation. During the course of the evening, he joked about his illness, reminisced, and lashed out at the insensitive way the tabloids were treating his family's predicament. Landon's final public appearance doubled the show's ratings and left the nation with a collective lump in its throat.

Two weeks later, he was hospitalized for treatment of a blood clot in his knee. Doctors reassured the public "it was a small surgical procedure not directly related to the cancer."

The June issue of *Life* magazine featured a cover story by Landon in which he vowed "If I'm gonna die, Death's gonna have to fight to get me." Later that month, Johnny Carson's son was killed in an

Michael Landon lost his fight to cancer on July 1, 1991.

auto accident, and ignoring his own pain, Landon called to console his friend.

On the afternoon of Monday, July 1, 1991, Michael Landon died at home, leaving behind his wife, Cindy, nine children from three marriages, and in the words of one television critic, a legacy of courage and grace.

A spokesman for Pernell Roberts said Landon's one-time TV brother was "deeply grieved."

The Friday following his death, Landon's ashes were interred at Hillside Memorial Park and Mortuary in Los Angeles, within fifty yards of Lorne Greene's final resting place.

Given the passings of Greene and Landon, as well as the total reluctance of Pernell Roberts to reprise the role of Adam, it appeared as though all prospects for reviving "Bonanza" were finally dead. But early in 1992, a syndicated series based on "Bonanza: The Next Generation" was announced, with production to begin at Lake Tahoe that June. Although Ben Johnson was originally scheduled to replace the late John Ireland as Aaron Cartwright, the role was changed to a character named Bronc Evans, a seasoned Ponderosa wrangler. Some shooting was done, and Johnson even hosted a promotional film, but the series, "Bonanza: Legends of the Ponderosa," never got off the ground. Budgets for syndicated programs are often based on the sale of broadcast rights to foreign markets, and funding of the updated Cartwright saga reportedly fell far short of the necessary $1.1 million-per episode Dortort and his team required.

However, in February of 1993, NBC, which had first been offered the series, had a change of heart, due largely to the recent ratings success of "Dr. Quinn, Medicine Woman" on CBS. While the network was not interested in a weekly series, they were willing to test the waters with a two-hour movie, to be preceded by a "Bonanza" documentary of sorts.

On November 28, viewers were first treated to "Back to Bonanza," a one hour hodgepodge of clips from the original series loosely structured around the 1963 episode "The Legacy." Hosted by Dirk Blocker and Michael Landon, Jr., it was a nostalgic overview rather than a definitive retrospective, as it pretty much ignored the post-Adam years of the show.

The movie, "Bonanza: The Return," was richer looking than "The Next Generation" and introduced Alistair MacDougall as Adam's son, A.C., and Brian Leckner (replacing Brian A. Smith) as Hoss' son, Josh, even though Dirk Blocker, a dead-ringer for his late father, was among the cast. Dortort felt he was too old for the part and gave him the role of a newspaper man instead. ("That's the reality of our business," Blocker reacted.) Back as Benj was Landon, Jr. (who co-wrote the story), but gone were Robert Fuller, Barbara Anderson, John Amos, and Gillian Greene. New supporting players included Richard Roundtree, Linda Gray and Jack Elam. And the Cartwright legend was further confused by the addition of Sara (Emily Warfield), Ben's granddaughter, and a change of dates on Hoss' gravestone. In "The Next Generation" the years of his birth and death were 1848 and 1881, but in "The Return" they have been amended to 1842 and 1878. Viewers with good memories also noted the fact that Ben Johnson's name was Jim Kelly in the 1971 episode "Top Hand" (which provides the first sepia-toned flashback used in "The Return"), not Bronc Evans.

Quibbles aside, the movie was a generally more entertaining production than "The Next Generation." A former Ponderosa ranch hand (Dean Stockwell, who appeared as a different character in the 1969 episode "The Medal") wants to acquire not only the Cartwright's land but also Sara. Of course he fails at both attempts, and is eventually run over by his own train.

For sentimentalists, the highlights of "The Return" were a scene in which the younger Cartwrights come across an album containing photographs of the original cast, and clips from "Top Hand," "Ponderosa Explosion" (1967) and "The Philip Diedeshiemer Story" (1959).

Ben Johnson remarked that the original show, on which he appeared three times, "was always decent. It was always something you could see with your family." As for how the elder Blocker and Landon might have felt about their sons' new version of the old legend, Johnson said, "I think their fathers would be proud of us, a-carryin' on the tradition."

Of Ben and his three sons, the only actor now alive is Roberts.

1959 publicity shot.

"The Return" doubled as a pilot for either a new series or more "Bonanza" movies, and despite a *TV Guide* preview calling it "a well-intentioned but pale sequel", the ratings were excellent.

A more engaging follow-up, originally entitled "The Ghosts" but changed to the more pedestrian "Under Attack," aired on January 15, 1995. This time Bronc and company defend the wounded Frank James (Leonard Nimoy) from renegade Pinkerton detectives, using an old cabin built by Ben Cartwright for cover.

Perhaps the only deficiency of "Under Attack" was the casting of Jeff Phillips, a Kevin Bacon lookalike, as Adam's son. According to David Dortort, NBC had signed Alistair MacDougall to another project without considering the fact that he would be needed for the next "Bonanza" film. Phillips did a sufficiently capable job of portraying A.C., but in the estimation of some critics,

MacDougall was more believable as the son of a character once played by Pernell Roberts. Sonia Satra, an actress who would have been Bronc Evans' granddaughter had "The Next Generation" series taken off in 1992, was introduced as A.C.'s love interest. But in the tradition of nearly all Cartwright women, she leaves by the end of the film.

Brian Leckner, again playing Josh, preferred "Under Attack" to "The Return" and hoped it would finally result in the long-planned series. "This one is a lot different. It's got a good script and Mark Tinker directed it. He's the one who did the 'ER' pilot."

Despite respectable ratings, "Under Attack" remains the most recent television effort based on "Bonanza." Ben Johnson, sadly, passed away in 1996, putting the "next generation" Cartwrights in limbo. And though there have been serious preparations for a feature film at Universal Studios, the future of that project appears cloudy. As of this writing, the only big screen appearances by the Cartwrights are a humorous bit in the 1961 Jerry Lewis feature "The Errand Boy" and the foreign theatrical version of "Ride the Wind."

As for other members of "Bonanza's" extended family:

MITCH VOGEL said in 1971: "I've been very lucky, but one day I would like to portray a character other than the good clean kid I have played to date. I would like to play a bad kid, maybe one from the ghetto who is an addict." In reality, he had guest roles on "Little House on the Prairie," "Wonder Woman," "Gunsmoke" and "The Quest," the latter a short-lived Western series with Tim Matheson and Kurt Russell, son of Bing "Clem Foster" Russell. Vogel also made a low-budget feature, "Texas Detour," and has abandoned acting for private life. He and his family reportedly enjoy watching him as Jamie Cartwright on the Family Channel.

DAVID CANARY is familiar to soap opera fans from his long-running role on the daytime drama "All My Children." After "Bonanza" he made commercials for everything from bread to television sets, and appeared on such series as "Alias Smith and Jones" and "The Rookies." He made the TV films "Incident on a Dark Street" and "Melvin Purvis, G-Man," and the theatrical releases "Shark's Treasure" and "Posse." In 1991, he hosted the "Bonanza" segment of "Michael Landon: Memories with Laughter and Love," which NBC aired in 1991.

TIM MATHESON has made feature films such as "National Lampoon's Animal House" and "Up the Creek," but shows up most often on the small screen. After his brief tenure as Griff King, he was a guest on numerous series ("Medical Center," "Police Story," "Hawaii Five-O," etc.) and a regular on the series "The Quest," "Tucker's Witch," "Just in Time" and "Charlie Hoover."

BING RUSSELL is retired today, but after nearly ten years on "Bonanza" did episodes of "Gunsmoke," "Mannix," "The Streets of San Francisco" and "Petrocelli." He was also in Michael Landon's television movie "The Loneliest Runner" and portrayed Vernon Presley in the 1979 TV biopic "Elvis" with son Kurt.

KATHIE BROWNE, a semi-regular as Adam Cartwright's near-bride in four episodes, co-starred on the short-lived "Hondo" series in 1967 and landed guest parts on dozens of shows, including the Westerns "Branded," "The Wild, Wild West," and "The Big Valley." A former president of the Screen Actors Guild, she has for years been married to actor Darren McGavin.

VICTOR SEN YUNG was wounded during a 1972 airline hijacking in California, but recovered to appear in the 1973 television adaptation of John Steinbeck's "The Red Pony" with Henry Fonda, Ben Johnson and Jack Elam. In addition, he had guest parts on "Kung Fu" and "How the West Was Won." On November 9, 1980, neighbors smelled natural gas leaking from Yung's North Hollywood home, from where he had been selling Chinese pottery by mail. The coroner estimated the actor's death to have occurred ten days earlier, and in January the incident was ruled as accidental. Yung was 65.

RAY TEAL, who portrayed Virginia City lawman Sheriff Roy Coffee for all but "Bonanza's" first and last seasons, died on April 2, 1976, at the age of 74.

LOU FRIZZEL was a regular on the series "Chopper One" and "The New Land" after his two seasons on the Ponderosa. He died at the age of 59 on June 17, 1979.

GUY WILLIAMS will no doubt always be best remembered as Zorro or Professor John Robinson on "Lost in Space," but in-between those gigs he came close to becoming a Cartwright, portraying cousin Will in five episodes of "Bonanza's" memorable fifth season. He eventually moved to Buenos Aires, Argentina, where in May of 1989 he suffered a fatal heart attack in his apartment. As in the case of Victor Sen Yung, Williams was also 65, and more than a week passed before his body was discovered.

BRUCE YARNELL, prior to portraying another Cartwright cousin, Muley Jones, in two episodes, was a regular on the series "The Outlaws." A native of Los Angeles, he died on November 30, 1973, at the age of only 35.

Several actors played other Cartwright relatives (Barry Coe, Nina Foch, Inga Swenson, to name a few), and many wonderful performers appeared as the same character in more than one episode

(Arthur Hunnicutt, Victor French, Dub Taylor, Ann Prentiss, Slim Pickens, Jack Kruschen, Wayne Newton), all contributing to the colorful tapestry that was "Bonanza."

In late 1994, David Dortort composed a set of guidelines for the producers of the potential feature film based on his creation. He called them "The Bonanza Credo," and they explain perfectly the enduring appeal of the show.

Millions of viewers the world over would doubtlessly flock to a major motion picture based on the most popular Western series in the history of television. One can only hope the film becomes a reality, and that it will compare favorably with the original classic. The producers have some awfully large boots to fill.

In the meantime, "Bonanza" fans can make the pilgrimage to the Ponderosa Ranch near Incline Village from April through October, as thousands have done each year since 1967, and ponder what once was. Better still, anyone with a television and a VCR can experience the legend as often as they like.

THE BONANZA CREDO
by David Dortort

*In the Old West, it meant a lot to be a Cartwright.
Being a family, loving the land, being honest and fair.
Giving every man and every woman a second chance.*

More than most television shows, "Bonanza" has a heart and a soul. To protect that heart and soul and to preserve the basic integrity of the show, the following are the essential values that must be maintained:

1. The Cartwright family, the good father and the good, loyal sons, are the center of gravity around which the movie revolves. They may disagree on any number of issues, but always, in the end, they are a family again, all for one, and one for all.

2. They stand for tolerance, compassion and concern for all endangered species, and that includes the stranger in need of sanctuary, the battered mother, the abandoned child, the wounded animal, as well as the forests, the mountain streams, the lakes and ponds. No woman, no child, no animal can be abused without swift and full-bore punishment for the abuser.

3. The Ponderosa, the home of the Cartwright family, should be treated as a special kind of place, a sort of mythical kingdom on the glistening crown of the Sierra. Good people, role models, are in charge here. People slow to anger, but tread lightly or suffer the consequences. Stern, formidable, when faced with injustice, but loose, relaxed, fun-loving, a family that can laugh at itself as easily as it can challenge a swindler, a bounty hunter, a slave master, or a robber baron, no matter how high the odds are stacked against them.

It's a whole new world today, but some things never change. Such as the high standards maintained by America's most-loved fictional family, the Cartwrights of the great Ponderosa Ranch.

BONANZA
September 12, 1959-
January 16, 1973

Above:The Cartwright knights at their "round table" ("Gabrielle" 1961). Lower left: Ben's three sons (1959). Lower right: At Lake Tahoe for "Showdown at Tahoe" (1967). Far right: at Incline Village (1967).

CHAPTER SEVEN

Bonanza Collectibles

Bonanza tin cup: a souvenir of The Ponderosa Ranch, Lake Tahoe, Nevada.

As the popularity of Bonanza grew, merchandising grew with it. The following pages represent a sampling of Bonanza memorabilia. These collectibles are by no means a complete record of the material produced, but they do help us to see how popular the show was and how much its memory is prized today. Much of the material shown here is bought, sold and traded by collectors around the world.

Comics

June-Aug. 1960–Dell #1110

Sep.-Nov. 1961–Dell #1221

Feb.-April 1962–Dell #1283

May-Jul. '62–Dell #01070-207

Aug.-Oct. '62–Dell #01070-210

December 1962–#1

March 1963–#2

June 1963–#3

September 1963–#4   *February 1964–#6*   *April 1964–#7*   *August 1964–#9*

October 1964–#10   *December 1964–#11*   *April 1965–#13*   *June 1965–#14*

August 1965–#15   *October 1965–#16*   *December 1965–#17*   *February 1966–#18*

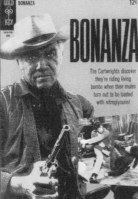

April 1966–#19   *June 1966–#20*   *August 1966–#21*   *November 1966–#22*

More Comics

February 1967–#23

May 1967–#24

August 1967–#25

May 1968–#28

August 1968–#29

November 1968–#30

February 1969–#31

May 1969–#32

August 1969–#33

November 1969–#34

February 1970–#35

May 1970–#36

TV Guide

June 25, 1960

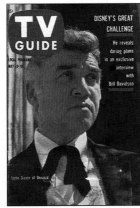

May 13, 1961

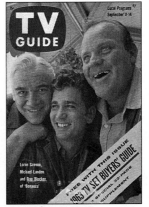

September 8, 1962

March 30, 1963

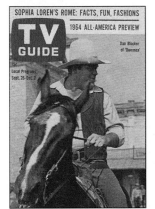

September 26, 1964

March 13, 1965

September 4, 1965

July 22, 1967

March 3, 1968

November 29, 1969

March 27, 1971

October 14, 1971

Additional Items

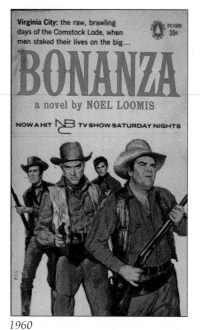

1960

A recent Bonanza book, 1992

1966

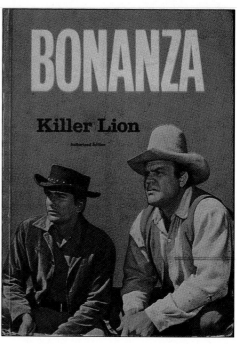

Above: The first of four Whitman Books for young readers, 1966.
Left: Bonanza Collectible Plates. Another late arrival to the collectible scene. This is an advertising flyer from 1990.

122

View-master stereo pictures, 1971

1964

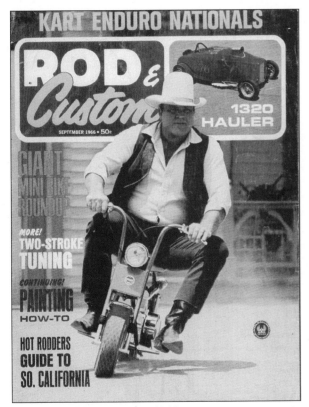

Rod and Custom, *September, 1966*

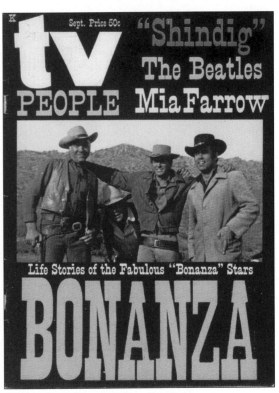

TV People, *Collector's Edition One 1964*

First of four two-episode videos (Republic, 1987). Front cover art is from "Ride the Wind" and the back cover is an NBC promotion poster from 1966.

An evening of songs and stories by Lorne Greene from 1964. This album was Greene's second and featured hits such as Ringo, the Ponderosa theme and the Saga of the Ponderosa. Other recordings are pictured on pages 19, 20, 26, 61 and 63.

First video release of "Ride the Wind" (NTA, 1984) with the orginal movie poster art.

A rare book of stories with cartoon illustrations. Published in England in 1965.

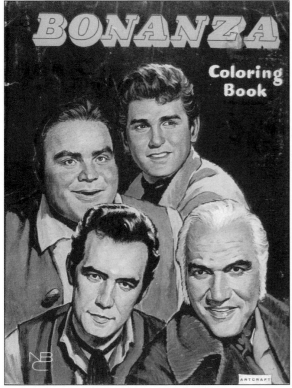

One of the many coloring books. This is from 1960.

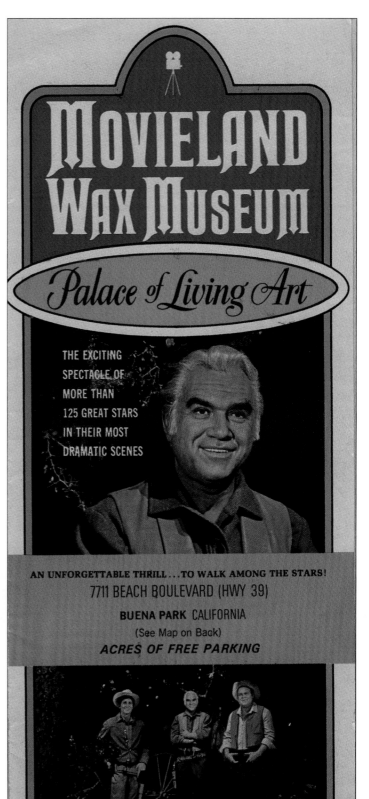

Many amusement and entertainment places made use of Bonanza's popularity. Here is an ad from 1968.

There were 428 episodes of "Bonanza," comprising 431 hours of broadcast time. For years the exact number has been inaccurately reported from as few as 260 to as many as 440. The most common figure cited is 430, counting "Ride the Wind" and "The Pursued" as two episodes apiece rather than one each because they were shown in two parts. Occasionally a source will state there are 431 episodes, due to "Forever" (originally aired as a single two-hour segment) being split in half in syndication.

NBC reran older episodes under the title "Ponderosa" from May through August 1972. The network also combined two thematically similar episodes ("The Strange One" from 1965 and "Second Sight" from 1972) into something called "Bonanza: The Movie," complete with annoying commentary by an anonymous narrator. That fall, 260 episodes were syndicated, enough for stations to show five days a week without a repeat for a full year. The 166 which remained in an NBC storage vault for several years became known as the so-called "lost" episodes.

In the fall of 1988, Republic Pictures distributed 120 of these to The CBN Family Channel. "We are rejuvenating the original 35mm color negatives through a process which removes scratches and dust from the original," Republic's Charles Larsen said when the agreement was announced. "Then, using the latest technology, the original 35mm interpositive and the original magnetic sound tracks are mastered in digital video. The results are incredible." One year later, the cable channel acquired the 47 episodes left in the package, but to date has refused to air "The Pursued" and "A Visit to Upright." They truly *are* "lost" episodes. Viewers should also be aware that the Family Channel routinely cuts three or more minutes from each episode to make time for more commercials. When "Forever" is chopped into two segments instead of being shown in its original form, up to five minutes are missing.

For a series of its classic stature, "Bonanza" has an unfortunately checkered history on home video. By the end of 1996, only 25 episodes had

Left: At Lake Tahoe (1967).
Right: Landon, Brenda Scott and Warren Vanders at Iverson Ranch for "The Far, Far Better Thing" (1965).

CHAPTER 8

EPISODE GUIDE

Lorne Green and Dan Blocker in a 1960 publicity shot.

been released, the majority of them selected on the basis of prominent guest stars or ratings performance rather than merit alone. In 1984, Republic issued the theatrical version of "Ride the Wind," followed three years later by four tapes containing two episodes apiece ("A Rose For Lotta," "The Underdog," "The Dark Gate," "The Honor of Cochise," "The Boss," "The Truckee Strip," "Hoss and the Leprechauns," "To Own the World"). The four highest rated episodes ("The Pure Truth," "The Cheating Game," "Bullet For a Bride," "The Trap") were released in 1990, with an additional four ("Enter Mark Twain," "Silent Thunder," "The Crucible," "Any Friend of Walter's") the next year. Both Columbia House Video and Time-Life Video attempted to repackage several of these seventeen episodes, meeting with only modest success.

Two other companies, Diamond Entertainment Corporation and Front Row Entertainment, have between them released another eight episodes, most from the first season ("The Stranger," "The Avenger," "Bitter Water," "Feet of Clay," "Escape to Ponderosa," "The Fear Merchants," "Blood on the Land," "The Spitfire"), but viewers are advised that unlike the Republic tapes, these are not mastered from original negatives or duplicated at the highest speed. Although they are unedited, the teaser of "The Fear Merchants," for example, is missing, and it is conceivable there could be other omissions.

What follows are concise summaries of all 428 episodes, along with airdates, significant guest stars and various notes of interest. I have made every attempt to correct titles, dates and names which have appeared incorrectly in other sources. The broadcast information given for "A Severe Case of Matrimony" and "Stage Door Johnnies" from Season Nine (1967-68) are their rerun dates. Both were first shown early in the season, but the exact dates could not be obtained by the time this book went to press.

SEASON 1 (1959-60)

1. A ROSE FOR LOTTA
September 12, 1959
The mine owners of Virginia City use chanteuse Lotta Crabtree and a hired killer in an attempt to extort Ponderosa timber from the Cartwrights. With Yvonne DeCarlo. Written by David Dortort.

2. DEATH ON SUN MOUNTAIN (THE SUN MOUNTAIN HERD)
September 19, 1959
Greedy opportunists stir up trouble between the Paiute tribe and the citizens of Virginia City until the Cartwrights intervene. Based on fact, with exteriors filmed at Iverson Movie Location Ranch. No landing constructed yet for the Ponderosa stairway. Lorne Greene's first voice-over narration. With Barry Sullivan, Leo Gordon and Karl Swenson. Written by Gene L. Coon and David Dortort.

3. THE NEWCOMERS
September 26, 1959

Ben orders a crew of hydraulic miners off the Ponderosa and assigns Hoss the task of making certain they leave. Hoss falls in love with the lone woman in the party, unaware she is dying. Filmed in Big Bear, California. First episode to reveal the exterior of the Ponderosa ranch house. With Inger Stevens.

4. THE PAIUTE WAR
October 3, 1959

The Cartwrights become involved when white men provoke an Indian uprising. Impressive battle scenes staged at Iverson. With Jack Warden and Anthony Caruso.

5. ENTER MARK TWAIN
October 10, 1959

Samuel Clemens arrives in Virginia City to write for the Territorial Enterprise at the same time a crooked politician tries to lay claim to the Ponderosa. First of three appearances by the character of Mark Twain, played this time by Howard Duff.

6. THE JULIA BULETTE STORY
October 17, 1959

Little Joe is infatuated with saloon owner Julia Bulette, whom he imagines is much like his late mother. First episode to reveal background details concerning Marie Cartwright, and inspired by the true story of a Virginia City madam. Also the first episode to showcase Michael Landon.The familiar music is "Aura Lee," a popular Civil War era folk ballad whose tune is better known to modern listeners as "Love Me Tender." Roy Engel makes his first of many appearances as the town doctor. With Jane Greer.

7. THE SAGA OF ANNIE O'TOOLE
October 24, 1959

Adam defends the mining claim of Annie O'Toole in a court presided over by Judge Ben Cartwright. First episode filmed in Griffith Park's Bronson Canyon, used frequently by the series all the way through the final season. With Ida Lupino and Alan Hale, Jr., whose father was "married" to Lupino in the 1940 film "They Drive By Night."

8. THE PHILIP DEIDESHEIMER STORY
October 31, 1959

Adam and Hoss assist a German engineer in developing the concept of "square set" mining. Based on fact, and the first episode not to include all four Cartwrights. Hoss refers to the character with whom he was in love in "The Newcomers." First episode to open with Lake Tahoe in the background. With John Beal, Mala Powers and R.G. Armstrong.

9. MR. HENRY COMSTOCK
November 7, 1959

In a flashback, the legendary prospector arrives on the Ponderosa and participates in the founding of Virginia City. Actually the second episode filmed, and an early classic. Coincidentally, guest star Jack Carson played a teller at the Comstock Bank and Trust in the 1942 film "Gentleman Jim." Written by David Dortort.

10. THE MAGNIFICENT ADAH
November 14, 1959

Virginia City is visited by actress Adah Issacs Mencken, who happens to be an old acquaintance of Ben's. Joe is badly beaten by Adah's jealous suitor, who is bested in a fight with an enraged Hoss. With Ruth Roman.

11. THE TRUCKEE STRIP
November 21, 1959

Western version of Romeo and Juliet as the Cartwrights feud with the Bishops and Joe falls in love with the enemy's daughter. In one emotionally charged scene, Joe actually pulls a gun on Ben, and in another slips and calls Hoss "Horse". Filmed near Big Bear. With James Coburn.

12. THE HANGING POSSE
November 28, 1959

Adam and Joe reluctantly join a group of vengeful townsmen bent on lynching a trio of fleeing outlaws, one of whom murdered a woman. The leader of the posse, Paiute Scroggs, is played by the superb Arthur Hunnicutt.

13. VENDETTA
December 5, 1959

In a variation of "High Noon," Ben and Hoss must face a gang of outlaws practically alone when most of Virginia City's citizens go into hiding. The most action-filled episode since "The Paiute War." With Mort Mills, Bill Quinn and Whitney Blake.

Landon in a 1960 publicity shot.

16. EL TORO GRANDE
January 2, 1960

Ben sends Hoss and Joe to Monterey to purchase an expensive seed bull. The first of Blocker and Landon's many comic misadventures, although the casual use of violence is oddly uncharacteristic for the series. Hoss reveals his real name to be Eric for the first time.

17. THE OUTCAST
January 9, 1960

Because she is related to criminals, a young woman is ostracized by everyone but the Cartwrights. She unwisely seeks solace with an ex-con friend of Joe's, and it's up to Ben to straighten everything out. Good story and direction by Thomas Thompson and Lewis Allen, respectively. With Jack Lord, Susan Oliver, Irene Tedrow and Edward Platt.

18. A HOUSE DIVIDED
January 16, 1960

As the Civil War approaches, Adam and Joe clash over which side to support. The situation is complicated by the arrival of Southern sympathizer Frederick Kyle, an old friend of Joe's mother. Viewers discover in this episode that Joe's middle name is Francis. With Cameron Mitchell, who later starred as Buck Cannon in David Dortort's "The High Chaparral."

19. THE GUNMEN
January 23, 1960

In the first all-out comic episode of the series, Hoss and Joe travel to Kiowa Flats, Texas, where they are mistaken for the notorious Slade Brothers, also played by Blocker and Landon. With Henry Hull and Ellen Corby.

20. THE FEAR MERCHANTS
January 30, 1960

The Cartwrights encounter racial bigotry in Virginia City and end up protecting a Chinese boy from mob violence. Victor Sen Yung, in his largest role to date, speaks normally in the presence of his fellow countrymen, but reverts to broken English when with the Cartwrights. With Gene Evans, Frank Ferguson and Philip Ahn.

21. THE SPANISH GRANT
February 6, 1960

The Cartwrights' ownership of the Ponderosa is thrown into question by an alleged Spanish noblewoman. With Patricia Medina and Sebastian Cabot. Script co-written by David Dortort.

14. THE SISTERS
December 12, 1959

In the space of one episode, Adam is challenged to a duel, involved with a woman against Ben's advice, accused of murder by the town drunk and jailed by a crooked sheriff. With Buddy Ebsen, Fay Spain and Malcom Atterbury, who played Michael Landon's father in "I Was a Teenage Werewolf."

15. THE LAST HUNT
December 19, 1959

Hoss and Joe come across a pregnant Indian woman while hunting bighorn sheep and must deliver her baby. Despite touches of humor, including a scene in which Joe refers to a meal as "cattle fodder", the story does not have an altogether happy ending. Locations filmed at Big Bear. With Raymond Bailey, Mr. Drysdale on "The Beverly Hillbillies."

22. BLOOD ON THE LAND
February 13, 1960
A shiftless sheepherder encroaches on Cartwright property and refuses to budge. Jeb Drummond is played by Everett Sloane, who appeared in the classic "Citizen Kane" with Orson Welles.

23. DESERT JUSTICE
February 20, 1960
When a tough U.S. marshal from California arrests a Ponderosa ranch hand for murder, Adam and Hoss go along to make sure their employee reaches Los Angeles alive. In one scene, Adam is dressed in black for the first time. In another, Hoss, upon seeing southern California for the first time, remarks, "It sure ain't never gonna amount to much." Later, Adam makes an amusing reference to the chow Joe says he was forced to eat in "The Last Hunt." With Claude Akins and Ron Hayes.

24. THE STRANGER
February 27, 1960
Nevada Territory is awaiting statehood, and Ben considers running for governor until he learns he is wanted for murder in New Orleans. Once again, there are several references to Joe's mother, and viewers are shown Marie's grave near the shore of Lake Tahoe. With Lloyd Nolan and Hank Worden.

25. ESCAPE TO PONDEROSA
March 5, 1960
Adam is attacked by three army deserters, and the Cartwrights tangle with the brutal captain pursuing them. With Grant Williams and Gloria Talbott.

26. THE AVENGER
March 19, 1960
Ben and Adam are going to be hanged for murder unless Hoss and Joe can wire the governor a petition with the names of 50 citizens. Although the town was ready to support Ben for governor in "The Stranger," no one will sign. Hope arrives in the form of a mysterious man called Lassiter. According to David Dortort, this episode was the pilot for a proposed series that never materialized. With Vic Morrow. Written by Clair Huffaker.

27. THE LAST TROPHY
March 26, 1960
Adam takes Ben's friends, Lord Marion Dunsford and wife Lady Beatrice, on a hunting expedition, and they are attacked by a crude gang of murderers and thieves. During one early scene, after listening to Ben reminisce, Hoss says, "Always like to hear Pa get wound up. He don't do it often." With Hazel Court and Bert Freed.

28. SAN FRANCISCO
April 2, 1960
In this comic episode, the first to take place far from the ranch, Ben, Hoss and Joe deliver a herd to San Francisco. Although he warns his sons to be careful in the big city ("This is not the Ponderosa!"), Ben is the one who is shanghaied and must be rescued. One of the last productions to use Paramount's huge water tank, which had to be excavated from under a parking lot in 1984 for the fourth "Star Trek" film. While immersed in the tank, Lorne Greene's hairpiece floated to the top, and he would not come up until he found it. Victor Sen Yung has even more screen time than in "The Fear Merchants." With Richard Deacon and Tor Johnson. Ironically, director Arthur Lubin made a 1940 film called "San Francisco Docks."

29. BITTER WATER
April 9, 1960
The Cartwrights save the day when Texas ticks infect area cattle herds with a deadly fever. With Don Dubbins, Merry Anders and Rhys Williams.

30. FEET OF CLAY
April 16, 1960
Hoss takes the young son of a convicted felon under his wing, then is forced to kill the boy's father. The most emotional Hoss story since "The Newcomers" and one of Blocker's best. With David Ladd.

31. DARK STAR
April 23, 1960
Joe falls in love with an undeniably strange gypsy girl who says she is cursed and never does seem to "snap out of it." The first episode of the series with a supernatural flavor, directed, appropriately enough, by Lewis Allen, who made the classic ghost film "The Uninvited" in 1944. Grandon Rhodes makes the first of numerous appearances as a Virginia City doctor. With Susan Harrison

32. DEATH AT DAWN
April 30, 1960
Virginia City is plagued by organized crime in an episode with a sterling cast, including Robert Middleton, Morgan Woodward and, in the first of several guest roles on the series, Gregory Walcott. Playing the part of Beth Cameron is Lorne Greene's second wife, Nancy Deale.

131

Greene was a stabilizing influence for the entire cast.

SEASON 2 (1960-61)

33. SHOWDOWN
September 10, 1960

A young bank robber hires on at the Ponderosa in order to keep his gang informed of the law's efforts to discover their whereabouts. First appearance of Ray Teal as Sheriff Roy Coffee. With Ben Cooper and Jack Lambert.

34. THE MISSION
September 17, 1960

On a trek across the desert, Hoss and a drunken scout must foil an attempt to steal army gold. Filmed entirely outdoors. With Henry Hull, Peter Whitney, John Dehner, Harry Carey, Jr., Lane Bradford and Don Collier.

35. BADGE WITHOUT HONOR
September 24, 1960

Adam's life is saved by an enigmatic U.S. marshal who has come to Virginia City to arrest a friend of the Cartwrights'. Outstanding performance by Dan Duryea.

36. THE MILL
October 1, 1960

The Cartwrights construct a grist mill to provide income for a crippled rancher who blames Ben for his predicament. Ben has to contend with the man's depraved caretaker, and finds himself attracted to his wife. "Sons can't be everything," Ben tells her. With Claude Akins and Harry Townes.

37. THE HOPEFULS
October 8, 1960

Adam guides a wagon train of Quakers and falls for the leader's daughter. The force Adam must employ to protect them conflicts with their passive philosophy of life.

38. DENVER MCKEE
October 15, 1960

Veteran actor Franchot Tone ("Mutiny on the Bounty") portrays a former lawman gone bad in a story directed by Jacques Tourneur, another Hollywood pro ("Cat People," Stars in My Crown"). Of course Joe is sweet on the old man's daughter.

39. DAY OF RECKONING
October 22, 1960

Prejudice erupts on both sides when Ben gives land to the Indian who saves his life. Intense performance by Ricardo Montalban. With Madlyn Rhue, Karl Swenson and Anthony Caruso.

40. THE ABDUCTION
October 29, 1960

Joe's latest girlfriend is kidnapped by the owner of a carnival in an episode filmed entirely on a soundstage. Reed is played by Gerald Mohr, who appeared infrequently as Doc Holliday on "Maverick."

41. BREED OF VIOLENCE
November 5, 1960

While tracking wolves responsible for killing Ponderosa cattle, Hoss and Joe become the captives of outlaws. The girlfriend of the gang's leader is the rebellious daughter of a strict sheriff, as well as a friend of Joe's.

42. THE LAST VIKING
November 12, 1960

Hoss meets his Uncle Gunnar for the first time, unaware that he commands a band of raiding comancheros. With Neville Brand.

43. THE TRAIL GANG
November 26, 1960

On a drive back to Nevada from Texas, Ben hires a young man who is both an outlaw and the son of the sheriff whose town the Ponderosa hands are entering. With Edgar Buchanan and Robert J. Wilke.

44. THE SAVAGE
December 3, 1960

Adam's life is saved by a woman known to the Indians as White Buffalo Woman, but who is actually the daughter of Norwegian immigrants. Filmed at Iverson's Ranch and Hollywood's Franklin Lake. With Anna-Lisa.

45. SILENT THUNDER
December 10, 1960

Joe teaches sign language to the deaf and dumb daughter of a widowed sheepman. First episode directed by Robert Altman, with imaginative touches (whiskey dripping off a bible, sequence of what woman sees from tilted angle) characteristic of his unique vision. With Stella Stevens and Albert Salmi.

46. THE APE
December 17, 1960

Hoss befriends a dull-witted giant whose temper scares everyone, including the rest of the Cartwrights. With Cal Bolder and Leonard Nimoy.

47. THE BLOOD LINE
December 31, 1960

Ben feels responsible for the son of a man he was forced to kill, but the young man is determined to get even. A professional gunman offers to do the job for him. With familiar screen heavy Lee VanCleef.

48. THE COURTSHIP
January 7, 1961

Hoss plans to marry the widow of one of Ben's friends, not knowing she is a compulsive gambler and refusing to believe it when the other Cartwrights confront him with the truth. With Julie London.

49. THE SPITFIRE
January 14, 1961

Joe becomes the target of vengeful squatters after he kills one of them in self-defense. With Jack Elam.

50. THE BRIDE
January 21, 1961

The Cartwrights' ownership of the Ponderosa is threatened by a woman claiming to be Ben's wife, her scheming partner and a crooked sheriff. With Adam West, John McIntire and Hank Worden.

51. BANK RUN
January 28, 1961

When they "rob" the bank in Virginia City to save depositors from being cleaned out by its president, Hoss and Joe wind up wanted by the law. A humorous episode directed by Robert Altman.

52. THE FUGITIVE
February 4, 1961

Adam goes to Mexico to find out how the son of a family friend was killed, only to learn the man is still alive. With Frank Silvera, who portrayed Don Sebastian on "The High Chaparral."

53. VENGEANCE
February 11, 1961

Hoss accidentally kills a drunk he is trying to disarm. The man 's brother bushwhacks Hoss, who has lost the will to live. The name of "Bonanza's" unit production manager, A.J. Durkus, is stamped on a crate in this episode's opening shot.

54. THE TAX COLLECTOR
February 18, 1961

The kindness Hoss extends to shiftless Jock Henry is not exactly repaid when Henry becomes an assistant assessor and raises the Ponderosa's annual tax bill from $375 to almost $1700. With Eddie Firestone and Kathie Browne.

55. THE RESCUE
February 25, 1961

The Cartwright boys are concerned that Ben might be getting on in years, yet it is he who saves them from rustlers. Filmed at Iverson's Ranch. With Ron Hayes, Lane Bradford and Leif Erickson, who played John Cannon on "The High Chaparral."

56. THE DARK GATE
March 4, 1961

Adam fears his friend has gone insane after he beats his wife to death and joins an outlaw gang. Climax shot at Red Rock Canyon. With James Coburn and Henry Dean Stanton.

On location for "The Quest" (1962).

57. THE DUKE
March 11, 1961

Hoss takes on The Duke of London, an arrogant, abusive bare-knuckle fighter, though his brawn is no match for the Duke's agile skills. With J. Pat O'Malley and Jason Evers. Directed by Robert Altman.

58. CUTTHROAT JUNCTION
March 18, 1961

When freight company detective Jed Trask is fired after a decade of loyal service, he joins the thieves preventing supplies from reaching Virginia City. Solid Western with all four Cartwrights and a great performance by guest star Robert Lansing.

59. THE GIFT
April 1, 1961

While crossing the desert with a white stallion intended as a birthday gift for Ben, Joe runs into a pack of merciless comancheros. A highlight of the series, filmed at Red Rock Canyon. With Martin Landau, Jim Davis and Jack Hogan.

60. THE RIVAL
April 15, 1961

Jim Applegate, Hoss' rival for the affections of Cameo Johnson, is a member of a vigilante group who lynched an innocent man and his wife. Directed by Robert Altman, who begins the episode with a close-up of a frog. With Charles Aidman, Peggy Ann Garner.

61. THE INFERNAL MACHINE
April 22, 1961

Hoss believes in his friend's primitive version of the automobile in this lighthearted yet sad episode. When the "car" uses up the last of its fuel, Hoss remarks, "Dadburn it, I still say it woulda worked." With Eddie Ryder, George Kennedy and Shug Fisher.

62. THE THUNDERHEAD SWINDLE
April 29, 1961

With Virginia City on the verge of economic ruin, out of work miners put their hopes in word of a strike at a mine everyone believed was played out. Ben suspects the new owners have been stealing silver from an adjoining mine also thought dry, and resolves to prove it. Filmed in Bronson Canyon. With Parley Baer and Vitto Scotti.

63. THE SECRET
May 6, 1961

Joe is the victim of an elaborate frame-up, accused of murdering a pregnant girl. When Ben is asked if Joe is telling the truth, he replies, "If I were to start doubting my son at this point, everything I've lived and worked for would be lost." Directed by Robert Altman. With Morgan Woodward as the town sheriff instead of Ray Teal.

64. THE DREAM RIDERS
May 20, 1961

To finance his dream of constructing an airship capable of crossing the Atlantic, Ben's friend plans to rob the Virginia City bank while diverting the citizens' attention with a hot air balloon. Directed by Robert Altman.

65. ELIZABETH, MY LOVE
May 27, 1961
At the bedside of a seriously ill Adam, Ben thinks back to his days as a first mate in the merchant marine and his marriage to Adam's mother, Elizabeth Stoddard. With Geraldine Brooks, Torin Thatcher and Ted Knight.

66. SAM HILL
June 3, 1961
Blacksmith Sam Hill fights to keep the land on which his mother is buried after his drunken father signs the deed over to a colonel and his private army. Poetic episode written by David Dortort and directed by Robert Altman. With Claude Akins, Edgar Buchanan and Ford Rainey

SEASON 3 (1961-62)

67. THE SMILER
September 24, 1961
A drunk is killed during a saloon brawl with Hoss, and though the man's brother insists there are no hard feelings, he is actually a silver-tongued devil bent on revenge. With Herschel Bernardi and Scatman Crothers.

68. SPRINGTIME
October 1, 1961
After they accidentally injure self-made tycoon Jedediah Milbank, the Cartwright boys must each tend to a different business transaction while he recovers at the Ponderosa. With John Carradine, Denver Pyle and John Qualen.

69. THE HONOR OF COCHISE
October 8, 1961
The Cartwrights and a bigoted army captain are pinned down by Cochise and his braves, who claim the officer poisoned 30 of their people. Exciting episode with DeForest Kelley, Jeff Morrow and a pre-Clem Foster Bing Russell.

70. THE LONELY HOUSE
October 15, 1961
Joe and a widow friend of the Cartwrights are held captive by a wounded outlaw and his men. With Paul Richards and Faith Domergue.

71. THE BURMA RARITY
October 22, 1961
In this comic episode involving a precious emerald, the Cartwrights turn the tables on a pair of land swindlers.

72. BROKEN BALLAD
October 29, 1961
Adam tries to help a reformed gunman who wants only to live peacefully near Virginia City. Good story without a tidy ending. Pernell's first chance to sing on the series. With Robert Culp and Dabbs Greer.

73. THE MANY FACES OF GIDEON FLINCH
November 5, 1961
Hoss and Joe become involved when "Bullethead" Burke vows revenge on an old man he claims cheated him in an investment deal. A hilarious comedy directed by Robert Altman, who uses Clem Bevans and Burt Mustin like a Greek chorus. With Harry Swoger, Ian Wolfe, Sue Ann Langdon and Arnold Stang.

74. THE FRIENDSHIP
November 12, 1961
Joe takes responsibility for a bitter young man who has been in prison from the age of 13. With Dean Jones.

75. THE COUNTESS
November 19, 1961
A woman whom Ben once loved returns and attempts to trick him into marrying her by ruining his business. At the end of the story, Ben says almost losing the Ponderosa will make him and his sons appreciate it more.

76. THE HORSE BREAKER
November 26, 1961
A professional wrangler working for the Cartwrights is paralyzed when thrown by a particularly mean bronco. The woman nursing him was once engaged to the late son of a neighboring rancher out to get Ben. With Ben Cooper, R.G. Armstrong and Sue Randall.

77. DAY OF THE DRAGON
December 3, 1961
In a card game, Joe unwittingly wins a servant girl belonging to a Chinese warlord. Alternately amusing and exciting. With Mort Mills, Philip Ahn, Richard Loo and Lisa Lu.

Roberts with Dawn Wells in the 1962 episode, "The Way Station."

78. THE FRENCHMAN
December 10, 1961

An irritating man who boasts of being the reincarnation of French poet Francois Villon shows up to cause trouble for the Cartwrights. At one point the date is said to be October 1860, though in the previous season's "The Courtship," the year is 1861.

79. THE TIN BADGE
December 17, 1961

Joe accepts the job of temporary sheriff in the town of Rubicon, unaware he is being used to facilitate a scheme involving murder. With Vic Morrow, Karen Steele and John Litel.

80. GABRIELLE
December 24, 1961

Hoss and Joe come across a blind girl whose family has been killed in a wagon wreck, learning later that her grandfather is a bitter hermit who spent 21 years in prison for a murder he did not commit. Shown on Christmas Eve, this was the first of the series' two holiday episodes. Filmed at Incline Village. With John Abbott, Diane Mountford and Kevin Hagen.

81. LAND GRAB
December 31, 1961

The Ponderosa is overrun with settlers bearing phony property deeds, and one of Ben's oldest friends is responsible. With John McGiver.

82. THE TALL STRANGER
January 7, 1962

Hoss loses Margie Owens to smooth-talking adventurer Mark Connors, but comes to her rescue when Connors leaves her broke and pregnant. A sad and memorable episode. With Kathie Browne, Sean McClory and Jacqueline Scott.

83. THE LADY FROM BALTIMORE
January 14, 1962

An overbearing friend of the family tries to force her daughter into marrying Joe, though she does not love him. The situation grows more complex when Adam stumbles onto the scheme. With Mercedes Mc Cambridge.

84. THE RIDE
January 21, 1962

Adam races against the clock to prove a man who was once his friend is guilty of a robbery and murder Adam is convinced he committed. Filmed at Iverson's Ranch. With Jan Merlin and Chubby Johnson.

85. THE STORM
January 28, 1962

Joe plans to marry the daughter of a man Ben once sailed with, but she is fatally ill. Ben consoles him with words spoken years before by the father of Adam's mother. With Brooke Hayward.

86. THE AULD SOD
February 4, 1962

The Cartwrights pretend the Ponderosa belongs to the town lush when his aging mother arrives from Ireland for a visit. With James Dunn and Cheerio Meredith.

87. GIFT OF WATER
February 11, 1962
The Cartwrights dig a well and rig a windmill for a drought-stricken farm family. With Royal Dano, Majel Barrett and James Doohan.

88. THE JACK KNIFE
February 18, 1962
Adam gives a second chance to a family man he suspects is one of the rustlers who have been hitting the Ponderosa herds. With John Archer and Bethel Leslie.

89. THE GUILTY
February 25, 1962
When Ben fails to prevent the death of a friend's son, Adam and Joe, concerned by their father's depression, attempt to prove there was nothing he could have done. With Lyle Bettger and Charles Maxwell.

90. THE WOOING OF ABAGAIL JONES
March 4, 1962
Classic comedy in which the Cartwright boys help an unhappy ranch hand with the affection of the woman with whom he is smitten. Hank is played by crooner Vaughn Monroe.

91. THE LAWMAKER
March 11, 1962
Ben supports the appointment of Asa Moran as Virginia City's temporary sheriff, but Moran goes overboard with his authority, jailing Adam in the process. With Arthur Franz, Les Tremayne and John Mitchum.

92. LOOK TO THE STARS
March 18, 1962
The Cartwrights step in when a brilliant student is expelled by a bigoted teacher. Based in part on the life of Nobel Prize winner Albert Michelson. With William Schallert, Joe DeSantis and Santon.

93. THE GAMBLE
April 1, 1962
In the town of Alkali, the Cartwrights are jailed on false charges of robbery and murder, but Joe escapes and returns with an army of Ponderosa hands. Location scenes filmed at Iverson's Ranch. First script co-written by Michael Landon. With Charles McGraw and Ben Johnson.

94. THE CRUCIBLE
April 8, 1962
Stranded in the desert by bandits, Adam's survival depends on the whims of a demented prospector. Allegedly Pernell Roberts' favorite episode. With Lee Marvin.

95. INGER, MY LOVE
April 15, 1962
Ben recalls meeting Hoss' mother, Inger Borgstrom, in Illinois as he and Adam were making their way West. Dan Blocker's arm is in a sling because of a real-life riding accident. First of two episodes concerning Inger. Script co-written by David Dortort. With Inga Swenson and Jeremy Slate.

96. BLESSED ARE THEY
April 22, 1962
When two feuding families argue over custody of two orphaned children, a reluctant Ben is called upon to straighten out the situation before real trouble erupts. With Irene Tedrow and Ford Rainey.

97. THE DOWRY
April 29, 1962
The Cartwrights get mixed up in the romance of a phony heiress and an equally phony land baron. With Luciana Paluzzi.

98. THE LONG NIGHT
May 6, 1962
Adam is forced to trade clothes with an escaped convict. A posse which includes the convict's partner does not believe his story. With James Coburn, Frank Ferguson, Whit Bissell and a pre-Clem Foster Bing Russell.

99. THE MOUNTAIN GIRL
May 13, 1962
Joe promises a dying sheepman he will make sure the old man's granddaughter gets her rightful inheritance from a wealthy San Francisco family. This episode was filmed immediately after "Inger, My Love," which explains why Blocker's arm is still in a sling. With Warren Oates.

100. THE MIRACLE MAKER
May 20, 1962
Hoss blames himself when a young woman is crippled in a wagon accident, and hopes a faith healer can help her walk again. Blocker's arm is still in a sling. With Ed Nelson, Mort Mills, Raymond Bailey and Bill Quinn.

Blocker with Chub at Vasquez Rocks.

SEASON 4 (1962-63)

101. THE FIRST BORN
September 23, 1962
New Ponderosa hand Clay Stafford turns out to be Joe's half-brother, but he ultimately decides life on a ranch is not for him. He is neither seen nor mentioned again. With Barry Coe.

102. THE QUEST
September 30, 1962
Determined to prove he can succeed at something without the other Cartwrights, Joe wins a contract for Ponderosa timber, then discovers that having a family to rely on can definitely be an asset.

103. THE ARTIST
October 7, 1962
Ben helps Matthew Raine, a famous painter who has gone blind and now wallows in self-pity, discover new purpose in life. "A creative man is not a one-sided man," he tells him. With Dan O'Herlihy, Virginia Grey and Arch Johnson.

104. A HOT DAY FOR A HANGING
October 14, 1962
Hoss is jailed for robbing the bank in Dutchman Flats, a town on the brink of economic collapse, even though the sheriff knows he is innocent. With Denver Pyle, Roy Roberts, Lane Bradford and John Mitchum.

105. THE DESERTER
October 21, 1962
An Indian-hating colonel comes to the Ponderosa in search of a deserter who happens to be his son. And who also happens to be married to an Indian. Maria is played by Gale Garnett, daughter of veteran director Tay Garnett. With Claude Akins, Robert Sampson and Anthony Caruso.

106. THE WAY STATION
October 29, 1962
With a storm brewing, Adam takes refuge at a stage stop run by a cantankerous old man and his restless granddaughter. They are soon joined by a wanted killer. With Robert Vaughn and Dawn Wells.

107. THE WAR COMES TO WASHOE
November 4, 1962
The Civil War once again divides the citizens of Nevada Territory, as well as Adam and Joe Cartwright. The plot involving British spy Bill Stewart is based on historical fact. With Harry Townes.

108. KNIGHT ERRANT
November 18, 1962
Hoss volunteers to pick up an injured neighbor's mail order bride, but by the time they return, she has fallen in love with him. With John Doucette and Judi Meredith.

109. THE BEGINNING
November 25, 1962

The Cartwrights help a young white man raised as an Indian adjust to "civilized" society. With Carl Reindel, Ken Lynch and Raymond Bailey.

110. THE DEADLY ONES
December 2, 1962

Mexican revolutionaries planning to rob a gold shipment en route to Emperor Maximilian take over the Ponderosa, blasting Joe in the back with a shotgun. With Leo Gordon and Jena Engstrom.

111. GALLAGHER'S SONS
December 9, 1962

Hoss has his hands more than full with two orphaned girls and the four outlaws who are after them. With Victor French and Ken Mayer.

112. THE DECISION
December 16, 1962

On a cattle drive, Hoss is seriously injured when his horse stumbles. The only doctor Ben can find is scheduled to hang at sundown. With DeForest Kelley.

113. THE GOOD SAMARITAN
December 23, 1962

Hoss plays matchmaker and helpful neighbor in this gentle, feel-good story. With Don Collier, Jeanne Cooper

114. THE JURY
December 30, 1962

When Hoss is responsible for causing a hung jury, Ben tells him "a man is never wrong doing what he thinks is right," and Adam attempts to validate his brother's reasonable doubt.

115. THE COLONEL
January 6, 1963

Frank Medford, a figure from Ben's "wild, misspent youth", shows up in Virginia City, and though down on his luck, creates trouble for the Cartwrights by claiming to be a successful businessman. With John Larkin, Edward Platt and Warren Kemmerling.

116. SONG IN THE DARK
January 13, 1963

Adam exposes the truth about a religious zealot who will stop at nothing to establish his own church. With Edward Andrews, Gregory Walcott, Virginia Christine and Mort Mills.

117. ELEGY FOR A HANGMAN
January 20, 1963

Adam aids a newspaperman in proving a senator was a party to murder. With Keir Dullea, Otto Kruger, Kevin Hagen and Ron Soble.

118. HALF A ROGUE
January 27, 1963

In this entertaining episode, laced with humor, Hoss first meets mountain man Jim Layton. Bing Russell makes his debut as Deputy Clem Foster.
With Slim Pickens.

119. THE LAST HAIRCUT
February 3, 1963

A vain outlaw murders a man in front of witnesses, including Joe, but a clever lawyer is able to get him acquitted. Though enraged, Joe has to convince the dead man's son it is wrong for them to take the law into their own hands. With Perry Lopez and Chubby Johnson.

120. MARIE, MY LOVE
February 10, 1963

When a horse falls on Joe, Ben cannot help but remember that is how Marie Cartwright was killed. He thinks back to meeting her in New Orleans in a rather confusing story not quite in sync with details discussed in "The First Born." With Felicia Farr and Eduard Franz.

121. THE HAYBURNER
February 17, 1963

For a change, it is Adam rather than Joe who becomes mixed up in one of Hoss' funny exploits. Together they purchase a thoroughbred horse, and end up competing against their little brother in the big Virginia City race. With William Demarest, Ellen Corby and Percy Helton.

122. THE ACTRESS
February 24, 1963

Joe becomes romantically involved with a woman who considers herself a serious dramatic actress. Unfortunately, she is the only one who does. With Patricia Crowley.

123. A STRANGER PASSED THIS WAY
March 3, 1963

Hoss develops amnesia after an outlaw knocks him out, and moves in with a Dutch couple. The woman regards him as a substitute for their dead son, and unless he recovers his memory, the other Cartwrights fear he will leave them forever. With Robert Emhardt and Signe Hasso.

Guy Stockwell and Landon in "Invention of a Gunfighter" (1964).

124. THE WAY OF AARON
March 10, 1963
Adam takes a shine to Rebecca Kaufman, the daughter of a Jewish peddler, and bandits are convinced the Kaufman wagon is worth robbing. With Aneta Corsaut and Harry Dean Stanton.

125. A WOMAN LOST
March 17, 1963
Ben's attempts to rehabilitate an alcoholic saloon singer he knew in better days are complicated by her involvement with a former prize fighter. With Ruta Lee and Don Megowan.

126. ANY FRIEND OF WALTER'S
March 24, 1963
Classic comedy in which Hoss first meets reclusive prospector Obie and his lazy but allegedly brilliant mongrel dog, Walter. With Arthur Hunnicutt, Steve Brodie and James Luisi.

127. MIRROR OF A MAN
March 31, 1963
The peaceful world of a Ponderosa hand is disturbed by the arrival of his no-good father and twin brother, who is a wanted man. With Ron Hayes and Ford Rainey.

128. MY BROTHER'S KEEPER
April 7, 1963
Adam's disgust with the hardships of Western existence is aroused after he accidentally shoots Joe. Filmed at Iverson's Movie Location Ranch.

129. FIVE INTO THE WIND
April 21, 1963
After their stagecoach crashes, Joe and five ragtag passengers must get out of the desert on foot. Filmed in Griffith Park. With Kathleen Crowley and Dabbs Greer.

130. THE SAGA OF WHIZZER McGEE
April 28, 1963
Hoss becomes concerned for the welfare of an insecure, belligerent fellow who is as small as Hoss is large. Interesting blend of comedy and pathos that ends unpredictably. With Burt Mustin and Med Florey.

131. THE THUNDER MAN
May 5, 1963
Ben sends for an explosives expert who has an equally volatile attitude toward women. With Simon Oakland and Bill Quinn.

132. RICH MAN, POOR MAN
May 12, 1963
Claude Miller, the laughingstock of Virginia City, gets even with everyone who has made fun of him when he strikes it rich. Filmed in Bronson Canyon. With John Fiedler and J. Pat O'Malley.

133. THE BOSS
May 19, 1963
Ben regrets that he helped Tom Slayden start a freight hauling business when Slayden sets out to ruin all competition, and Joe is shot in the process. Co-written by actor Leo Gordon. With Carroll O'Connor and Denver Pyle.

134. LITTLE MAN 10 FEET TALL
May 26, 1963
An Italian immigrant has dreams of his son becoming a guitar virtuoso, but the boy would rather be a cowboy like Hoss. With Ross Martin, Denver Pyle, Lane Bradford.

SEASON 5 (1963-64)

135. SHE WALKS IN BEAUTY
September 22, 1963
Hoss wants to marry mysterious Regan Miller, a woman with a less than pristine past. When he thinks Adam is trying to steal her away, he loses control and beats him up. With Gena Rowlands and Jeanne Cooper.

136. A PASSION FOR JUSTICE
September 29, 1963
Charles Dickens visits Virginia City and is appalled to discover his work being reprinted in the local paper without his permission. With Jonathan Harris.

137. RAIN FROM HEAVEN
October 6, 1963
A destitute rainmaker and his family arrive in drought-stricken Virginia City. While Ben helps him try to create rain, Hoss tends to the man's seriously ill little girl. With John Anderson.

138. TWILIGHT TOWN
October 13, 1963
Joe is bushwhacked and awakens to find himself in a town that may or may not be populated by ghosts. An eerie, well-produced episode.

139. THE TOY SOLDIER
October 20, 1963
Adam encounters drunken artist James Callan, branded a "squaw man" because he is married to an Indian, and whose talent is going to waste in the town of Sheep Head. Directed by Tay Garnett ("The Postman Always Rings Twice"). With Philip Abbott and Morgan Woodward

140. A QUESTION OF STRENGTH
October 27, 1963
Hoss and a pair of nuns, the younger one having a difficult time training for the order, are robbed and stranded at a way station. With Judy Carne and John Kellogg.

141. CALAMITY OVER THE COMSTOCK
November 3, 1963
Joe runs into the legendary Calamity Jane and eventually her jealous beau, who is none other than Doc Holliday. With Stefanie Powers and Christopher Dark, who also appeared in the "Bonanza" pilot.

142. JOURNEY REMEMBERED
November 10, 1963
In this sequel to "Inger, My Love," Ben recalls his journey West and the birth of Hoss. Perhaps the best of the series' four flashback episodes. With Inga Swenson, Gene Evans, Kevin Hagen and Ken Lynch.

143. THE QUALITY OF MERCY
November 17, 1963
Joe wrestles with his conscience after his friend commits a supposed mercy killing. With Richard Rust, who was in "The Legend of Tom Dooley" with Michael Landon.

144. THE WAITING GAME
December 8, 1963
Adam becomes involved with the recently widowed Laura Dayton and her little girl Peggy. Filmed at Golden Oak Ranch. Frank Dayton is played by Wayde Preston, who starred in his own series, "Colt .45." With Kathie Browne and Katie Sweet. Good direction by actor Richard C. Sarafian.

145. THE LEGACY
December 15, 1963
Convinced Ben is dead, the Cartwright boys split up to seek vengeance in one of the most outstanding episodes of the series. With James Best, Percy Helton, Philip Pine and James Doohan.

146. HOSS AND THE LEPRECHAUNS
December 22, 1963
In what is arguably the series best-loved comedy, Hoss swears he has seen green elves running around the Ponderosa. Nels Nelson and Harry Monty played Munchkins in the classic "The Wizard of Oz." With Sean McClory.

Dan Duryea and Greene in "Logan's Treasure" (1964).

147. THE PRIME OF LIFE
December 29, 1963

Ben becomes irritable and reckless when the completion of an important timber project is hindered by an old rival. With Jay C. Flippen, Roy Jenson and Butch Patrick.

148. THE LILA CONRAD STORY
January 5, 1964

Joe and Adam protect a saloon girl who has killed in self-defense from a lynch mob. Filmed at Golden Oaks. With Patricia Blair and Andrew Duggan.

149. PONDEROSA MATADOR
January 12, 1964

The Cartwright boys are infatuated with the daughter of a bull breeder, and with the help of one of the beasts, manage to tear up most of Virginia City. With Marianna Hill, Nestor Paiva and Frank Ferguson.

150. MY SON, MY SON
January 19, 1964

Ben's plans to marry Katherine Saunders are upset when her son Eden is accused of killing his former girlfriend. Climax filmed in Bronson Canyon. With Theresa Wright and Dee Pollack.

151. ALIAS JOE CARTWRIGHT
January 26, 1964

Joe is mistaken for an army deserter in this seriocomic episode. Michael Landon also plays Joe's double, Angus Borden. Filmed at Vasquez Rocks. With Keenan Wynn.

152. THE GENTLEMAN FROM NEW ORLEANS
February 2, 1964

The new stranger in town claims to be the famous pirate Jean Lafitte, and Hoss believes him. Coincidentally, Lorne Greene appeared in the 1958 film "The Buccaneer," featuring Yul Brynner as Lafitte. With John Dehner.

153. THE CHEATING GAME
February 9, 1964

In this sequel to "The Waiting Game," Laura Dayton resents Adam's advice on how she ought to be running her ranch. With Peter Breck and Katie Sweet.

154. BULLET FOR A BRIDE
February 16, 1964

Remorseful after accidentally blinding Tessa Caldwell, Joe asks her to marry him. She regains her sight, and her penniless father fears the marriage will be called off if Joe finds out. Filmed at Golden Oaks. With Marlyn Mason and Denver Pyle.

155. KING OF THE MOUNTAIN
February 23, 1964

When mountain man Jim Layton decides to marry, he asks Hoss to be his best man in this follow-up to the previous season's "Half a Rogue." With Slim Pickens, Robert Middleton and Byron Foulger.

156. LOVE ME NOT
March 1, 1964
A Western version of "My Fair Lady" as Ben struggles to teach the social graces to a white woman raised by the Paiutes. She falls in love with him and is hurt when he tells her all she has is a schoolgirl crush. A humorous yet touching episode. With Anjanette Comer.

157. THE PURE TRUTH
March 8, 1964
Hoss, suffering from spring fever, goes to the wrong town to pick up a prisoner for Roy Coffee and finds himself accused of bank robbery. The highest-rated episode of the series. With Glenda Farrell and Lloyd Corrigan.

158. NO LESS A MAN
March 15, 1964
The town council of Virginia City feels Roy Coffee is no match for the marauding Wagner Gang, but Adam and Ben do not agree. With Parley Baer and John Kellogg.

159. RETURN TO HONOR
March 22, 1964
Ben is summoned to another town to pick up the body of his brother's dead son, only to discover him alive and being hunted by counterfeiters who want the engraving plates he has stolen. Guy Williams makes his first appearance as Ben's nephew, Will. With Arch Johnson and Robert J. Wilke.

160. THE SAGA OF MULEY JONES
March 29, 1964
The Cartwrights are visited by their second cousin, Muley Jones of Weedville, Missouri, who sings with a window-shattering voice. With Bruce Yarnell, Jesse White, Strother Martin and Jerome Cowan.

161. THE ROPER
April 5, 1964
Will has second thoughts about staying on at the Ponderosa, but before he definitely makes up his mind, outlaws hit the ranch and take him with when they leave. With Scott Marlowe, Julie Sommars.

162. A PINK CLOUD COMES FROM OLD CATHAY
April 12, 1964
Hoss orders fireworks from a trading company, only to be sent a hard headed Oriental girl who proceeds to interfere with the construction of a railroad spur being built across the Ponderosa. With Marlo Thomas, Benson Fong and Philip Ahn.

163. THE COMPANEROS
April 19, 1964
Just as he is getting accustomed to life on the Ponderosa, Will is tempted to go to Mexico with an old friend he met while fighting for Juarez. This rather talky episode is the only one to feature Guy Williams almost exclusively. With Frank Silvera and Faith Domergue.

164. ENTER THOMAS BOWERS
April 26, 1964
A black opera singer is invited to perform in Virginia City and faces prejudice and suspicions about his past. Landmark episode with William Marshall, who went on to portray Blacula in a pair of Seventies horror films and the King of Cartoons on "Pee-Wee's Playhouse."

165. THE DARK PAST
May 3, 1964
Moody bounty hunter Dev Farnum shows up on the Ponderosa, where the Cartwrights are harboring the wife of the man he is after. Edgy, offbeat performance by a young Dennis Hopper.

166. THE PRESSURE GAME
May 10, 1964
Adam's relationship with Laura Dayton is complicated by her scheming Aunt Lil and her apparent attraction to Will Cartwright. With Kathie Browne and Joan Blondell and Katie Sweet.

167. TRIANGLE
May 17, 1964
Adam is secretly building a home for himself and Laura. She, however, has fallen in love with Will. But when Adam injures his back and must get around in a wheelchair, everyone's plans are put on hold. Filmed at Golden Oaks. With Kathie Browne and Katie Sweet.

168. WALTER AND THE OUTLAWS
May 24, 1964
Hilarious sequel to "Any Friend of Walter's" in which Obie leaves his dog in Hoss' care. Filmed at Iverson's Ranch. With Arthur Hunnicutt, Steve Brodie and James Luisi.

Blocker with James Gregory in "A Man to Admire" (1964).

SEASON 6 (1964-65)

169. INVENTION OF A GUNFIGHTER
September 20, 1964
Joe eventually regrets teaching John Chapman how to handle a gun, as Chapman soon begins abusing the skill. With Guy Stockwell.

170. THE HOSTAGE
September 27, 1964
Ben is held for ransom by outlaws holed up in an abandoned mine. Filmed at the Baldwin Gold Mine in Holcomb Valley, near Big Bear. This episode was originally aired without commercial interruption. With Harold J. Stone, Jacqueline Scott, Buck Taylor and Conlan Carter.

171. THE WILD ONE
October 4, 1964
Hoss tangles with ornery, opinionated horse wrangler Lafe Jessup, who is reluctantly married and about to become a father. Filmed at Red Rock Canyon. With Aldo Ray.

172. THANKS FOR EVERYTHING, FRIEND
October 11, 1964
Adam has to help track down a murderer to whom he owes his life. With Rory Calhoun, star of the series "The Texan."

173. LOGAN'S TREASURE
October 18, 1964
A man Ben helped send to prison twenty years before insists he does not know where the gold he and his partner stole is buried. Others, including a bounty hunter and his partner's son, do not believe him. Filmed at Golden Oak. With Dan Duryea, John Kellogg, Tim McIntire and Virginia Gregg.

174. THE SCAPEGOAT
October 25, 1964
Hoss prevents bumbling Waldo Watson, a fighter running from eastern gamblers, from committing suicide. Filmed at Iverson's Ranch. With George Kennedy and Richard Devon.

175. A DIME'S WORTH OF GLORY
November 1, 1964
An opportunistic journalist causes trouble for Ben, Adam and an aging lawman whose best days are behind him. With Bruce Cabot, Walter Brooke and Charles Maxwell.

176. SQUARE DEAL SAM
November 8, 1964
A good-hearted conman and his wife end up running Virginia City's orphanage, thanks mainly to the efforts of Hoss.

177. BETWEEN HEAVEN AND EARTH
November 15, 1964
Ben helps Joe deal with his fear of heights in this psychological story inspired by one of Michael Landon's real life phobias. Filmed at Vasquez Rocks. With Richard Jaeckel.

178. OLD SHEBA
November 22, 1964
Hoss fills in for a professional wrestler he injures, and the promoter pays him off in livestock—an elephant. With William Demarest.

179. A MAN TO ADMIRE
December 6, 1964
Hoss relies on a clever attorney with a drinking problem to clear him of a murder charge. In one of the series' historical inaccuracies, Abraham Lincoln sends a wire saying he needs Hoss' lawyer for cases in Illinois, although by this time (it was 1861 in the previous season's "The Waiting Game") Lincoln was president. With James Gregory.

180. THE UNDERDOG
December 13, 1964
The Cartwrights put their trust in a half-breed who is, in reality, leader of the horse thieves no one has been able to catch. With Charles Bronson.

181. A KNIGHT TO REMEMBER
December 20, 1964
Mexican bandits who rob the stagecoach Adam is riding in are frightened off by an armor plated rider who claims to be King Arthur. With Henry Jones, Rodolfo Acosta, Robert Sorrells and Charles Watts.

182. THE SAGA OF SQUAW CHARLIE
December 27, 1964
A peaceful Indian is framed for the kidnapping of a young girl, a stunt which ends in tragedy. With Anthony Caruso, Virginia Christine, Myron Healey, John Mitchum and Donald "Red" Barry.

183. THE FLAPJACK CONTEST
January 3, 1965
Joe puts Hoss on a strict diet so he will be ravenous enough to win the $500 prize offered in Virginia City's flapjack eating contest, during which a bank robbery takes place.

184. THE FAR, FAR BETTER THING
January 10, 1965
On their way to prevent a young woman from encountering renegade Paiutes, Joe and a friend are captured. Filmed at Iverson's Ranch. With Warren Vanders, Brenda Scott and X Brands, a regular on TV's "Yancy Derringer."

185. WOMAN OF FIRE
January 17, 1965
Adam vs. a hot tempered young lady in this frontier "Taming of the Shrew." Filmed at Golden Oak Ranch. With Joan Hackett, Jay Novello and Cesare Danova.

186. THE BALLERINA
January 24, 1965
Hoss helps a saloon dancer attain her dream of becoming a ballerina. With Warren Stevens and Barrie Chase.

187. THE FLANNEL-MOUTH GUN
January 31, 1965
Adam becomes involved with a quick-trigger range detective hired by the Virginia City Cattleman's Association to find out who is responsible for all the rustling going on in the area. With Earl Holliman, Robert J. Wilke, Harry Carey, Jr., Don Collier and I. Stanford Jolley.

188. THE PONDEROSA BIRDMAN
February 7, 1965
Ever the sucker for the wild notions of the underdog, Hoss "flies" in this silly but amusing episode. With Ed Wynn and Marlyn Mason.

189. THE SEARCH
February 14, 1965
Adam sets out to track down the man who has been impersonating him. With Lola Albright and Kelly Thordsen.

190. THE DEADLIEST GAME
February 21, 1965
The Cartwrights play host to Guido Borelli, a world renowned aerial acrobat who once saved Ben's life in Italy. Borelli's troupe, beset by internal strife, is in Virginia City for a performance. With Cesar Romero.

191. ONCE A DOCTOR
February 28, 1965
Hoss' latest acquaintance, an Englishman named Professor Poppy, is actually Percival Alexander Mundy, M.D., who has given up the practice of medicine. However, when Hoss is shot in the back, only Mundy's skill can save him. With Michael Rennie.

192. RIGHT IS THE FOURTH R
March 7, 1965
While working as a substitute teacher, Adam uncovers an ugly secret about the territory's past that others would prefer remain hidden. With Mariette Hartley and Everett Sloane.

193. HOUND DOG
March 21, 1965
Cousin Muley Jones returns to the Ponderosa, along with a pack of noisy hound dogs, in this funny sequel to "The Saga of Muley Jones." With Bruce Yarnell, Sue Ane Langdon and Chubby Johnson.

From "The Lonely Runner (1965).

194. THE TRAP
March 28, 1965

One of Joe's old girlfriend's thinks he killed her husband so they could be together. Unfortunately, that is what her husband's twin brother also believes. In another chronological inaccuracy, the year is given as 1859. Highest-rated episode of the season. With Joan Freeman and Steve Cochran.

195. DEAD AND GONE
April 4, 1965

Adam tries to find the good in Howard Mead, a talented troubadour who refuses to stay on the right side of the law. Dramatic debut of singer/songwriter Hoyt Axton. Last episode Pernell Roberts worked on, although he was in a couple aired after this.

196. A GOOD NIGHT'S REST
April 11, 1965

Unable to get any peace and quiet under his own roof, Ben checks into the Virginia City hotel but fares even worse. With Eddie Firestone, Lloyd Corrigan, Robert Ridgley and Clegg Hoyt.

197. TO OWN THE WORLD
April 18, 1965

One of the wealthiest men in the world, Charles Augustus Hackett, offers to buy the Ponderosa, price no object. Ben says the ranch is not for sale, but Hackett refuses to give up. With Telly Savalas.

198. LOTHARIO LARKIN
April 25, 1965

Ladies' man Lothario Larkin creates havoc whenever he hits Virginia City, so Roy Coffee orders him out of town. Naturally, Hoss takes him in. Only "lost" episode from the Pernell Roberts years of the series, though he does not appear. With Noah Berry, Jr., Frank Ferguson and Morgan Woodward.

199. THE RETURN
May 2, 1965

No one in Virginia City is happy to see ex-con Trace Cordell, especially the man he crippled in a gunfight, now married to Cordell's former girlfriend. Filmed at Golden Oak Ranch. With John Conte, Joan Blackman, Phil Chambers and Tony Young, who was a regular on the series "Gunslinger."

200. THE JONAH
May 9, 1965

The Ponderosa hands are upset when the Cartwrights hire George Whitman, who is supposed to be jinxed. Hoss tells George to ignore such foolishness, but a gypsy fortune teller says otherwise. With Andrew Prine, Angela Clark and Ken Mayer.

201. THE SPOTLIGHT
May 16, 1965

Ben invites opera singer Angela Bergstrom to sing at Virginia City's anniversary celebration. She accepts but does not tell him her famous singing voice is long gone. In one amusing scene, Hoss begins to recite Shakespeare, to which Joe responds, "Nah, we got rid of him" in reference to Pernell. Filmed at Golden Oak Ranch. With Viveca Lindfors, Robert Foulk and Ron Randell.

202. PATCHWORK MAN
May 23, 1965
Hoss offers a job to cowardly Albert Saunders, who goes by the name Patch, just as a hydraulic mining outfit endangers the Ponderosa. With Grant Williams, Bruce Gordon, Lane Bradford and Sue Randall.

SEASON 7 (1965-66)

203. THE DEBT
September 12, 1965
Wanting to restore their family's once-respected name, a young man and his sister offer to work on the Ponderosa for free. Several years before, their outlaw father, whom they believe to be dead, stole from Ben. However, their father is not dead, and Roy Coffee has just arrested him. With Tommy Sands, Brooke Bundy and Ford Rainey. Filmed at Incline Village.

204. THE DILEMMA
September 19, 1965
Ben is made a temporary judge at the same time a man he once helped receive a parole admits to robbing the bank. He tells Ben he will reveal where the money is if allowed to go free. With Tom Tully and Kelly Thordsen.

205. THE BRASS BOX
September 26, 1965
Jose' Ortega claims to have papers which state most of the territory belongs to him, including all but a small corner of the Ponderosa. And Ben's attorney says the document could be legal. With Ramon Navarro, Michael Dante, Roy Jenson and Adam Williams.

206. THE OTHER SON
October 3, 1965
The Cartwrights help a blasting expert and his two sons transport nitroglycerine, needed for blasting open flooded mines, across the mountains. Ben makes a reference to writing Adam, the first time he has been mentioned since leaving the series. Bing Russell appears as a lawman other than Clem Foster. Filmed at Incline Village and Toiyabe National Forest, this episode looks more like a movie than a television show. With Ed Begley.

207. THE LONELY RUNNER
October 10, 1965
Sad tale of a man falsely accused of murder while trying to regain possession of his beloved mare. Filmed at Toiyabe National Forest and Incline Village. With Gilbert Roland, Pat Conway, Ken Lynch and Roy Barcroft.

208. DEVIL ON HER SHOULDER
October 17, 1965
Ben is attracted to Sarah Reynolds, member of a religious order led by her fanatical uncle. When she is accused of being a witch, the Cartwrights step in. With Ina Balin, John Doucette and Angela Dorian.

209. FOUND CHILD
October 24, 1965
Hoss comes upon an overturned stagecoach and discovers a little girl suffering from shock. After the Cartwrights succeed in bringing her around, Hoss is disappointed to learn she has relatives and cannot stay. With Eileen Baral and Gerald Mohr.

210. THE MEREDITH SMITH
October 31, 1965
Ben must determine who is the rightful heir to a fortune that includes water rights vital to the Ponderosa. A funny episode highlighted by the always entertaining Strother Martin. With Robert Sorrells, Eddie Firestone, Winnie Coffin and Guy Lee, who went by the name "Buddy Lee" when he appeared in the first season's "The Fear Merchants."

211. MIGHTY IS THE WORD
November 7, 1965
Virginia City's newest preacher is an ex-gunfighter who wants only to build a new church, but the brother of one of his victims has other ideas. The blueprints for the church are said to be a gift from Adam. With Glenn Corbet, Michael Witney, Sue Randall and Julie Gregg.

212. THE STRANGE ONE
November 14, 1965
Hoss and Joe find a woman abandoned by a wagon train because her gift of prophecy is considered a curse. "Wouldn't it be wonderful," says Ben, "if everybody made a real effort to understand whatever's strange and unfamiliar rather than fear it and try to destroy it?" Filmed at Iverson's Ranch. With Louise Sorel and Robert McQueeney.

From "Three Brides for Hoss" (1966).

213. THE RELUCTANT REBEL
November 21, 1965
The Generation Gap, Western-style, as Hoss tries to bring a young man and his father closer together. With Tim Considine and Royal Dano.

214. FIVE SUNDOWNS TO SUNUP
December 5, 1965
The mother of a young outlaw condemned to hang threatens to have her gang's hostages killed if her son is not set free. One of the hostages is Joe. Good direction by Gerd Oswald helps this seem more like a feature film than a series. With John Hoyt, Marie Windsor and Roy Jenson.

215. A NATURAL WIZARD
December 12, 1965
Hoss finds a kindred spirit in Skeeter Dexter, a lonesome young man who feels closer to animals than to most people. With Eddie Hodges, Jacqueline Scott and Karl Swenson.

216. ALL YE HIS SAINTS
December 19, 1965
Little Michael Thorpe heads to the high country to ask God to spare his critically wounded father, believing he has found Him in the form of longtime fugitive Tom Cain. Filmed in Toiyabe National Forest and Incline Village. With Leif Erickson, Clint Howard, Rodolfo Acosta and Simon Scott.

217. THE DUBLIN LAD
January 2, 1966
After sitting on a jury that has convicted a man of murder, Joe has second thoughts about the verdict and decides to do some investigation of his own. Good story, not as predictable as others of this sort. With Liam Sullivan, Tim McIntire, Paul Birch and Maggie Mahoney.

218. TO KILL A BUFFALO
January 9, 1966
A wounded young Indian Hoss finds on the prairie is torn between accepting the ways of the white man or returning to his old life.

219. RIDE THE WIND
Part One:January 16, 1966
Part Two:January 23, 1966
The Cartwrights lend a hand to the struggling Pony Express in this fact-based episode, the first "Bonanza" to be shown in two parts. Filmed at Red Rock Canyon and Vasquez Rocks, released theatrically to foreign markets in 1967. With Victor Jory, Rod Cameron, Warren Vanders, Tom Lowell and DeForest Kellley.

220 .DESTINY'S CHILD
January 30, 1966
After his only friend is killed, the Cartwrights take in a slow-witted man who, Roy Coffee informs them, is wanted for murder by Arizona authorities. With Dick Peabody, Walter Burke and Steve Raines.

221. PEACE OFFICER
February 6, 1966
Virginia City's acting sheriff is a no-nonsense lawman who thinks nothing of going to extremes to maintain order. With Eric Fleming ("Rawhide"), Ron Foster, Dee Pollock, Roy Barcroft and Ted Knight.

222. THE CODE
February 13, 1966

Joe is goaded into facing gunman Dan Taggart, unaware there is more to the prearranged duel than he realizes. With George Montgomery.

223. THREE BRIDES FOR HOSS
February 20, 1966

Not one but three mail order brides show up unexpectedly at the Ponderosa, all of them believing they are to marry Hoss.

224. THE EMPEROR NORTON
February 27, 1966

Joshua Norton, an eccentric and formerly wealthy San Francisco merchant who considers himself the Emperor of the United States and Protector of Mexico, comes to the Ponderosa. Authorities want to have him committed, and Ben contacts Mark Twain to testify as to Norton's sanity. Based on fact. With Sam Jaffe, Parley Baer and William Challee.

225. HER BROTHER'S KEEPER
March 6, 1966

Ben and Claire Armory fall in love, but their future is jeopardized by her disabled brother. To explain the eye patch Lorne Greene wears for a real life mishap, the script says Ben was injured in a hunting accident. Filmed at Golden Oak Ranch. With Nancy Gates and Wesley Lau.

226. THE TROUBLE WITH JAMIE
March 20, 1966

The Cartwrights attempt to straighten out the snobbish young son of Ben's cousin. With Michael Burns ("Wagon Train") and Ross Elliott ("The Virginian").

227. SHINING IN SPAIN
March 27, 1966

An adoring daughter is crushed to learn her father is not the big success she thought he was. With Judi Rolin, Gene Lyons and Woodrow Parfrey.

228. THE GENIUS
April 3, 1966

Hoss chooses a difficult task when he decides to rehabilitate a famous poet who has crawled inside the bottle. With Lonny Chapman.

229. THE UNWRITTEN COMMANDMENT
April 10, 1966

Everyone feels Andy Walker is an outstanding singer but his father, who feels the boy should concentrate on ranch work instead. Joe mentions receiving a letter from Adam, currently in Paris. First of two appearances by Wayne Newton as Andy. With Malcom Atterbury.

230. BIG SHADOW ON THE LAND
April 17, 1966

Italian immigrants are determined to establish their own vineyard on Ponderosa property. First of three appearances by Giorgio Rossi and family. With Jack Kruschen, Penny Santon and Robert Foulk.

231. THE FIGHTERS
April 24, 1966

Feeling guilty for unintentionally ending the career of a professional boxer, Hoss vows never to fight again. But things change when Joe is nearly beaten to death. With Michael Conrad, Phillip Pine and Cal Bolder.

232. HOME FROM THE SEA
May 1, 1966

A sailor claiming to be one of Adam's closest friends is given a warm welcome by the Cartwrights, who have no way of knowing the man and an accomplice plan to rob them. With Alan Bergmann.

233. THE LAST MISSION
May 8, 1966

Ben and Hoss unwittingly aid a vengeful army colonel who plans to wipe out every Indian he can with a Gatling gun. Filmed at Vasquez Rocks. With R.G. Armstrong, Tom Reese, Brendan Boone, Ken Mayer and Clay Tanner.

234. A DOLLAR'S WORTH OF TROUBLE
May 15, 1966

Hoss finds himself in another mess, this one involving a beautiful blonde, a moonshiner and a nearsighted outlaw allergic to flowers and chocolate. With Sally Kellerman, Elisha Cook and Robert Foulk.

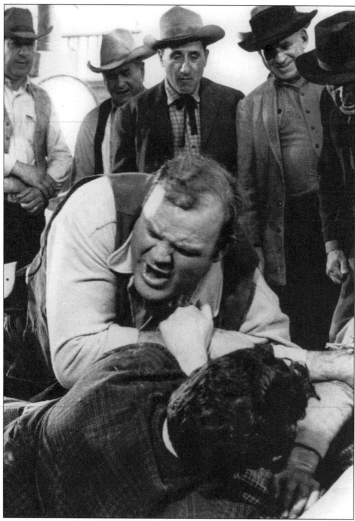

From "The Fighters" (1966).

SEASON 8 (1966-67)

235. SOMETHING HURT, SOMETHING WILD
September 11, 1966
The Cartwrights' longtime friendship with a neighboring rancher is threatened by his mentally unstable daughter. Filmed at Golden Oak Ranch. With Lyle Bettger, Lynn Loring.

236. HORSE OF A DIFFERENT HUE
September 18, 1966
So the Cartwrights will not be killed, one of Ben's oldest friends must make sure Joe does not win a horse race. Filmed at Golden Oak Ranch. With Charles Ruggles, Skip Homeier and Julie Parrish.

237. A TIME TO STEP DOWN
September 25, 1966
After the Cartwrights put him out to pasture, an embittered old wrangler plans to take part in robbing the Ponderosa. With Ed Begley, Audrey Totter and Donald "Red" Barry.

238. THE PURSUED
Part One:October 2, 1966
Part Two: October 9, 1966
The Cartwrights encounter religious prejudice when they travel to Beehive, Nevada, to buy horses from a Mormon rancher and his two wives. Filmed at Lone Pine, this excellent episode has regrettably been out of circulation for years. With Eric Fleming, Dina Merrill and Lois Nettleton.

239. TO BLOOM FOR THEE
October 16, 1966
Hoss is engaged to Carol Attley, a troubled woman with a past darker than he imagines. Generally unsung highlight of the series, with excellent performances by Blocker and Geraldine Fitzgerald, a lovely score by David Rose and a good story by June Randolph. Filmed at Golden Oak Ranch.

240. CREDIT FOR A KILL
October 23, 1966
Though his friend is badly in need of the reward money, Joe insists it belongs to him in order to protect his friend from the dead outlaw's brother. With Don Collier, Luana Patten, Charles Maxwell and Troy Melton.

241. FOUR SISTERS FROM BOSTON
October 30, 1966
The Cartwrights come to the rescue of four inexperienced homesteaders when devious cattlemen try to run them off their property. David Rose's music was later used as the theme of "The High Chaparral." With Vera Miles, Morgan Woodward, Melinda Plowman and Owen Bush.

242. OLD CHARLIE
November 6, 1966
A young cowpoke is killed during a fight with Hoss, but the harmless blowhard who runs the Virginia City stable takes the credit, placing him in danger from the dead man's brothers. With John McIntire, Jeanette Nolan, Tim McIntire and Hal Baylor.

243. BALLAD OF THE PONDEROSA
November 13, 1966
A young troubadour who blames Ben for the death of his father returns to Virginia City. In one scene, Ben says the man is welcome to use Adam's guitar. Script co-written by Michael Landon. With Randy Boone, Ann Doran, Roger Davis, Lane Bradford and John Archer.

244. THE OATH
November 20, 1966
On the trail, a half-breed tells Joe about his plan to kill Ben, unaware of who Joe is. Filmed at Vasquez Rocks. With Tony Bill, Douglas Kennedy and Ben Gage.

245. A REAL NICE, FRIENDLY LITTLE TOWN
November 27, 1966
During his quest to discover who shot Joe in the rear end, Hoss tangles with two rascals and their long suffering mother. With Louise Latham, Mark Robert Doyle, Clegg Hoyt and Mark Slade, who played Blue on "The High Chaparral."

246. THE BRIDEGROOM
December 4, 1966
Joe plays matchmaker in this story of a rancher attempting to marry off his supposedly unremarkable daughter. With Jeff Corey, Joanne Linville and Ron Hayes.

247. TOMMY
December 18, 1966
The Cartwrights protect a woman and her deaf and dumb little son from the boy's outlaw stepfather. With Michael Witney and Hank Worden.

248. A CHRISTMAS STORY
December 25, 1966
Warbling Andy Walker returns to Virginia City a big success, along with his shifty Uncle Thaddeus. With Wayne Newton, Jack Oakie, Dabbs Greer and Mary Wickes.

249. PONDEROSA EXPLOSION
January 1, 1967
Two Virginia City oldtimers fool Hoss and Joe into raising rabbits for profit. With Dub Taylor, Chubby Johnson and Chick Chandler.

250. JUSTICE
January 8, 1967
When the woman he was planning to marry is strangled, Joe forces the only suspect to confess. With Beau Bridges and Roy Roberts.

251. A BRIDE FOR BUFORD
January 15, 1967
Hoss is sure a beautiful singer is only after a prospector's money when she shows an interest in him. With Lola Albright, Jack Elam, Richard Devon and Paul Brinegar ("Rawhide").

252. BLACK FRIDAY
January 22, 1967
In another town, Joe encounters a former Ponderosa hand who is now a gunfighter and expecting to be killed on Friday the 13th. With John Saxon, Ford Rainey and Robert McQueeney.

253. THE UNSEEN WOUND
January 29, 1967
Ben discovers that his friend, Sheriff Paul Rowan, is suffering from stress brought on by his wartime experiences. With Leslie Nielsen, Paul Lambert, Nancy Malone, Percy Helton and Douglas Henderson.

254. JOURNEY TO TERROR
February 5, 1967
Joe visits married friends in Arizona Territory and learns the husband has become a criminal. With Jason Evers, John Ericson and Kevin Hagen.

255. AMIGO
February 12, 1967
A wounded comanchero sides with the Cartwrights when the rest of the band shows up to rob and burn the Ponderosa. Originally written for Sammy Davis, Jr., who was replaced by Henry Darrow, Manolito on "The High Chaparral." With Gregory Walcott, Anna Navarro and Warren Kemmerling.

256. A WOMAN IN THE HOUSE
February 19, 1967
Mary Wharton, an old friend of the family, comes to live on the Ponderosa with her shiftless husband, Russ. When Ben learns Mary is the victim of domestic abuse, he sends Russ packing. With Diane Baker, Paul Richards, Raymond Guth and Robert Brubaker.

From "The Deed and the Dilemma" (1967).

259. DARK ENOUGH TO SEE THE STARS
March 12, 1967
Ben hires a drifter who is running from a murder that was actually self-defense. Filmed at Golden Oak Ranch. With Richard Evans and Linda Foster.

260. THE DEED AND THE DILEMMA
March 26, 1967
Ben assists Giorgio Rossi in his battle for rights to water on an adjoining property. A follow-up episode to "Big Shadow on the Land." With Jack Kruschen, Penny Santon, Chris Alcaide and Donald Woods.

261. THE PRINCE
April 2, 1967
The Cartwrights play host to Russian royals, who are the target of jewel thieves. With Warren Stevens, Lloyd Bochner and Adam Williams.

262. A MAN WITHOUT LAND
April 9, 1967
The foreman of a neighboring ranch frames Joe for murder as part of a scheme to get his employer's property. With Royal Dano, Jeremy Slate and James Gammon.

263. NAPOLEON'S CHILDREN
April 16, 1967
A gang of juvenile delinquents, led by an intelligent runt who calls himself Napoleon, terrorizes Virginia City. With Robert Biheller, Michael Burns and Woodrow Parfrey.

264. THE WORMWOOD CUP
April 23, 1967
A woman arrives in Virginia City and tacks up posters offering $1,000 to the man who kills Joe in a fair fight. Script co-written by Michael Landon. Fine score by David Rose. With Judi Meredith and Frank Overton.

265. CLARISSA
April 30, 1967
The Cartwrights' well-meaning but irritating eastern cousin causes trouble for them wherever she turns. Hoss mentions Giorgio Rossi's wine. Good example of how a woman would have upset the series' equilibrium. With Nina Foch, Roy Roberts, Ken Mayer and Robert Foulk.

257. JUDGEMENT AT RED CREEK
February 26, 1967
Hoss and Joe have their doubts as to who really robbed a way station, suspecting the two men they have captured are innocent. With John Ireland, James B. Sikking and Harry Carey, Jr.

258. JOE CARTWRIGHT, DETECTIVE
March 5, 1967
Joe becomes fascinated by detective literature and drags Hoss into the picture when he suspects the bank is going to be robbed. The script for this comic episode was written by Michael Landon, based on a story by Oliver Crawford. Fight scene deliberately imitative of the "Batman" series. With Mort Mills and Ken Lynch.

266. MAESTRO HOSS
May 7, 1967

Hoss is conned into buying a violin from a gypsy fortune teller, and everyone on the Ponderosa–except for Hop Sing—suffers the consequences. Filmed at Golden Oak Ranch. With Zsa Zsa Gabor and Kathleen Freeman.

267. THE GREEDY ONES
May 14, 1967

The Ponderosa is in danger of being overrun by gold hunters. The episode appropriately concludes the season with one of Lorne Greene's infrequent voice-overs: "The gold rush was over, gone like a soap bubble in the sun. The Ponderosa was just as it has always been. And we went home." With Robert Middleton, Lane Bradford and George Chandler.

SEASON 9 (1967-68)

268. SECOND CHANCE
September 17, 1967

Rampaging Indians trap Hoss and Joe in a way station with a group of failed pioneers who are headed east rather than west. Traditional, exciting Western. With James Gregory and Joe DeSantis.

269. SENSE OF DUTY
September 24, 1967

Ben, leader of the reactivated Virginia City militia, is responsible for escorting an Indian prisoner across hostile territory. This episode introduces "Special Guest Star David Canary" who announces: "My name's Candy. I'm from any town within 500 miles east of here." Another solid Western, filmed at Red Rock Canyon. With Kip Whitman, Michael Forest and Richard Hale.

270. THE CONQUISTADORS
October 1, 1967

Mexican prospectors take Joe prisoner and demand $100,000 in gold for his return. Outlaws plan to steal the ransom money before Ben and Hoss can deliver it. With John Saxon, John Kellogg and Eddie Ryder.

271. JUDGEMENT AT OLYMPUS
October 8, 1967

Candy is arrested for committing murder in the town of Olympus. Ben says the Cartwrights will back him, and sends Joe along to make sure everything is all right. Prototype for several episodes over the next few seasons. With Barry Sullivan, Dabbs Greer, Brooke Bundy, Arch Johnson, Robert Brubaker and Vaughn Taylor.

272. NIGHT OF RECKONING
October 15, 1967

A sadistic outlaw and his gang hold Hoss, Joe and Candy prisoner at the Ponderosa while they try to learn where a traitor has stashed the loot. With Richard Jaeckel, Ron Hayes and Joan Freeman.

273. FALSE WITNESS
October 22, 1967

After completing a cattle drive, Candy announces he is headed for Chicago, but he, Hoss, and Joe are placed in protective custody in the town of Sand Dust after they witness a robbery and murder. With Michael Blodgett, Robert McQueeney, Russ Conway and Davey Davison.

274. THE GENTLE ONES
October 29, 1967

Most people consider Mark Cole a coward, but he does not hesitate to step forward when his brother attempts to break a horse by torturing it. With Robert Walker, Jr., Lana Wood and Douglas Henderson.

275. DESPERATE PASSAGE
November 5, 1967

Driving horses to Utah, the Cartwrights and Candy discover only two people left in a town wiped out by Indians. Filmed at Incline Village. With Steve Forrest and Tina Louise.

276. THE SURE THING
November 12, 1967

A young girl's ownership of a beloved stallion is jeopardized by the "big plans" of her scheming father. With Kim Darby and Tom Tully.

277. SHOWDOWN AT TAHOE
November 19, 1967

A cunning band of outlaws plan to rob a large currency shipment and make their getaway across Lake Tahoe on Ben's steamboat. Filmed at Incline Village. With Richard Anderson, Karl Swenson, Kevin Hagen, Christopher Dark and Sheila Larken.

Landon in "Black Friday (1967).

280. JUSTICE DEFERRED
December 17, 1967
Hoss cannot convince Andy Buchanan they convicted the wrong man of murder, and when Andy will not testify against the real killer, the results are grim. With Simon Oakland, Nita Talbot, Carl Reindel and Tol Avery.

281. THE GOLD DETECTOR
December 24, 1967
Hoss wants to buy a mine thought to be worthless, and orders a fancy invention to prove it is not. With Paul Fix, Wally Cox, Dub Taylor, Chubby Johnson and Kelly Thordsen.

282. THE TRACKERS
January 7, 1968
Ben helps hunt down an ex-con he helped convict of bank robbery five years before when the bank is robbed again. The man claimed he was innocent the first time and had nothing to do with the latest heist. With Bruce Dern, Warren Stevens, Warren Vanders, Ted Gehring.

283. A GIRL NAMED GEORGE
January 14, 1968
Trick photography is employed to help a killer beat a murder rap, but the camera also proves to be his undoing. With Gerald Mohr, Jack Albertson, Steve Raines, Andy Devine and Shelah Wells.

284. THE THIRTEENTH MAN
January 21, 1968
The ranchers are once again losing stock to rustlers, and not everyone agrees with range detective Marcus Alley's preventive methods. Filmed at Vasquez Rocks. With Richard Carlson, Albert Salmi, Kenneth Tobey, Myron Healey, Bill Quinn and Anna Navarro.

285. THE BURNING SKY
January 28, 1968
A pair of bigots make life rough for a new Ponderosa hand and his Indian wife. With Victor French, Dawn Wells, Gregg Palmer and Michael Murphy.

286. THE PRICE OF SALT
February 4, 1968
To his dismay, Ben finds that his friend's niece intends to exploit the ranchers' desperate need of salt for their dying herds. With Kim Hunter, James Best and John Doucette.

278. SIX BLACK HORSES
November 26, 1967
Ben's old friend has stolen money from corrupt politicians in New York and plans to invest it in Nevada. Script co-written by Michael Landon. With Burgess Meredith, Richard X. Slattery, Hal Baylor and Don Haggerty.

279. CHECK REIN
December 3, 1967
The Cartwrights help prevent a young man's uncle from wrongfully acquiring a remarkable stallion. With James MacArthur, Ford Rainey and Charles Maxwell.

287. BLOOD TIE
February 18, 1968
Joe is tricked into hiring a charming thief who plans to take part in robbing the Ponderosa. With Robert Drivas, Conlan Carter and Leo Gordon.

288. THE CRIME OF JOHNNY MULE
February 25, 1968
Hoss is the only one who believes rather simple-minded Johnny Mule when he swears he had nothing to do with killing a local rancher. With Noah Berry, Jr., Jack Ging and Colleen Gray.

289. THE LATE BEN CARTWRIGHT
March 3, 1968
Ben allows everyone to conclude an attempt on his life was successful in order to ruin the plans of a corrupt politician. First use of the music later used as the end credit theme for "Little House on the Prairie." With Sidney Blackmer, Bert Freed, William Campbell and Simon Scott.

290. STAR CROSSED
March 10, 1968
Candy falls in love with a woman being blackmailed by a lawman from another town. David Canary's fourteenth episode, and the first in which he is given the spotlight. Filmed at Franklin Lake. With Tisha Sterling and William Windom.

291. TROUBLE TOWN
March 17, 1968
Passing through River Bend on a cattle drive, Candy decides to quit his job at the Ponderosa and stay with a friend, saloon girl Lilah Holden, who seems upset. Before long, the Cartwrights are involved with River Bend's cold-blooded sheriff. With Elizabeth MacRae, Robert Wilke, Tol Avery and Steve Brodie.

292. COMMITMENT AT ANGELUS
April 7, 1968
Joe and Candy come to the aid of miners who are striking due to unsafe working conditions. Filmed at Bronson Canyon. With Peter Whitney, Ken Lynch, Greg Mullavey and Marj Dusay.

293. A DREAM TO DREAM
April 14, 1968
Hoss brings happiness to the family of a bitter, alcoholic rancher. A return to the "heart" of the series, written by Michael Landon, who later recycled the story as "Someone Please Love Me" for "Little House on the Prairie." Filmed at Franklin Lake. With Julie Harris, Steve Inhat and Johnnie Whitaker.

294. IN DEFENSE OF HONOR
April 28, 1968
A half-breed who works for Ben falls in love with a Ute woman who is already promised to a warrior of her tribe. Filmed at Bronson Canyon. With Lou Antonio, Arnold Moss, Ned Romero, John Lodge, Troy Melton, Lane Bradford and Cherie Latimer.

295. TO DIE IN DARKNESS
May 5, 1968
After Ben and Candy have been missing for over a month, everyone assumes they must be dead. In reality they are being held prisoner in a mine shaft by an ex-con wrongly convicted on Ben's testimony. Filmed in Bronson Canyon. Written and directed by Michael Landon. With James Whitmore.

296. THE BOTTLE FIGHTER
May 12, 1968
Hoss is accused of stabbing a man to death, and his only hope of acquittal is a once great trial lawyer who is now a hopeless drunk. With Albert Dekker.

297. THE ARRIVAL OF EDDIE
May 19, 1968
A young man rejects an offer to work on the Ponderosa because Hoss shot his father, but a rancher intent on making trouble for the Cartwrights blackmails him into taking the job. With(Jan-)Michael Vincent and Jim Davis.

298. THE STRONGHOLD
May 26, 1968
Joe and Candy sell a herd to two brothers in Arizona, but are paid with a worthless draft. The widow of a man one of the brothers killed helps them get their money. With Michael Witney, Lynda Day, Paul Mantee, Hal Baylor, Robert Brubaker and William Bryant.

299. PRIDE OF A MAN
June 2, 1968
Joe reluctantly takes a job as substitute teacher and must contend with two older students who have no use for education. With Morgan Woodward and Anne Helm.

300. A SEVERE CASE OF MATRIMONY
July 7, 1968
An untalented gypsy girl tries to get the Cartwrights to finance her career as an opera singer. Filmed at Franklin Lake. With Susan Strasberg and J. Carrol Naish.

Landon on location at Incline Village for "Different Pines, Same Wind" (1968).

SEASON 10 (1968-69)

302. DIFFERENT PINES, SAME WIND
September 15, 1968

An old woman thinks Joe is after her land when he actually wants to help her keep it out of the hands of a destructive strip miner. Filmed at Incline Village. With Irene Tedrow, John Randolph, G.D. Spradlin and George Murdock.

303. CHILD
September 22, 1968

Hoss is saved from a lynch mob by a black cowboy named Child Barnett. With Yaphet Kotto, John Marley and Charles Maxwell.

304. SALUTE TO YESTERDAY
September 29, 1968

The Cartwrights, Candy and an army detail take cover when they are attacked by bandits. Among the defenders is the woman who used to be Candy's wife. Filmed at Incline Village. With Pat Conway, Sandra Smith and John Kellogg.

305. THE REAL PEOPLE OF MUDDY CREEK
October 6, 1968

Ben is in charge of a vicious prisoner and gets virtually no help from the cowardly citizens of the town where he is holding him for the law. With Joe Don Baker, Clifton James and Mitch Vogel.

306. THE PASSING OF A KING
October 13, 1968

The son of a rancher to whom the Cartwrights are selling a prize bull is trying to get his father ruled mentally incompetent. With Denver Pyle, Jeremy Slate, Diana Muldaur, Dan Tobin and Russ Conway.

307. THE LAST VOTE
October 20, 1968

Hoss and Joe back different candidates in Virginia City's mayoral election. With Wally Cox, Tom Bosley, Robert Emharhardt and Lane Bradford.

308. CATCH AS CATCH CAN
October 27, 1968

Everything goes wrong for the Cartwrights and Candy in the town of Tin Bucket where, rumor has it, the Ponderosa is about to go under. With Paul Richards and Slim Pickens.

301. STAGE DOOR JOHNNIES
July 28, 1968

Hoss and Joe vie for the affections of visiting entertainer Mademoiselle Denise, though she is concerned more for her little dog than anything else. With Kathleen Crowley, Walter Brooke, Mike Mazurki and Shug Fisher.

309. LITTLE GIRL LOST
November 3, 1968
Life on the ranch is disrupted by the arrival of a young brat who happens to be distantly related to the Cartwrights. Filmed at Franklin Lake, though this episode features the first shot of the Ponderosa Ranch house built at Incline Village.

310. THE SURVIVORS
November 10, 1968
A white woman abducted years before by the Paiutes is reunited with her husband, who is less than pleased to learn she has given birth to an Indian baby. With Mariette Hartley and John Carter.

311. SOUND OF DRUMS
November 17, 1968
In the third and final appearance of the Rossi family, Giorgio Rossi does not understand why he cannot allow Indians who have left the reservation to live on his land. With Jack Kruschen and Penny Santon.

312. QUEEN HIGH
December 1, 1968
Joe and Candy win a stamping mill in a poker game, but the fact that they know nothing about running it is the least of their worries. Filmed in Bronson Canyon. With Celeste Yarnell, Paul Lambert and Dabney Coleman.

313. YONDER MAN
December 8, 1968
An army scout Ben once knew comes to the Ponderosa and asks Ben to stake him to a cattle ranch in Mexico. With John Vernon and Rodolfo Acosta.

314. MARK OF GUILT
December 15, 1968
Hop Sing tells Hoss and Candy they can use the ancient Chinese art of fingerprinting to prove Joe is innocent of murder. With Dick Foran, Alan Bergmann and Lou Frizzel.

315. A WORLD FULL OF CANNIBALS
December 22, 1968
Candy warns the Cartwrights they are asking for trouble by allowing a government witness to hide at the Ponderosa. With James Patterson and Mark Richman, villain of "Bonanza: The Next Generation."

316. SWEET ANNIE LAURIE
January 5, 1969
Hoss comes to the aid of a frightened young woman trying to run from her outlaw husband. With Joan Van Ark and James Olson.

317. MY FRIEND, MY ENEMY
January 12, 1969
Only the testimony of an Indian wanted for horse theft can clear Candy of murder. Hoss makes a reference to the death of Custer, which took place in 1876, several years after the time in which this episodes takes place. Filmed at Franklin Lake. With John Saxon, Gregory Walcott, Chick Chandler and Woodrow Parfrey.

318. MRS. WHARTON AND THE LESSER BREEDS
January 19, 1969
Candy sets out to help an elderly British woman recover the jewels stolen from her in a stage holdup. With Mildred Natwick.

319. ERIN
January 26, 1969
The romance between Hoss and Erin O'Donnell, an Irish woman who lives with the Sioux, is threatened by a rancher considerably less open-minded than the Cartwrights. With Mary Fickett and Harry Holcombe, who makes his first appearance as Doc Martin.

320. COMPANY OF FORGOTTEN MEN
February 2, 1969
Army veterans led by a sergeant whom Candy knows camp on the Ponderosa while plotting to rob the U.S. mint in Carson City. With James Gregory, Ken Lynch, Charles Maxwell, John Kellogg and William Bryant.

321. THE CLARION
February 9, 1969
Ben's friend is struggling to keep her newspaper going in the face of harassment by the town boss of Gunlock, so without telling her, Ben buys the business. With Simon Oakland, Phyllis Thaxter, Hamilton Camp and Ken Mayer.

322. THE LADY AND THE MOUNTAIN LION
February 23, 1969
A shady magician with twin daughters comes to Virginia City. With Richard Haydn and Dabbs Greer.

323. FIVE CANDLES
March 2, 1969
The floor of the Virginia City courthouse collapses, trapping Ben in the basement with three other people, one of whom may or may not be guilty of murder. With Don Knight, Ted Gehring, Tiffany Bolling and Eddie Firestone.

Hoss pursues a favorite pastime.

324. THE WISH
March 9, 1969
Hoss spends his two-month vacation helping a black family get their farm in shape, and deal with racism in the neighboring town. Written and directed by Michael Landon. With Ossie Davis, George Spell and Roy Jenson.

325. THE DESERTER
March 16, 1969
Candy comes upon a soldier who is running from charges of desertion, and with Joe's help they foil a plan to sell guns to the Indians. With Ben Johnson, Ford Rainey and Ellen Davalos.

326. EMILY
March 23, 1969
Joe's former fiancee returns to Virginia City and conveniently neglects to tell him she is now a lawman's wife. With Beth Brickell and Ron Hayes.

327. THE RUNNING MAN
March 30, 1969
Joe and Candy travel to Butlerville and learn that one of Ben's old friends is burning out new settlers, whom he regards as squatters. With Will Geer, Robert Pine and Larry Casey.

328. THE UNWANTED
April 6, 1969
Feeling unloved, a marshal's daughter runs off with a Ponderosa hand her father thinks may be related to a man that shot him. The scene in which Dan Blocker and Bonnie Bedelia go on a picnic gives a hint of what their scenes in 1972's "Forever" may have been like had Blocker lived. With Charles McGraw and (Jan-) Michael Vincent.

329. SPEAK NO EVIL
April 20, 1969
Coley Clayborn, who has always thought his mother abandoned him and his father, thinks she is only after the gold mine he has inherited when she returns to Virginia City. With Dana Elcar and Gregg Palmer.

330. THE FENCE
April 27, 1969
On a trip to buy back a mine from their friend Sam Masters, Ben and Hoss discover he was once in charge of a Confederate prison camp, and is now the target of former inmates wanting revenge. Filmed at Big Bear. With John Anderson, J.D. Cannon, Larry Linville, Gary Wallberg and Charles Dierkop.

331. A RIDE IN THE SUN
May 11, 1969
A trio of particularly insidious thieves rob the bank and leave Ben with a bullet in his back. Joe heads off across the desert in pursuit. With Anthony Zerbe, Robert Hogan, Marj Dusay and Jack Collins.

Season 11 (1969-70)

332. ANOTHER WINDMILL TO GO
September 14, 1969
An Englishman with a passion for challenging ridiculous laws shows up on Ponderosa grazing land–rowing a boat mounted on a wagon. With Laurence Naismith, Gregg Palmer, Jill Townsend and, yes, that is comedian Foster Brooks as the judge.

333. THE WITNESS
September 21, 1969
A young woman prone to telling tall tales claims she witnessed a stagecoach holdup. With Melissa Murphy, Stefan Gierasch and Bo Hopkins.

334. THE SILENCE AT STILLWATER
September 28, 1969
A young boy positively identifies Candy as the man wanted in Stillwater for robbery, arson and murder. With Pat Hingle and Strother Martin.

335. A LAWMAN'S LOT IS NOT A HAPPY ONE
October 5, 1969
As acting sheriff of Virginia City, Hoss must contend with land swindlers and a reluctant bridegroom. With Tom Bosley, Robert Emhardt, Melinda Dillon and Helen Kleeb.

336. ANATOMY OF A LYNCHING
October 12, 1969
The Cartwrights face another lynch mob when an unpopular rancher beats a murder charge. With Guy Stockwell, Ted Ghering and Mills Watson.

337. TO STOP A WAR
October 19, 1969
Dan Logan, a former army scout and lawman who works for the Cartwrights, has his hands full with rustlers, a range war and a one-time prostitute whose devotion is questionable. With Steve Forrest, Miriam Colon, Warren Kemmerling and Richard Bull, better known as Mr. Oleson on "Little House on the Prairie."

338. THE MEDAL
October 26, 1969
Ben lends a hand to a down-and-out veteran who received the Congressional Medal of Honor. "Some wounds take a long time to heal," Ben tells him. "I have a few of those myself." Filmed in Los Padres National Forest. With Dean Stockwell, Harry Townes, Susan Howard and John Beck.

339. THE STALKER
November 2, 1969
Candy helps the widow of a man he was forced to kill, unaware she is plotting to get revenge. With Charlotte Stewart who played Miss Beadle on "Little House on the Prairie."

340. MEENA
November 16, 1969
Joe and Candy run into Meena Calhoun, a smart but slightly loopy prospector's daughter, and a trio of claim jumpers. Filmed at Iverson's Ranch. First of three episodes featuring Ann Prentiss and Dub Taylor as Meena and Luke Calhoun. With Victor French, Robert Donner and George Morgan.

341. A DARKER SHADOW
November 23, 1969
A Virginia City store clerk decides to take advantage of his co- worker's paralyzing sensitivity to bright light. Filmed at Los Padres National Forest. With Gregory Walcott, Dabney Coleman and Sandra Smith.

342. DEAD WRONG
December 7, 1969
In Sunville, Hoss and Candy are mistaken for a pair of infamous bank robbers, and with the help of the town loudmouth, stage Hoss' "death". A funny episode written and directed by Michael Landon. With Arthur Hunnicutt, Mike Mazurki, Robert Sorrells and John Carradine.

343. OLD FRIENDS
December 14, 1969
Ben is sorry to learn that two of his oldest friends are now on opposite sides of the law. Hoss makes the first reference to Adam in years. Filmed at Franklin Lake and Vasquez Rocks. With Morgan Woodward and Robert J. Wilke.

344. ABNER WILLOUGHBY'S RETURN
December 21, 1969
Joe agrees to help the man who tried to steal his horse find a box of gold he buried years before. With John Astin and Irene Tedrow.

Greene and David Cassidy in "The Law and Billy Burgess" (1970).

345. IT'S A SMALL WORLD
January 4, 1970

Ben attempts to help a recently widowed circus midget make a new start in Virginia City. Written and directed by Michael Landon, and redone as "Little Lou" on "Little House: The Next Generation." With Michael Dunn who made several appearances as Dr. Loveless on "The Wild, Wild West."

346. DANGER ROAD
January 11, 1970

Ben has conflicting feelings about helping a man he considers a traitor and deserter compete for a job hauling freight. Filmed in Los Padres National Forest. With Robert Lansing, William Sylvester and Anna Navarro.

347. THE BIG JACK POT
January 18, 1970

Everyone believes Candy has inherited a fortune, but Hoss and Joe have their doubts. With Walter Brooke.

348. THE TROUBLE WITH AMY
January 25, 1970

Ben knows that Amy Wilder, who is fiercely protective of the wildlife on her property, is eccentric, not senile, and must convince a judge of that when a competency hearing is ordered. With Jo Van Fleet, Donald Moffatt and John Crawford.

349. THE LADY AND THE MARK
February 1, 1970

A newly wealthy Ponderosa employee with a weakness for women becomes the target of con artists. With Christopher Connelly, Ralph Waite, Lou Frizzel and Elaine Giftos.

350. IS THERE ANY MAN HERE . . . ?
February 8, 1970

When the daughter of a friend declares her love for him, Ben agonizes over what to do. Adam is mentioned again, five years after his departure. With Mariette Hartley, John McLiam and Burr DeBenning.

351. THE LAW AND BILLY BURGESS
February 15, 1970

Ben seriously doubts an angry young man is guilty of several murders to which he has confessed. With David Cassidy, Les Tremayne, Mercedes McCambridge, Foster Brooks and Sam Melville.

352. LONG WAY TO OGDEN
February 22, 1970

Ben gambles the future of the Ponderosa to defeat a conniving Chicago meat packer who is threatening to ruin the local cattle industry. With Walter Barns, Kathleen Freeman and Billy Greenbush.

353. RETURN ENGAGEMENT
March 1, 1970

Lotta Crabtree returns to Virginia City, and Hoss, bitten by the acting bug, winds up accused of murder. With Sally Kellerman, Joyce Bulifant and William Bryant.

354. THE GOLD MINE
March 8, 1970

Joe helps a young man recover his gold claim from the two outlaws to whom he has been enslaved. Filmed at Vasquez Rocks. With Bruce Dern, Ross Hagen and Tony DeCosta.

355. DECISION AT LOS ROBLES
March 22, 1970

After Ben is critically wounded in a shootout with the vicious town boss of Los Robles, Joe tries to convince the citizens to stand up to the boss' private army. Written and directed by Michael Landon. With Joe DeSantis, Ted Cassidy an Lee deBroux.

356. CAUTION: EASTER BUNNY CROSSING
March 29, 1970

Hoss reluctantly agrees to play the Easter Bunny for the local orphans. At the same time a quartet of bumbling thieves comes to town. Filmed at Iverson's Ranch. With Marc Lawrence, Art Metrano, Len Lesser, Vic Tayback and James Jeter.

357. THE HORSE TRADERS
April 5, 1970

Hoss and Joe's plan to sell horses to the livery stables in town is thwarted by none other than Meena and Luke Calhoun. First appearances of Lou Frizzel as semi-regular Dusty Rhoades. With Ann Prentiss, Dub Taylor, Victor French, Robert Donner and George Morgan.

358. WHAT ARE PARTNERS FOR?
April 12, 1970

Hoss defends himself against bank robbery charges when he gets mixed up with a pair of inept cowboys who consider themselves desperados. With Slim Pickens, Dabbs Greer, Richard Evans, John Beck and Hamilton Camp.

359. MATTER OF CIRCUMSTANCE
April 19, 1970

Joe, left alone at the Ponderosa, is stomped by a horse and forced to consider amputating his own arm. Last regular appearance of Candy until September 1972. With Ted Ghering, Vincent Van Patten and Harry Holcombe.

Season 12 (1970-71)

360. THE NIGHT VIRGINIA CITY DIED
September 13, 1970

An arsonist is striking the town, and the only suspect is innocent. One of only a few episodes to feature both Roy Coffee and Clem Foster. With Angel Tompkins.

361. A MATTER OF FAITH
September 20, 1970

The Cartwrights discover that Dusty Rhoades has joined up with the young son of a rainmaker. First episode with Mitch Vogel as Jamie Hunter. With Bruce Gordon, Dabbs Greer, Geoffrey Lewis and Jack Collins.

362. THE WEARY WILLIES
September 27, 1970

The Cartwrights become aware of the hard time Civil War veterans are having as they struggle to reenter society. Written by Oscar-winning screenwriter Robert Pirosh. With Richard Thomas, Lonny Chapman, Lee Prucell, Elisha Cook and Harry Holcombe.

363. THE WAGON
October 5, 1970

After being taken into custody by a sheriff who does not care if he is guilty or innocent of any crime, Hoss escapes from a prison wagon with a woman he is convinced has gotten a raw deal. With Denver Pyle, Salome Jens, George Murdock and Jonathan Lippe

364. THE POWER OF LIFE AN DEATH
October 11, 1970

Wounded by Indians, Ben must rely on a fugitive murder suspect while Joe crosses the desert on foot in search of help. First episode filmed in Old Tucson, Arizona. With Rupert Crosse and Ted Gehring.

365. GIDEON THE GOOD
October 18, 1970

In Black River, Joe is ambushed by a sheriff trying to cover up his wife's crime. With Richard Kiley, Terry Moore, A. Martinez and Carmen Zapata.

366. THE TROUBLE WITH TROUBLE
October 25, 1970

Hoss volunteers to be acting sheriff of Trouble, California, a town which more than lives up to its name. Later, with Joe's help, Hoss manages to jail the entire population. With Gene Evans, E.J. Andre, G.D. Spradlin, Jeff Morris and Lane Bradford.

367. THORNTON'S ACCOUNT
November 1, 1970

Ben's horse throws him down a steep slope, injuring his back. Joe tries to round up some help, but can do no better than the lowlifes who are harassing the local settlers. Filmed at Big Bear. With Gregory Wolcott, Carl Reindel, Heather Menzies, Ken Mayer and Chick Chandler.

Greene as Ben's crooked look-alike in "A Deck of Aces" (1971).

368. THE LOVE CHILD
November 8, 1970

A dying young woman and her son are rejected by her father because she had the child out of wedlock. Written and directed by Michael Landon, who reused the story as "Child of God" on "Highway to Heaven." David Rose's music won an Emmy. With Carol Lawson, Will Geer, Josephine Hutchinson and Michael-James Wixted.

369. EL JEFE
November 15, 1970

Ben and Hoss come to the rescue of Mexican farmers who are being forced off their land by the greedy mine owner who runs the town of Prince River. Joe appears in one scene wearing a red shirt rather than his usual attire. Good surprise ending. With Warren Stevens, Rodolfo Asosta, Shug Fisher and Anna Navarro.

370. THE LUCK OF PEPPER SHANNON
November 22, 1970

Ben gives a job to Pepper Shannon on the condition the one-time outlaw stays away from Jamie, who happens to admire him. Another episode featuring a rare appearance of both Roy and Clem. With Neville Brand, Walter Brook, Dan Tobin and Harry Holcombe.

371. THE IMPOSTORS
December 13, 1970

Hoss and Joe pretend to be a stage robber's partners in order to recover stolen Cartwright money. All goes well until the wife of one of the thieves shows up. With Strother Martin and Anthony James.

372. HONEST JOHN
December 20, 1970

Jamie forms a bond with a bum and his tame crow. Before long, Jamie suggests they repair an old wagon and hit the road together. With Jack Elam.

373. FOR A YOUNG LADY
December 27, 1970

A girl's uncle and aunt want custody of her only because they believe she has the rights to her late grandfather's mine. With Jewel Blanch, Paul Fix, Madeleine Sherwood and Peggy Rea.

374. A SINGLE PILGRIM
January 3, 1971

Settlers from Virginia argue over Hoss' fate after one of them accidentally shoots him. Filmed in Los Padres National Forest. With Jeff Corey, John Schuck and Beth Brickell.

375. THE GOLD-PLATED RIFLE
January 10, 1971

When Jamie runs off after breaking a rifle he was told to leave alone, Ben follows and tells him, "I didn't pick my sons—they were born to me. But I did pick you. I didn't have to, but I did. You might consider that a point in your favor. Hoss and Joe and I want you to be part of our family."

376. TOP HAND
January 17, 1971

Ben gives a veteran wrangler who once had "bottle trouble" a job as ramrod of a major cattle drive. The man's former employer, whose herd is joining the Cartwright's, thinks his younger foreman should be in charge. Filmed at Old Tucson. Marvelous performance by expert horseman/actor Ben Johnson. With Roger Davis and Richard Farnsworth.

377. A DECK OF ACES
January 31, 1971

A con artist with an uncanny resemblance to Ben gladly sells a portion of the Ponderosa to the Central Pacific Railroad, a deal the real Ben has just turned down. Lorne Greene, of course, portrays Ben's "twin", Bradley Meredith. With Alan Oppenheimer, Charles Dierkop, Jeff Morris and Linda Gaye Scott.

378. THE DESPERADO
February 7, 1971

Hoss is taken prisoner by a fugitive black couple who admit they hate white people and have nothing to lose by killing him. Filmed at Old Tucson. With Lou Gossett, Marlene Clark, Ramon Bieri and Warren Vanders

379. THE RELUCTANT AMERICAN
February 14, 1971

An English couple comes to Nevada to learn why a ranch owned by a British investment firm is the only company holding not showing a profit. Directed by Philip Leacock, a former "Gunsmoke" producer. With Daniel Massey, Jill Haworth and J. Pat O'Malley.

380. SHADOW OF A HERO
February 21, 1971

Ben is shocked to learn the army general he is backing as governor advocates a policy of genocide toward all Indians. Filmed at Vasquez Rocks. With Dean Jagger, Laurence Luckinbill, Lane Bradford and John Randolph.

381. THE SILENT KILLER
February 28, 1971

An epidemic of influenza hits the Ponderosa, and the only person who seems sure of what to do is the wife of a doctor that Doc Martin claims is a fraud. This episode contains a stock shot of Virginia City from the Paramount Days, though the series was now produced at the Burbank Studios. With Meg Foster, Louise Latham and Harry Holcombe.

382. TERROR AT 2:00
March 7, 1971

Assassins, bent on making certain a treaty with the Indians is not signed, steal a Gatling gun and go to Virginia City posing as newspapermen. Suspenseful episode written and directed by Michael Landon. With Steve Inhat, Dabbs Greer, Chubby Johnson, Iron Eyes Chody and Helen Kleeb.

383. THE STILLNESS WITHIN
March 14, 1971

Blinded by an explosion, Joe wallows in self-pity, and at first resists the efforts of the woman trying to teach him to live without sight, not knowing she is also blind. Poignant highlight of the series, written by Suzanne Clauser and directed by Michael Landon, with the assistance of the Braille Institute of America. With Jo Van Fleet.

384. A TIME TO DIE
March 21, 1971

Ben's friend April Christopher is bitten by a rabid wolf and must accept the reality that nothing can be done to save her. Actress Vera Miles, who probably would have made an excellent Mrs. Cartwright had Ben been allowed to take the plunge, also appeared in a particularly sad episode of "Gunsmoke" this season. Directed by a former "Gunsmoke" producer Philip Leacock. With Melissa Newman, Henry Beckman and Rance Howard, father of Ron and Clint.

385. WINTER KILL
March 28, 1971

The foreman of a neighboring ranch shoots a special steer belonging to the Cartwrights, and his scheming boss plots to take unfair advantage of the mistake. Filmed at Incline Village. Script co-written by Robert Pirosh. With Glenn Corbett, Clifton James and Sheilah Wells.

386. KINGDOM OF FEAR
April 4, 1971

The Cartwrights and Candy are put on a chain gang and forced to work in a mining camp from which no one has ever escaped. Filmed at Incline Village in 1967, Hoss mentions Adam, and David Canary's sudden "return" to the series is billed as a special appearance. Written by Michael Landon. With Alfred Ryder, Richard Mulligan and Luke Askew.

Season 13 (1971-72)

David Dortort called Greene "The Perfect 'Bonanza' image."

387. AN EARTHQUAKE CALLED CALLAHAN
April 11, 1971

The only person who can get Dusty out of jail is a professional fighter who will not return to Virginia City, so Joe stays on the man's heels no matter where he goes. With Victor French, Sandy Duncan, Dub Taylor and Ted Gehring.

388. THE GRAND SWING
September 19, 1971

To teach Jamie responsibility after he wrecks a wagon and kills a horse, Ben takes him on an extended tour of the Ponderosa. A mini- epic filmed at Incline Village and Old Tucson with a touching conclusion. With Lane Bradford, Med Florey, Charlotte Stewart, Ted Gehring and Ralph Moody.

389. FALLEN WOMAN
September 26, 1971

A resentful woman forces Hoss to accept responsibility for her small son after his testimony sends her husband to prison. Exterior of the doctor's house was used later for "The Waltons." With Susan Tyrrell, Arthur O'Connell and Ford Rainey.

390. BUSHWACKED!
October 3, 1971

Two cowboys find Joe on the prairie, backshot and delirious in one of the most visually creative episodes of the series. Good script by Preston Wood, imaginative direction by William Wiard. With David Huddleston, Richard O'Brien, Peggy McCay and Keith Carradine.

391. ROCK-A-BYE-HOSS
October 10, 1971

Hoss is roped into being one of the judges of a beautiful baby contest, with not entirely predictable results. Humorous but also sobering, with Hoss telling the citizens of Virginia City that all babies are beautiful until their parents start teaching them bad ways. With Edward Andrews, Patricia Harty and Ellen Moss.

392. THE PRISONERS
October 17, 1971

Joe volunteers to help an old lawman escort a slick outlaw to jail, but when their prisoner kills the sheriff and escapes, he must face the task alone. Filmed in Los Padres National Forest. With Morgan Woodward, Michael Witney and Manuel Padilla, Jr.

393. CASSIE
October 24, 1971

To help the hapless wife and daughter of a lazy dreamer, Hoss arranges a "fixed" horse race. Filmed in Los Padres National Forest. With Jack Cassidy, Diane Baker, Lisa Gerritsen and Harry Holcombe.

394. DON'T CRY, MY SON
October 31, 1971
The wife of Virginia City's newest doctor leaves him after their son dies during childbirth. The doctor snaps and abducts another woman's baby. Written and directed by Michael Landon. With Richard Mulligan and Diana Shalet.

395. FACE OF FEAR
November 14, 1971
One of Jamie's classmates witnesses the aftermath of a murder and is too terrified to tell anyone, including her militant father, who suspects her of improper behavior. With Donald Moffatt, Bradford Dillman and Chick Chandler.

396. BLIND HUNCH
November 21, 1971
A veteran, blinded in the last battle of the war, returns to Virginia City to solve his brother's murder. Clever story by Robert Pirosh. With Rip Torn, Don Knight and Charles Maxwell.

397. THE IRON BUTTERFLY
November 28, 1971
Hoss takes the blame when a visiting actress kills her former suitor, a senator's son. With Mariette Hartley, Stefan Gierasch, Mills Watson, Allen Garfield and Peter Whitney.

398. THE RATTLESNAKE BRIGADE
December 5, 1971
Jamie is one of four young people abducted and held for ransom by dangerous convicts. Unusually grim episode. With Neville Brand.

399. EASY COME, EASY GO
December 12, 1971
Luke Calhoun loses his fortune to bad stock investments, and when Ben reluctantly allows him and Meena to stay at the Ponderosa, they proceed to disrupt the ranch's orderly operation. With Dub Taylor and Ann Prentiss.

400. A HOME FOR JAMIE
December 19, 1971
Just as Ben prepares to formally adopt Jamie, the boy's grandfather shows up to take him away. "He's not a boy," Ben tells the old gentleman. "He's a young man with his roots deep in Ponderosa soil. This is the life he knows, the life he loves, the life he wants." The episode contains a flashback to the final scene of "The Grand Swing." With Will Geer, Ford Rainey, Robert Carradine and Phyllis Love.

401. WAR BONNET
December 26, 1971
To die with honor, an old war chief who has saved Joe's life is determined to take back the warbonnet a man has had hanging on a saloon wall for fifteen years. Filmed in Bronson Canyon. With Forrest Tucker, Linda Cristal, Chief Dan George and Lee deBroux.

402. THE LONELY MAN
January 2, 1972
While panning for gold on his vacation, Hop Sing meets and falls in love with a shy young woman. Their future plans are dashed when a judge confirms what Ben has told Hop Sing: the law specifically prohibits interracial marriages. An outstanding change-of-pace episode as well as the only one to feature Victor Sen Yung exclusively. With Kelly Jean Peters.

403. SECOND SIGHT
January 9, 1972
Hoss enlists the aid of a clairvoyant woman when Jamie is missing and cannot be found. Hoss refers to Jamie as his "little brother" for the first time. With Joan Hackett

404. SADDLE STIFF
January 16, 1972
When Cactus, a Ponderosa hand, suggests Ben is getting too old for ranch work, Ben fires him and gets a job as "Ben Brown" to prove to himself he can still cut it. Filmed at Golden Oak Ranch. With Buddy Ebsen, Don Collier and Richard Farnsworth.

405. FRENZY
January 30, 1972
Ben must fight to protect a Serbian woman and her son when her mentally unstable husband snaps. With Michael Pataki and Kathleen Widdoes.

406. CUSTOMS OF THE COUNTRY
February 6, 1972
In the Mexican town of Agua Santos, Joe is arrested for taking his hat off in church, and Hoss encounters other odd community rulings when attempting to get Joe released from jail. Rare voice-over narration by Dan Blocker. With Alan Oppenheimer, Alfonso Arua, Pilar Seurat and Tony DeCosta.

At Red Rock Canyon for "Ride the Wind" (1966).

407. SHANKLIN
February 13, 1972

Hoss is shot by the leader of a band of ex-Confederate soldiers and lingers near death. Ironically, the only one who can save his life is the same man who wounded him. Sadly, Dan Blocker died exactly three months after the episode aired. With Charles Cioffi, Woodrow Parfrey, Dehl Berti, Eddie Little Sky and Rance Howard.

408. SEARCH IN LIMBO
February 20, 1972

In Mountain City, Ben is jailed on suspicion of murdering a man he admits he hated, but cannot remember where he was when the crime occurred. With Pamela Payton-Wright, Albert Salmi and Kenneth Tobey.

409. HE WAS ONLY SEVEN
March 5, 1972

A crippled old man's grandson is killed during a bank robbery, and Joe and Jamie hit the trail to help the man track down the killers. (In one of the series' few gaffes, there is a shot containing a Roosevelt dime.) Written and directed by Michael Landon, who used the basic story again for "He Was Only Twelve" on "Little House on the Prairie." With Roscoe Lee Browne, William Watson, Robert Doyle and Richard Farnsworth.

410. THE YOUNGER BROTHERS' YOUNGER BROTHER
March 12, 1972

Hoss is jailed by a sheriff who believes he is in cahoots with a trio of bungling outlaws, and when Ben and Joe try to bail him out, they are jailed as well. Written and directed by Michael Landon. With Strother Martin, Chuck McCann, Henry Jones, Ted Gehring, Ken Lynch and, yes, that is "The Tonight Show"'s Doc Severinsen in a brief cameo.

411. A PLACE TO HIDE
March 19, 1972

The Cartwrights arrange for the honorable surrender of a hunted Confederate officer and his men. Although he would be seen in the next two episodes aired, this was the last show Dan Blocker filmed. It is also the final one done by Ray Teal, but not the last time he appeared. Filmed at Franklin Lake. With Susanne Pleshette, Jon Cypher and Jodie Foster.

412. A VISIT TO UPRIGHT
March 26, 1972

Believing it may contain a hidden stash of gold, Hoss and Joe are reluctant to give up their ownership of a rundown saloon. However, if they keep it, a potential cattle deal Ben is hoping to finalize may be ruined. Along with "The Pursued," this is truly one of the "lost" episodes. With Loretta Swit, Anne Seymour, Alan Oppenheimer, Dan Tobin and Fran Ryan.

413. ONE ACE TOO MANY
April 2, 1972

In his absence, Ben's "evil twin", Bradley Meredith, pretends to be dying and starts selling off the Ponderosa's assets. With Greg Mullavey, Kate Jackson and Jack Collins.

Season 14 (1972-73)

414. FOREVER
September 12, 1972
Joe marries Alice Harper, and shortly after they begin their new life, thugs appear to collect money owed by Alice's indolent brother, with tragic results. Perhaps the most atypical and emotional episode of the series, as well as the first without Dan Blocker, whose absence is acutely felt. David Canary returns as Candy for the final ten of his 81 appearances, though there is no explanation of where he has been for the past two seasons. Filmed in Stanislaus National Forest. Written and directed by Michael Landon. With Bonnie Bedelia, Larry Golden, Andy Robinson, Roy Jenson, Lee deBroux and Robert Doyle.

415. HERITAGE OF ANGER
September 19, 1972
Ben helps a bitter ex-con readjust to life on the outside, a task complicated by the man's former business partners, who were responsible for setting him up. With Robert Lansing, Fionnula Flanagan, Warren Kimmerling and Len Lesser.

416. THE INITIATION
September 26, 1972
One of Jamie's friends is blamed when a boy accidentally dies during a ceremony for a secret club. Ben makes two references to losing Hoss. Filmed in Bronson Canyon. Many of the young guest stars had appeared in the John Wayne feature "The Cowboys," which was turned into a series produced by David Dortort in 1974. With Ron Howard, Sean Kelly and Phillis Love.

417. RIOT
October 3, 1972
Inspecting conditions in Nevada State Prison at the governor's request, Ben is taken hostage by rioting inmates. This episode introduces Tim Matheson as Griff King. Written by Robert Pirosh. With Aldo Ray, Gregory Walcott, Denver Pyle, William Bryant and Marco St. John.

418. NEW MAN
October 10, 1972
Paroled in Ben's custody, a belligerent Griff refers to the Ponderosa as "the classiest prison I've ever been in" as soon as they arrive there. The episode opens with the final scene from "Riot," to which this is a sequel. With Ronny Cox, Charles Dierkop and Jeff Morris.

419. AMBUSH AT RIO LOBO
October 24, 1972
Ben and a pregnant young woman are held hostage by outlaws waiting to rob a stage. Directed by Nicholas Colasanto, better known as Coach on the sitcom "Cheers." With James Olson, Sian Barbara Allen and Albert Salmi.

420. THE TWENTY-SIXTH GRAVE
October 31, 1972
Mark Twain ruffles dangerous feathers in Virginia City with accusations of claim-jumping and murder. First episode filmed for the final season. With Ken Howard, Dana Elcar, Walter Burke, Stacy Keach, Jr., Richard Bull and Sean Kelly.

421. STALLION
November 14, 1972
After a drifter steals Joe's new horse, Joe is forced to ride the animal to death in order to save the man's son. Filmed at Incline Village. Music later used for "Little House on the Prairie." First episode shown after "Bonanza"'s cancellation. With Clu Gulager, Vincent Van Patten and Mitzi Hoag.

422. THE HIDDEN ENEMY
November 28, 1972
The welfare of Virginia City is compromised by a new doctor addicted to morphine. With Mike Farrell (M*A*S*H), Melissa Murphy, Gary Busey, David Huddleston and Harry Holcombe.

423. THE SOUND OF SADNESS
December 5, 1972
A lonely old man opens his home to two orphan boys but runs into bureaucratic opposition when attempting to adopt them. Written and directed by Michael Landon, who actually appears wearing blue jeans in one scene. With Jack Albertson, John Randolph, Irene Tedrow and Harry Holcombe.

BONANZA

424. THE BUCKET DOG
December 19, 1972

Jamie acquires an Irish Setter, unaware that its rightful owner considers the dog an inferior example of the breed and wants it destroyed. Joe once again wears blue jeans. Filmed at Golden Oak Ranch. With Don Knight, William Sylvester and John Zaremba.

425. FIRST LOVE
December 26, 1972

Jamie is attracted to the abused young wife of Virginia City's unpopular new schoolmaster. Ben offers Jamie a paternal observation in a poetic scene reminiscent of speeches to his other sons in the series' earlier days. Filmed at Golden Oak Ranch. Written by producer Richard Collins. With Pamela Franklin and Jordan Rhodes.

426. THE WITNESS
January 2, 1973

An elderly widow suffers a fatal heart attack when a man posing as Candy robs her. Candy is arrested and must rely on a confident but inexperienced young attorney for his defense. The only time in the series' history where an episode title had been used before ("The Witness," 9-21-69).

427. THE MARRIAGE OF THEODORA DUFFY
January 9, 1973

Griff goes undercover as the "husband" of a government agent working to snare a gang of war criminals. Last episode ever filmed, containing one quick, final glimpse of the Ponderosa's exterior. With Karen Carlson and Ramon Bieri.

428. THE HUNTER
January 16, 1973

In the last episode aired, Joe is chased across the desert by a deranged soldier who has escaped from prison. A Western take on "The Most Dangerous Game." Written and directed by Michael Landon. Ben and Jamie appear briefly during the final look at the Ponderosa's interior. Filmed in Arizona's Coronado National Forest and Old Tucson. With Tom Skerritt.